War of
Another Kind

War of Another Kind

A Southern Community in the Great Rebellion

WAYNE K. DURRILL

New York   Oxford
OXFORD UNIVERSITY PRESS
1990

Oxford University Press

Oxford   New York   Toronto
Delhi   Bombay   Calcutta   Madras   Karachi
Petaling Jaya   Singapore   Hong Kong   Tokyo
Nairobi   Dar es Salaam   Cape Town
Melbourne   Auckland

and associated companies in
Berlin   Ibadan

Published by Oxford University Press, Inc.,
200 Madison Avenue, New York, New York 10016

Oxford is a registered trademark of Oxford University Press

Library of Congress Cataloging-in-Publication Data
Durrill, Wayne K. (Wayne Keith)
War of another kind : a southern community in the great rebellion
/ Wayne K. Durrill.
p.   cm.
Includes bibliographical references.
ISBN 0–19–506007–5
1. North Carolina—History—Civil War, 1861–1865.   2. Plantation
life—North Carolina—History—19th century.   3. Plantations—
North Carolina—History—19th century.   I. Title.
E573.9.D87   1990
975.6′03—dc20   89–36159   CIP

Map on page 192 courtesy of North Carolina Collection,
University of North Carolina Library at Chapel Hill.

246897531
Printed in the United States of America
on acid-free paper

To the memory of my mother
Beverly Jean Durrill

and to
A. L. W.

Acknowledgments

The road from a glimmer of an idea to a book in print is a long one for any author, but in my case, that journey has included more than the usual number of detours, dead ends, and potholes. But that, it turns out, is not bad news, for along the way I have met an astonishing number of people who were willing to share their time, knowledge, sound judgment, and good cheer—all of which proved to be essential (the good cheer especially) in completing this book. I would thank each of them here if I thought my readers had the patience and Oxford the budget to stand it; instead, I will mention only those whom I owe for special favors and buy the rest a beer the next time we meet.

In Chapel Hill, I wish to thank Jim and Dianne Leloudis for years of good companionship, conversation, dinners, and God knows what else that is a part of being best friends. I also thank Krista and Andy Carlson and Ann Sims and Bob Korstad for much the same. For his good counsel on all manner of professional and intellectual matters and for his friendship, I am grateful as well to Tom Reefe. I wish to thank my dissertation committee for their close reading of an earlier version of this book: Jacquelyn Hall, Colin Palmer, George Brown Tindall, William Barney, and especially my advisor Donald G. Mathews, to whom I owe extra thanks for letting me do just as I please. I am grateful, in addition, to the University of North Carolina for helping this project along with a Joseph E. Pogue Research Fellowship and a University

Teaching Fellowship and to H. G. Jones and his staff at the North Carolina Collection and Carolyn Wallace and her staff at the Southern Historical Collection.

In Washington, D.C., my debts grow so great that they would approach peonage if it were not for the generous and forgiving spirit of Pete Daniel, my advisor during a stint at the National Museum of American History, Smithsonian Institution, where I held a dissertation fellowship in 1986. His friendship, gentle criticism, and nationally acclaimed parties set a high standard for me and the other fellows, which manifested itself in a community of scholars gathered around the table at Gallagher's on Capitol Hill. That community has been my family in many ways for the past few years, and I value all who have lifted a glass with me in good cheer. But I feel a special debt to three of the founders and eldest stalwarts: Colleen Dunlavy, Stephanie McCurry, and Grace Palladino; to more recent members, Jo Ann Brown, Vernon Burton, Christine Hoepfner, Lu Ann Jones, Joni Kinsey, Lynn Kirby, Karen Linn, Charlie McGovern, Mary Panzer, Ron Radano, John Wettenhall, Jeannie Whayne; and to a still more recent visitor, Linda Przybyszewski.

During the past two years, I have had the good fortune to labor in a veritable workshop of historical research at the University of Maryland, College Park, alongside Ira Berlin, Steven F. Miller, and Leslie S. Rowland, each of whom with great patience taught me the craft of editing historical documents and deepened my knowledge of the Civil War era—both of which, I hope, are reflected in the story told here.

I am also indebted to the University of North Carolina, the American Historical Association, and the American Association for State and Local History for small research grants that helped move this project forward at crucial times. And I wish to thank the staff at Oxford University Press—especially Sheldon Meyer and Rachel Toor, and Scott Lenz for his thoughtful copy editing.

Finally, I am grateful to my father, Kenneth E. Durrill, for his unfailing support of my many unlikely and unpromising projects, this one of which at least made its way into print.

College Park, Md.   W. K. D.
May 1989

Contents

War of
Another Kind

Prologue: The Beginnings of a Plantation Community

· I ·

In 1851, ten years before secession, Samuel Newberry, a yeoman farmer and resident of Washington County, North Carolina, stood before a crowd of his neighbors and spoke of the grim future he foresaw: "Let this monstrous doctrine [secession] never come to maturity. This ill-timed step once taken can never be retraced, and you will bring upon the country all the horrors of civil war." "[Y]ou will see your country overrun by a ravaging soldiery . . . your now flourishing land will be desolated . . . your slaves will be wrenched from you by military force, and made your equals." "Oh, that the picture I have here drawn may never come to pass," he continued, "nevertheless, if this treasonable scheming and plotting cannot be uprooted, and is allowed to progress, all I have pointed out will happen in ten years from this day."

Samuel Newberry spoke those prescient words on behalf of Edward Stanly, the Whig candidate for a seat in Congress that encompassed several counties around the Albemarle Sound in northeastern North Carolina. Stanly and his party based their appeal to planters and yeoman farmers on the protection of property. Whigs argued that both land and slaves could be preserved best within the Union. Stanly's opponent, Thomas Ruffin, a secessionist Democrat, believed this not to be the case. According to Newberry's

3

account, "Col. Ruffin says we are driven to the wall; there is a monster [abolition] above head in the clouds." But local Whigs saw no such threat. "We have always had a vast majority of the officers of Government from the President to the lowest Government officer, and last year we had the fugitive slave law granted us." Why, then, the movement to destroy the Union?

Samuel Newberry thought he knew. "Gentlemen," he addressed his neighbors, "there is a deep laid scheme at the bottom of all this; it is no other than for the purpose of setting up a land and negro oligarchy to untenant the poor, and make them subserve to the will of the few." If war came then, it would not be over the "rights" that Democrats claimed had been trampled underfoot by Northerners. Neither would it be in defense of Southern society as Newberry and his friends knew it. Instead, civil war would be directed by a handful of planters who hoped to secure for themselves the powers of the state in order to serve their interests in land and labor.[1]

Historians have not viewed the Civil War in such terms. In a recent survey of the Confederacy, one scholar summarized the conventional wisdom this way: "The Confederate quest for home rule never became a contest over who should rule at home." In this view, conflict among Southerners, the little that occurred, was simply incidental to the larger "War Between the States," as Southerners came to call it in the twentieth century. It is this struggle between two nations that has obsessed historians. They have focused on affairs of state, on the words and actions of generals and politicians; theirs are stories of legislation and massive battles, of constitutional difficulties, and of strategy and tactics. These are important matters. But such histories frame accounts of the war in terms of the concerns articulated by national politicians and generals. They do not address issues that would be raised in Washington County during the war by slaves and white wage laborers, and they do not refer to the concerns of Samuel Newberry and his yeoman friends.[2]

Between the fall of 1860 and the summer of 1865, the residents of Washington County, North Carolina, fought a civil war among themselves. Certainly, they contributed to the War Between the States; the county sent roughly 350 men into the Confederate army and the same number into the Union army. For a time,

Plymouth was itself a federal army post and played a minor role in the conflict between Confederate and Union armies and navies. But the real war for most Washington County residents took place at home, literally on every person's doorstep. That war will be chronicled here.

Washington County's war at home was not merely an enactment of the national war at the local level. Sometimes, the two wars seemed to have little connection indeed. After Bull Run, a peculiar peace settled upon North and South as the great national armies took a long rest in order to reorganize and prepare for a lengthy war. But at the same time in Washington County, a political battle broke out of a kind and violence never before seen in that place. An alliance between planters and yeoman farmers, which had endured since the first nullification crisis in 1832, suddenly broke apart. Former allies turned against each other. Both sides began to compete for a constituency of poor white wage laborers and tenant farmers—a polarization totally inconceivable only months earlier.

Yet at other times, Washington County's war at home had everything to do with the national struggle. When in September 1862 President Abraham Lincoln announced that he would emancipate all slaves within federal lines after the first of the new year, local residents reacted swiftly. Planters, predictably, removed their slaves upcountry. Yeoman farmers immediately recognized the deeper implications of Lincoln's act, if not the president's intentions—the proclamation was not merely a manifesto for black freedom but also an attack on property and, as such, rendered the planters' claims to productive resources of all kinds untenable. Moreover, it implicated the federal government, specifically the Union army, in efforts to dispossess planters of their property. Hence, in January 1863, Washington County unionists confidently launched a property war against local planters that would continue for two years.

From secession to Lee's surrender, Washington County's white residents divided into three distinct groups—planters, yeoman farmers, and white laborers. Secessionist planters succeeded in attracting to their cause men who had been clients before the war—shinglers, tenant farmers, artisans, and small farmers who depended on plantation stores for supplies, credit, and marketing.

Yeoman leaders also found a constituency, men like themselves who farmed or hunted mainly for a subsistence and, thus, remained independent of the outside world. These alliances broke down in the crucible of war. Confederate soldiers from the county deserted in droves; later they hid in the swamps to avoid conscription officers. Landless unionists eventually turned on the county's yeomen and seized their lands as well as parcels belonging to planters. In the end, a guerrilla war ensued that arrayed each group against the others, a local war which so disrupted Confederate efforts to supply Lee's army in Virginia that Jefferson Davis himself authorized the total destruction of Plymouth by an army of ten thousand men in 1864.

In the midst of this three-cornered conflict, Washington County's slaves moved cautiously but deliberately to secure their freedom. Most were removed in 1862 or 1863 to the North Carolina piedmont. There they found themselves leased out to new masters who might be manipulated or intimidated. At the least, Washington County's slaves succeeded in renewing the rules by which they had worked and lived at home. But in many cases, they extended their limited liberties within slavery, and sometimes they escaped to federal lines or simply defied their masters' authority. Those slaves who remained in Washington County took the greatest advantage of the proximity of federal power. They seized plantations for their own use; bought and sold crops, livestock, tools, and other supplies; and many joined the federal army, some serving in Plymouth.

The local war chronicled here was as much a part of the Great Rebellion as Gettysburg and Lincoln's reelection. There were, in fact, many different wars fought between 1861 and 1865 in the United States—one between two national governments and their armies, one for land and labor in the South, and others. The conflict between national governments was a distinctly bourgeois affair. It proceeded by mutually respected rules of war that sacrificed the bodies of men to preserve all manner of possessions—land, slaves, personal property, women, and children. By contrast, the war for land and labor fought in Washington County soon became an attack on property itself. Most men there sought to preserve—not to sacrifice—themselves. They hoped to acquire by force possessions which could be distributed equitably among themselves, not to protect property that had become concentrated in the hands of a few planters and well-to-do yeomen. Washington County planters justifiably feared their unionist opponents and called them "levellers" and "agrarians."

The story of Washington County during the Great Rebellion is not a chronicle of great battles and momentous political debates. It is the story of ordinary people who fought over the means by which to make a living. Sometimes, local residents responded to national events—the outcomes of major battles and political decisions made in Washington or Richmond. But most often, the county's war took its own course, working out conflicts that had plagued the county for decades and raising issues that had not been matters of public discussion since the American Revolution. In this sense, Washington County's war was part of the national conflict; as in other communities throughout the North and South, the war provided opportunities to redress past grievances and lay new ones on the table. But unlike the national conflict, the Washington County war had no rules; no quarter would be given at home. The ties that bound local residents together, however tenuously in 1859, suddenly dissolved a year later. Brother fought brother. Neighbor attacked neighbor. Friends and allies alike turned on each other. Washington County's war at home proved to be, above all, an uncivil war, war of another kind.

· **II** ·

Washington County, North Carolina, is located at the mouth of the Roanoke River on the Albemarle Sound in northeastern North Carolina. The county in 1860 measured about twenty miles east to west and fifteen miles north to south. On the northern edge of the county, the land was flat and muddy, rising at three places to form dry savanna and elsewhere sinking to the southeast to form a large swamp. Washington County shared a common border to the east with Tyrrell County and to the south with Hyde and Beaufort counties. The lands along these borders consisted in 1860 almost entirely of cypress swamps. To the west lay Welch Creek and the Roanoke River which divided Washington County from Martin and Bertie counties.

Most of Washington County in the mid-nineteenth century lay

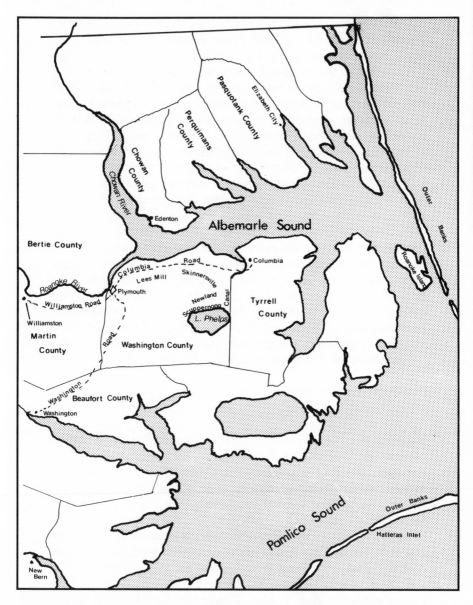

Washington Country area in 1865.

under water at least part of the year. The terrain stood at its highest point only about nine feet above sea level. As a result, rain water seldom drained quickly, collecting instead in low-lying troughs that supported impenetrable woodlands. Land that sloped even slightly became grassy marsh, in the midst of which small ridges created what Washington County residents called "islands" in the swamp. Those islands taken together formed a crescent shaped archipelago along the western, northern, and eastern edges of the county and in 1860 supported communities of yeoman farmers and swampers.

In the center of the county was the East Dismal Swamp, where no one lived. To the west, a ridge ran parallel to Welch Creek between the southern border of the county and Plymouth. On top of the ridge was the Washington Road, alongside which lay a narrow strip of open savanna occupied by subsistence farmers. Plymouth itself was located to the north on three small rises along the Roanoke River. To the west of town, a ridge supported the Williamston Road, and to the east, the Columbia Road connected Plymouth to an adjoining ridge. That ridge ran parallel to the Sound shore and supported two communities of small farmers called Lees Mill and Skinnersville. From Skinnersville, the Columbia Road continued southeast to the Scuppernong community.[3]

Scuppernong was the largest and most important of Washington County's rural neighborhoods in 1860. All the county's largest planters lived there. Josiah Collins's plantation set the pace. Located in the southeast corner of the neighborhood, Somerset Place included about three thousand acres of prime black soil and nearly three hundred thousand acres of cypress woodlands. There, nearly five hundred slaves cultivated corn in an intricate patchwork of irrigated fields. In addition, poor white men cut cypress shingles on these lands for sale in the Northern states on contract to Collins. Collins's planter neighbors, among others, included Charles Pettigrew's sons—Charles L. and William S.—and Henderson Phelps, each of whom ran plantations that worked over one hundred slaves.[4]

The land in Scuppernong lay on both sides of a river of the same name. That river flowed northwards from the East Dismal Swamp to the Albemarle Sound and was navigable for seven miles by small coastwise vessels. It was also connected by several canals to Lake Phelps, a body of fresh water that stood in a crater on the southern border of the county. The lake had no apparent source, except for rain water; and it possessed no natural outlet. Therefore, planters in 1860 found it to be a convenient source of water with which to irrigate their fields. Each planter in the neighborhood built a canal from the lake to his plantation. Those canals fed a network of ditches that allowed planters to divert water into the fields and then later to drain away the excess into the Scuppernong River.

The Albemarle Sound provided access for Washington County residents to the Atlantic Ocean. Shallow draft ships (thirty to sixty tons) left ramps on the county's two rivers, the Roanoke in the west and the Scuppernong in the east, and then proceeded through the Sound. From there, ships' captains could sail their vessels north through the Great Dismal canal to Norfolk and the Chesapeake Bay, or they could sail south past Roanoke Island, through the Pamlico Sound, over the sand bar at Hatteras inlet, and into the Atlantic Ocean. Washington County residents used these routes to ship corn and shingles to New York, Charleston, Baltimore, and Norfolk.

At the center of this trade lay the port of Plymouth, the county seat, located on the Roanoke River about four miles upstream from the Albemarle Sound. In 1860, it was one of the busiest ports in the state and boasted the only federal customs house in northeastern North Carolina. Its economic hinterland extended more than one hundred miles up the Roanoke River valley and included some of the richest corn-producing plantations in the state. In 1860, Plymouth had a total of 872 residents—409 whites, 401 slaves, and 62 free colored persons, most of whom worked in the merchandising trades or as artisans. Others were lawyers, one a boardinghouse keeper, two were ministers, one a steam sawmill manager, one a ship captain, and several were local government officials, housekeepers, washerwomen, and day laborers.[5]

Most Washington County residents, 5,485 out of a total population of 6,357 in 1860, lived in the countryside; 3,184 whites, 2,064 slaves, and 237 free blacks were distributed through five neighborhoods—from west to east, in Plymouth, Lees Mill, Skinnersville (also called Germanton), Newland, and Scuppernong. Virtually all of these people were connected with farming. A handful of planters ran the largest places. Meanwhile, perhaps five hundred white men operated smaller farms; some owned the land they worked and perhaps a slave or two, while others rented land. The remainder worked as contract laborers—on large plantations, while others labored for friends or relatives—and as shingle makers in the swamps. Most white women worked at home. Slaves, of course, worked as farm laborers and sometimes as artisans for their masters. Very few appear to have been hired out.[6]

· **III** ·

The dominance of planters over their neighbors, black and white, was something relatively new in Washington County. Before 1780, local residents counted no planters among their number and few slaves. They lived in a yeoman's community, the very embodiment of the republican values for which so many local residents had fought in the Revolution. But all that changed in the 1780s. After the Revolution, several planters in Edenton, a town on the north side of the Albemarle Sound, formed the Lake Company, an investment group that speculated in real estate. The planters concentrated their efforts on what was then Tyrrell County (later divided into Washington and Tyrrell counties) where a large freshwater lake, later named Lake Scuppernong and then Lake Phelps, had only recently been discovered deep in the cypress swamps. The lake stood some nine feet above sea level and, therefore, could, the Lake Company hoped, be used to irrigate rice fields if canals could be dug and plantations cleared in the wilderness. The surrounding land also could be timbered to produce lumber and shingles for sale in the North.

In 1787, the first efforts began to carve plantations out of the swamps near Lake Phelps. One of the Lake Company partners, the first Josiah Collins, sent two ships to western Africa to purchase slaves, who, when they landed at Edenton in June, were sent to Lake Phelps. There, confined at night to wooden stockades, the slaves built a seven-mile-long canal that connected the lake with the Scuppernong River. That canal supplied water to grow rice and later corn at Collins's Somerset Place plantation. Shortly thereafter, Charles Pettigrew, another of the Lake Company partners,

brought slaves from Edenton to clear and build Bonarva plantation. But the Lake Company planters' main resource was the more
than three hundred thousand acres of woodland that they purchased in Washington and Tyrrell counties before 1800. They contracted with poor white men to cut timber there and sawed the
lumber in their own mills.[7]

In establishing their plantations, large slaveholders challenged
the dominance of yeoman farmers over Washington County. By
1802, that conflict had led to a political crisis. During the spring,
rumors spread of a plot among the region's slaves. There may have
been some truth to the allegations; local slaves could have taken
Prosser's revolt around Richmond in 1800 as their model, and
they had just participated in the Albemarle region's version of the
Great Revival. Those religious exercises had propagated an equali-
tarian ethos that was central to evangelical thought and practice.
The revival produced a regional slave leadership, preachers who
moved from one plantation to another, spreading the gospel and,
perhaps, more. Whatever the case, a certain slave preacher living
in Bertie County across the river from Plymouth, Dr. Joe, had supposedly conspired with runaway slaves who had hidden in the
swamps "to kill the white people."[8] At the same time, however,
poor whites, both yeoman farmers and "swampers" (mostly wage
laborers) went through a similar experience. They, too, became
caught up in the Great Revival, and they, too, produced new leaders who organized poor white people across county lines.

Planters became alarmed. To reduce the danger, they mobilized
white farmers and laborers with rumors of slave insurrections and
race war. Thomas Blount, a leading politician in the Sound area,
made an especially outrageous claim: "[W]hen all the white men
were killed the Black men were to take their places, have their
wives, &c. &c." Planters also sought out black "conspirators" to
legitimate such charges and organized poor whites into slave patrols. In the end, white vigilantes in Washington County shot "6 or
7 blacks . . . on their way to Williamston," supposedly to join
the insurrection.[9]

These incidents had the effect of precluding a confrontation between planters and poor whites—for the moment. Between 1802
and 1830, planters, yeoman farmers, and white laborers lived more
or less peaceably. Many more planters established themselves and

their slaves in the county, chiefly in the Plymouth and Scuppernong neighborhoods. Yeoman farmers, too, cleared new land, especially in Skinnersville and Lees Mill, and they established an entirely new settlement in a place they named Newland—literally on new land cleared west of the Scuppernong neighborhood. Most white men in the county prospered as the local economy expanded rapidly.

But by the mid-1830s, troubling new political and economic questions had arisen in the county and the nation. Whigs argued that economic expansion could best be promoted by government intervention—by regulating tariffs to promote the export of manufactured goods and by financing commercial development through government-backed banks. Jacksonian Democrats thought this was all nonsense, that economic development would be best served by simply letting small holders—yeoman farmers and artisans—continue to expand their existing production. In Washington County, these conflicting views became joined in a struggle between yeomen and planters for political dominance.

Planters in Washington County managed a small political miracle. The county had voted mainly for Jeffersonian Democrats in the 1810s and 1820s. Therefore, it was reasonable to suppose that local yeoman farmers would become Jackson men when the second-party system formed. Yet, they did not. Planters in Washington County used the nullification crisis of 1832 to draw a yeoman constituency into the newly formed Whig party, which subsequently dominated the county's politics through 1860. How they did so is not clear. We do know that the basis of this coalition was a common interest in land. Planters and yeoman farmers both wished to protect their property, and both became convinced that that could best be done in supporting the Whig party. Landless whites and slaves, of course, could not vote and, therefore, did not participate in this compromise.[10]

At about the same time, planters also actively sought out clients among poor whites in their neighborhoods, men who had been left out of the political settlement based on a common interest in property. At both Somerset Place and Bonarva, planters ran stores and extended credit to small farmers and laborers who sought to buy cloth, household items, tools, knives, gun powder, and all manner of other necessities and luxuries. Uriah Bennett, an eight-year-old slave at Somerset Place plantation in 1860, recalled in later years: "The poor white people, who did not have land enough to support them, would come and work for [Josiah] Collins, and take earnings in trade, like flour and other things they needed." Planters also leased land to poor men who agreed to cut timber and then to have it sawed in the planter's sawmill and ferried to the North on his ship. (The Collins and Pettigrew families both owned their own coastwise ships from the 1830s to 1860.)[11]

Similarly, planters in Washington County hired an enormous number of white laborers. Some worked temporarily as coopers, sawyers, overseers, carpenters, machinists, boat makers, gin builders, ironmongers, or millwrights; but most labored for planters in unskilled occupations. Charles L. Pettigrew employed poor white neighbors to spay livestock, clear ground, cut and roll logs, run errands, hunt runaway slaves, and dig or clean canals and ditches. In all this, Pettigrew took care to create the greatest obligation to himself among his neighbors. He hired poor white men mainly in years when crops had gone bad; the men, of course, worked for very low wages then, but they were also exceedingly grateful for the crumbs that Pettigrew let fall from his table. In one year, Pettigrew, who was by no means the county's largest planter, alone employed nearly one hundred men, or about one-seventh of the county's adult males.[12]

Finally, planters took care to defer to lesser white men when it cost them nothing. During court week, planters smoothed their relations with yeoman farmers through ritual displays of mutual respect. On such occasions, Josiah Collins III (grandson of the founder of Somerset Place) always treated "the poor man with the same politeness that he does the rich." He saluted any small farmer he met because "not to lift your hat to a poor *white* man would be giving mortal offence." Collins hoped by the gesture to enforce the idea that *"colour* alone makes caste here." Planters also intervened on behalf of poor people in court, and they mediated relations between poor whites and slaves who could not adjudicate their disputes in an ordinary court of law, slaves being considered incompetent under law to testify in cases involving whites.[13]

In these ways, Washington County planters produced a constituency for themselves. Yet, all was not peace and prosperity in the county. Most of the land lay in the hands of a very few wealthy planters, who also owned and operated the county's sawmills, controlled access to water from Lake Phelps by their canals, held all the credit available, dominated the county's government, and had exclusive connections to markets for corn through factors in Charleston, Norfolk, and New York. If yeoman farmers and white laborers prospered, it would be only through the encouragement of local planters. If slaves lived at all, it would be as a result of their masters' beneficence. Not surprisingly then, poor whites and blacks both resented planters and their engrossment of resources and power.

Most poor whites, whether yeoman farmers or laborers, expressed their resentment in oblique ways. Those who could do so simply distanced themselves from planters. Subsistence farmers in the Newland neighborhood refused to join the Episcopal church founded by the Collins and Pettigrew families and formed the Concord Church instead. White laborers employed by planters often failed to do a job properly here and cheated on a contract there.

However, there were some bolder fellows among the county's poor whites. In 1859, Durham Lassiter, a thirty-nine-year-old illiterate sawmill hand living in the Newland neighborhood, had begun leasing out rights to lands adjoining his own which belonged to Josiah Collins. When a question arose about his possession of the timber, Lassiter "suggested claims" of his own and "alleged licence" from Collins. Moreover, when Collins threatened to sue or have him arrested, Lassiter told the planter that he could not "be staid by legal process." In fact, a survey of Collins's swamplands completed in 1860 showed that Lassiter and another man had "made some 20,000 shingles" there during the previous year. Moreover, other poor white men recently had cut over five hundred thousand shingles on the same lands.[14]

Blacks, given their extreme dependence, had fewer opportunities to express their objections. William Pettigrew's head driver, Henry, sometimes pointedly informed his absent master in a dictated letter that he needed no further instructions in order to run the plantation. But slaves faced a more direct enforcement of inequality than did poor whites. Uriah Bennett recalled: "The overseers were pretty cruel sometimes" at Somerset Place. And the county's slaves remained under the surveillance of the slave patrol. "For months and months, at a time, we were never allowed off the farm," remembered Bennett, "sometimes we would get as far as the gate and peep over. We were told that if we got outside the Padirollers would get us."[15]

The county's slaves, however, did not remain entirely under the thumb of local planters. In the mid-1830s, they participated in a second regional revival that produced another generation of local black leaders. Some, like Henry, ran away to the swamps, sometimes for years at a time, and formed maroon communities that became occasional sanctuaries for the county's slaves. Others led local revolts. On Charles Pettigrew's plantation, Bonarva, slaves took over the plantation while the planter served for two years in Congress. They sold the plantation's corn and livestock and pocketed the proceeds, and they defied the authority of an overseer with whom Pettigrew had contracted to manage his estate. In the summer of 1836, the overseer quelled the disturbance by administering one thousand lashes to various slave leaders, one hundred of which were applied directly to Henry.[16]

Between 1836 and 1860, planters and yeoman farmers ruled the county without much difficulty. Conflict remained muted, carried out clandestinely and without producing a serious challenge to the power of propertied men. Planters and yeoman farmers succeeded by forming a leadership based on a common interest in the protection of property and by bringing several constituencies to bear on public issues. Planters marshaled their clients, mostly poor white men whom they employed or to whom they leased land or lent money and other goods, and yeoman farmers brought themselves and their families and friends. Slaves became the foil on this wider political stage. They were the excuse to mobilize white men, whatever their differences, under a planter leadership in the drama of supposed local and regional slave revolts.

All of this worked well enough for local planters until the late 1850s. Then, national issues began to impinge on local political arrangements, especially the question of an extension of slavery into the territories and the implications of the fugitive slave law. Those national disputes brought into local public discussion all manner of questions regarding slaves in particular and property in general. For the first time in three decades, differences among planters, yeoman farmers, and white laborers surfaced, as did the possibility of a new allocation of power benefiting different interests.

· **IV** ·

In the spring of 1860, one local planter noted that the "political affairs of Washington County" had become "somewhat disturbed." Local Democrats had split along sectional lines. In early May, Captain M. Bowan, a planter who would remain a unionist throughout the war, held a meeting of Douglas Democrats in the Lees Mill militia district. Unionist sentiment ran high there. And a few days later during court week, Breckinridge Democrats met in Plymouth to consider the possibility of secession. Each meeting nominated candidates for the General Assembly election that would be held in July. Meanwhile, Whigs, who dominated politics in Washington County, all favored remaining in the Union. But they struggled among themselves for control of a new constituency of poor white men.[17]

Some in the local Whig party, which for years had relied for its constituency on an alliance of property holders, proposed to add white wage laborers to their fold. They hoped to do so through the so-called ad valorem tax bill. This legislation would require slaveholders to pay a standard poll tax for every slave they owned, not just for the traditional three-fifths. The increase in revenue thus produced would enable the state to lower overall poll-tax rates. Laboring white men, thereafter, would pay less tax and, con-sequently, be able to vote more often (the payment of the poll tax being a prerequisite to receiving the privilege of casting a ballot). In Washington County, J. J. Lindsey held ad valorem meetings throughout the county. But that threatened to divide the local Whig party because many planters still preferred to rely on the alliance of property holders.[18]

At the core of these conflicts lay the question of slave labor. Democrats debated among themselves how best to preserve it, within or without the Union. Whigs differed over whether the planters' value in slaves ought to be compromised in favor of wage earners who would ensure the party's voting dominance. Such questions had the potential to disrupt local routines of power. One planter complained: "As slavery is the great question of the day, & is indeed one of mighty moment, it is seized upon with the avidity of a dying grasp by the ambitious, by the fanatical & by the mis-chievous, both north & south."[19]

By late 1860, the stage was set for local war. Planters feared a national government that seemed hostile to the possession of their most valuable property—slaves. Yeoman farmers began to feel uncomfortable in a political alliance with planters who appeared bent on destroying the nation in order to save the one species of property in which most yeomen had little interest. Finally, white laborers sensed an opportunity as planters and yeomen vied for their votes. It became apparent that the county's alliance of property holders had begun to disintegrate. Only the timing of open conflict remained to be determined. Lincoln's election in November 1860 settled that question.

1

Secession

· I ·

On Tuesday evening, October 16, 1860, about twenty Washington County slaves assembled at a shingle-maker's camp in McRae's swamp. The slaves proposed among themselves to "collect together about 300" who would join them, "march towards Plymouth at about 11 o'clock on some night," "murder & destroy all they might encounter on the road, set fire to the town, kill all of the inhabitants that might oppose them, [and] seize what money there might be, also what ammunition & weapons" they might require. They then hoped to "take possession of vessels" which would take them to an unspecified destination where, presumably, they would find freedom. The group's leader was a slave, probably a shingle maker hired out to himself, belonging to a man in Norfolk. He and some others had brought firearms and ammunition to the camp.[1]

The plan drew opposition from at least one slave present who warned that they all "would have their necks broken" if they attempted such an escape. The plan's advocates, however, told him that he "had no sense," swore at him, and called him a "Tyrrell negro," implying that he was little more than a backwoods bumpkin from the swamps of adjacent Tyrrell County. The man called a "Tyrrell negro" remained unconvinced. He was a "swamper" or shingle maker and a slave owned by a man named Spruill. Spruill had lent the slave to his daughter, who was married to a man

19

named Blount. The Blounts lived on the main road between Mackey's Ferry and Plymouth to the west along which the insurrectionists planned to travel.

The black swamper feared the worst. He, therefore, told his "young mistress," Mrs. Blount, of the plan "under apprehension" for her safety. Perhaps, he feared as well for his own life. Whatever the case, Mrs. Blount informed her husband of the plot, and he immediately took the slave to Plymouth. On Monday, October 22, the "Tyrrell negro" was examined by a magistrate privately and then again in public. The same day, based on that testimony, local constables arrested four slaves who had attended the meeting and imprisoned them in Plymouth. Finally, the magistrates bound their prisoners over for trial at the March 1861 term of the Washington County Superior Court.[2]

The report of a "slave insurrection" produced a "panic" among some whites in Washington County. On Monday morning, Plymouth was "in the greatest commotion." Some went about the streets arguing that those charged should be "hung without judge or jury." One woman who lived in Plymouth brought her family to the town hotel to spend the night, "she being afraid to remain in her own house." As a result, a planter explained: "At Plymouth it was necessary to put the negroes in jail to keep them from being killed by the negroless people of Washington County." Persons in the county's outlying districts also became alarmed. Some "country people" were reported "so much excited" that they "avow[ed] themselves as ready to slaughter the negroes indiscriminately." In the southern portion of Washington County, reports circulated of "as many as 50 persons on guard at night." That week, the local slave patrol, moribund for years, began to "guard roads & bridges" near the plantations, anticipating "an attack" from the slaves at Lake Phelps."[3]

After the initial scare, local patrols continued their vigilance. In the first week of November 1860, a group of thirty men visited Charles Pettigrew's plantation, Bonarva, while he was in South Carolina on business. They examined "everything" on the place. Moreover, they informed Pettigrew's overseer, Jacob Spiers, that they had assigned a permanent three-man patrol to the neighborhood that would cost Pettigrew $1.25 for each taxable slave he owned. On November 7, the patrol went a step further. On that day, Pettigrew, after his return home, sent several slaves with some damaged corn to another plantation that he owned nearby. In the past, the slaves at Lake Phelps always had moved freely in the neighborhood. Therefore, Pettigrew issued no passes. But when this group attempted to travel, the patrol "whipped the people." In addition, the officers informed Spiers that in the future the slaves "should have passes" if Pettigrew wished them to move among his plantations.[4]

Did the meeting at McRae's swamp constitute an insurrection? Did the whites in Plymouth and elsewhere respond in order to enforce racial fears? How can we interpret the actions taken by Washington County slaves, farmers, and planters in the fall of 1860? Charles Pettigrew gives a clue. On October 20, two days before news of the slave meeting became known, the planter wrote: "I really see no reason to apprehend any difficulty among the negroes. It is mainly resulting from the panic on the part of the whites. I think there is a profound agitation in the south, a feeling as if something was going to happen."[5] That agitation had mobilized poor whites, ostensibly on behalf of planters. But, in fact, the slave patrol acted against planters' wishes and interests by harassing their slave property, invading plantations, conducting unauthorized searches, and then taxing slaveowners for the inconvenience. The Washington County insurrection scare did not signal the beginning of a black uprising, although some blacks did plot an escape. Moreover, it did not mobilize poor white men behind planter leadership as had earlier supposed "slave revolts." Instead, it marked the advent of a contest among whites over who might rule at home.

· **II** ·

North Carolina's political "agitation" came to a boil in the presidential election of 1860. A strong showing by Whigs in state elections the previous summer encouraged that party's leaders to campaign actively for the Constitutional Union candidate, John Bell. Moreover, they were heartened by the national Democrats' recent division into Northern and Southern wings at their second party convention in Baltimore. North Carolina's Whigs boasted that they offered the "only national candidates for President & Vice-President in the United States." Meanwhile, North Carolina Democrats held two conventions. The first consisted of Douglas supporters who, like the Whigs, sought a national compromise over slavery. The second Democratic meeting supported Breckinridge for the presidency. At that meeting, North Carolina's governor warned of war if Lincoln were elected.

In this contest, Washington County planters were divided. Local Breckinridge Democrats believed the Union already destroyed and prepared for war, although men of a similar cast of mind elsewhere in the South remained cautious. Josiah Collins, the county's largest planter, his wife and his sons, George and Arthur, all declared themselves secessionists. Charles Pettigrew, in the past a staunch Whig, also supported Breckinridge, but with great reluctance. He saw the national leaders among the Breckinridge Democrats as "moderate" men who vowed secession only in case of Lincoln's election.[6] By contrast, Bell's Whig advocates in Washington County took a more sanguine view of the political situation. William Pettigrew, for one, believed it "wisest for the South to fight her battles in the Union." He argued that the Republican party "will probably be shattered into pieces in the course of the next four years: After which we may again be in the ascendancy." In the meantime, however, should Lincoln win and then attack slavery, the South would be justified in "punish[ing] the aggressor."[7] Finally, a handful of Douglas Democrats sent Uriah W. Swanner to a Democratic anti-secessionist convention held in Raleigh.[8]

On November 8, 1860, Breckinridge defeated Bell in North Carolina by a small margin, 48,539 to 44,900 votes. But in Washington County, Bell polled a strong majority, as he did in most counties around the Albemarle Sound. Bell received 413 votes, Breckinridge 159, and Douglas 44. Lincoln, of course, did not appear on any ballot. The vote confirmed the Albemarle Sound area's opposition to secession and set it at odds with the governor and General Assembly. But it also placed the region in opposition to the new Lincoln government.[9]

In Washington County, Lincoln's election had a profound effect. On Saturday, November 10, the news reached Charles Pettigrew. He predicted a "great commotion," which, in fact, began immediately. After word of the election's results reached Plymouth, many of the Bell men rejoiced and became filled "with such violent party dislike" that they had an "exhibition of fireworks." Other unionists, men "mostly in the society No. 2," as one planter put it, began to show red, white, and blue badges. In contrast, the Breckinridge men in Plymouth, who began to wear blue cockades, remained calm but now advocated secession openly. Politics in Washington County had polarized between secessionists and anti-secessionists, with those supporting the federal government in the majority.[10]

The consensus of Southerners working within the Union had dissolved. Charles Pettigrew lamented, "It is a great misfortune to the country that the south cannot be united; I fear it will be ruin and bring civil war."[11] But the polarization of local politics threatened to undo more than merely the relation of states in the Union—it could undermine the local antebellum political leadership. Planters feared that the "better class of the people will have very little to do in forming" a government now. Should secession come, they expected "much violence and much lawlessness."[12]

After the election, "the whole talk of the country" around the Albemarle Sound focused on "the condition of politics." South Carolina's secession became the point of contention.[13] There seemed "little to hope for from the General Government." It appeared to planters that "the intention of the North [is] to reduce the South to the condition of a conquered provence." One planter warned that "when we become convinced that there is nothing but subjugation before us, we will not hesitate to adopt such measures as will be necessary for the security of our rights."[14] To this end, North Carolina's governor called for a February vote to approve or reject a constitutional convention to be held in March 1861. The convention's members would be selected in the same election and have unlimited powers.[15]

· **III** ·

In early February 1861, Whigs across the state turned their attention to the proposed state secession convention which they hoped to prevent by defeating the proposal in the upcoming referendum. Charles Latham, a prosperous yeoman farmer and Washington County's representative in the legislature, organized the local effort. Before the war, he more than any other man had engineered the county's Whig coalition between planters and yeoman farmers. He, thereby, manipulated his election to local office throughout the 1850s. But times had changed after 1859. A reduction in property qualifications enacted in North Carolina had shifted the center of power in the county toward smaller farmers. That antagonized planters who now in the midst of political crisis wanted one of their own, not a yeoman farmer, to represent the county's interests at the convention.[16]

During the fall of 1860, Latham had attempted initially to interest Henry Short, a fellow yeoman farmer, in running for the convention seat, but Short flatly refused. Perhaps, he could hear the murmur of disgruntled planters in the political background. Whatever the case, Short suggested William Pettigrew as a compromise candidate. Latham agreed and told Short, "Get Pettigrew if you can"; then "you will have no trouble in the County."[17]

To this choice, the county's large planters responded enthusiastically. In a letter to Pettigrew, a committee of Washington County Whigs pledged their "hearty support," and another forty-three local residents signed a petition requesting that he stand for election.[18] These men ranged from the very wealthy to the miserably poor. A. H. Garrett owned nineteen hundred acres of land valued at $22,000 and produced ten thousand bushels of corn in 1859. By contrast, J. W. Davis farmed sixteen acres of land worth $20 and grew only 110 bushels of corn. Most of Pettigrew's supporters, however, fell somewhere in the middle range of farmers. More typically, John Durden owned fifty acres of cleared land for planting and 150 acres of timber, useful for making cypress shingles and grazing livestock. Durden valued his farm at $1,200.[19]

To the entreaties of these men, William Pettigrew acceded. The planter had never held public office. He always had preferred to work his will in state and local government through his friends and associates. But a secession convention would debate and alter fundamental issues in North Carolina as no other body had done since the Revolution. Pettigrew felt the matter deserving of his personal attention. On February 14, therefore, Pettigrew wrote a gracious letter to C. H. Willis, a planter who lived in Plymouth, setting forth the basis on which he proposed to attract local voters to his candidacy.

Pettigrew began with a reaffirmation of classical republican values. The planter stressed that he did not seek office, the office sought him. But now he owed his services in "this day of trial" to his "state & country." He, therefore, would accept the nomination, not for his own advancement, but for the good of the community. Moreover, he argued that "changes are constantly occurring, a month being as full of great events as years formerly were; which disqualifies one from saying to-day what will be wisest or safest for North Carolina by the middle of March." Therefore, he must "go untrammeled" to the convention. Finally, William Pettigrew outlined his position toward secession. If North Carolina's "citizens and property" could be protected within the Union, then the state's interests might be served best there. If not, North Carolina must be considered "a subjugated province at the mercy of a lawless, unprincipled, unrestrained, dominant party, trampling upon the Constitution, and refusing such additional Guarantees as our safety at home as well as abroad demand." In such a case, something must be done, but he declined to say what that might be.[20]

The planter directed his artful letter to both planters and small farmers who had two interests in common—civil liberties and property in land. He promised to both groups happiness and security for their interests, whether in the Union or out of it. More telling is what Pettigrew chose not to say. The planter neglected to mention the possibility of war. In such a case, poor men would fight while planters commanded, a prospect not likely to produce many votes for Pettigrew. The planter also failed to mention slaves or slavery, choosing instead to subsume that topic under general references to the protection of property. This was a letter calculated to appeal to Washington County planters and yeomen both, to unite the two groups around common interests, and to bury potentially divisive issues. In limiting the scope of public discussion, the planter acted on a knowledge of potential challenges from both opponents and proponents of secession.

On the one hand, Pettigrew anticipated trouble from property-less whites. He knew of a similar situation in Badwell, South Carolina, where his uncle, James L. Petigru, a much abused anti-secessionist, and a cousin lived. His cousin warned that "in our country to go against the *sovereign* voice is to be a target for every leveller to discharge his vituperation." The reference to "levellers" doubtless reminded Pettigrew of Washington County's slave patrol and its invasion of local plantations. Moreover, he surely recalled that since the easing of voting restrictions, the yeomanry, always an important part of the local Whig constituency, had become an essential counterweight to the opinions and actions of swampers and laborers. The difference between levellers and yeomen lay in property owning, if only of land. Pettigrew, therefore, astutely stressed the protection of property, if somewhat vaguely so as not to offend yeomen who had little interest in slaveholding.[21]

On the other hand, Democrats threatened to identify the Union with the Republican party, thus making secession inevitable. William Pettigrew's friend James C. Johnston, a planter who lived in Edenton across the Albemarle Sound, provided useful arguments to counter the Democrats' efforts. He told Pettigrew that South Carolinians, dominated as they were by elitists, could never "live under any other form of Government than a Despotism." "Davis will act the part of 'pro-*consul*,'" Johnston warned, "and rule [the South] with a rod of iron." "I know no man so well calculated to be first emperor of the Southern Confederacy." Therefore, should secessionists dominate the constitutional convention with its unrestricted powers, Washington County planters, mostly Whigs, might find themselves obeying the dictates of a handful of Democratic politicians in Raleigh without recourse to an electorate.[22]

To counter such a possibility, Washington County Whigs proposed to bind local planters and yeoman together, as they had done before the secession crisis, in opposition to elitist Democrats and leveling poor whites. In the effort, William Pettigrew foresaw little difficulty. His brother's wife stated flatly that "William . . . will have no opposition."[23]

· **IV** ·

The secession campaign did not turn out as the Pettigrews had anticipated. On February 19, 1861, Washington County Whigs met in the courthouse at Plymouth. About three hundred men gathered, many of whom had come to town for the spring session of the county Superior Court. At an appointed time, Captain M. Bowen, a prominent Whig planter, motioned that Uriah W. Swanner be elected to chair the meeting. After a voice vote, Swanner took the chair and entertained a motion by Colonel E. W. Jones, an attorney and the county's militia commander. Jones proposed that a committee of three from each of the county's four militia districts be formed "to report resolutions for action of the Convention."[24]

All of this appeared routine enough, but it was not. The chairman, Uriah Swanner, had run for the legislature as a Douglas Democrat the previous fall. He was strongly pro-Union. Moreover, Swanner got himself appointed chairman by a group of his yeoman friends who had entered the courthouse early and voted with few others present. William Pettigrew considered Swanner "hostile to my election." Moreover, only two of the twelve men appointed to the resolutions committees could be considered Pettigrew supporters. One man, John C. Johnston, had signed the original petition drafting Pettigrew for the Whig nomination, and the other, D. G. Cowand, a Plymouth merchant, was a close friend, business ally, and occasionally personal secretary to William Pettigrew. The remaining ten men had no evident public or private connection to the planter. These arrangements did not bode well for Pettigrew's candidacy.[25]

After the committees had been formed, each left the courtroom to consider resolutions in private. In the meantime, the chair recognized Henry A. Gilliam, an attorney and friend to William Pettigrew, and allowed him to speak on the candidate's behalf. Then the planter himself rose to address the audience.[26]

William Pettigrew began by stressing the experiences all Washington County residents shared. He appeared before his audience not "as a politician, but rather as one of yourselves, one whose thoughts & feelings & interests are all closely identified with yours." Moreover, he reaffirmed the value of legitimate opposition. "In a free country like ours we must be permitted to differ on questions of minor importance." Having honored the disagreements among local residents, he now argued that a question of fundamental importance lay before the voters in which they all had a single interest. "It is a matter of political existence."[27]

Pettigrew then outlined the central question he proposed to address in the coming campaign. In the planter's view, power had been produced in North Carolina since the Revolution by means of a constitutional compromise. "The great & good men of the Revolution" induced these "13 sovereign, independent states to enter into a confederacy, with the express understanding that each was to retain all its rights except those that were relinquished to the General Government." "Gentlemen," he went on, "this is a government of concessions & compromises. It was formed by them & cannot last without them." But what those compromises included Pettigrew did not say.[28]

The difficulty now lay in efforts by Northerners, particularly abolitionists and Republicans, to redefine the terms of that compromise. "Why for 30 years," Pettigrew complained, Northern reformers had been "instituting aggressive measures against the Rights of the South," measures that in recent years had "increased in bitterness & malignancy, until they resulted the 6th Nov. in the election of Abram Lincoln." "Now fellow citizens," Pettigrew argued, "the time has arrived when this ever disturbing question of northern aggression upon the South must *cease.*"

He stopped short of saying how it should cease. Instead, the planter launched into a detailed exposition of the standard constitutional unionist plea for national unity and a lengthy history of efforts to compromise the interests of the North and South. He concluded: "I love this union & desire its preservation if it can be preserved honorably; if it cannot be, I love my country, my state & her institutions."[29]

Pettigrew had spoken for an hour. In that time, he had managed to mention the Constitution's three-fifths compromise, the extension of "southern rights" into the territories, and "other propositions"—meaning the fugitive slave law—without once referring to slavery. His speech constituted a masterful effort to sweep under the political rug all of the issues that divided planters and yeomen in Washington County. But his focus on national issues and a thinly disguised defense of secession drew him away from themes that earlier he had used to persuade yeomen of their ties to planters. Gone were references to the sanctity of property or the importance of defending civil liberties. Now the planter attempted to invoke vague loyalties—common residence and attachment to the state of North Carolina. Pettigrew himself had moved significantly toward the firebrand position he had ridiculed earlier among South Carolinians. As he and other large planters dug in to defend slavery, they had less to concede to yeoman farmers.

When William Pettigrew sat down, his friend Henry Gilliam rose to commend the planter's lengthy remarks and to place Pettigrew's name in contention for the Whig nomination. Then to the astonishment of Pettigrew and his friends, a man named Hanks nominated Charles Latham for the same position. Latham was the county's Whig representative in the legislature and the very man who had arranged Pettigrew's nomination just two weeks earlier. A moment later, one of Latham's friends proposed that "the Latham men should go on the left-side of the aisle & Pettigrew men on the right." Pettigrew sat on the judge's bench to observe the result. The planter "had no doubt but that a large majority" favored his nomination. On Latham's side, he observed "25 to 50 town boys not entitled to a vote." But at that point, Latham's men "became very noisy," while Pettigrew's men remained quiet. After much milling around, it became impossible to correctly count the votes.

Pettigrew insisted that "the Latham men should go out at one door & the Pettigrew men at the other." "This was disregarded," however, and "entire disorder prevailed." No one could make an accurate count, and soon most of the men had moved out onto the street. At that point, Swanner took it upon himself to declare Charles Latham the Whig nominee. William Pettigrew charged that Swanner had made no count and had no knowledge of whom those in attendance actually favored. Then, Pettigrew's supporters announced his candidacy. The race was on. Two Whigs would contest for the convention seat.[30]

What had gone wrong? How could Latham have changed his course in the space of a few days? What did the challenge to Pettigrew mean? Evidently, Latham had noted the shift of opinion toward secession among Whig planters only days before the caucus in Plymouth. He knew that such a position would not sit well with yeoman farmers in Washington County and threatened to split the yeoman constituency from planters, which would mean the end of the local Whig party. Latham, therefore, set out to reshape the local party in an image appealing to yeoman farmers. He became an unconditional unionist.

Meanwhile, William Pettigrew inadvertently aided Latham's efforts by accepting the support of local Democrats. This enabled unionists to portray the planter as an enthusiastic secessionist. Latham pointed to Pettigrew's relatives, chiefly brother Charles, an avowed secessionist, and brother James Johnston Pettigrew who already had accepted an officer's commission in the South Carolina army. (The unionists again conveniently chose to ignore James L. Petigru.) In addition, Latham had taken the precaution of posting notice of the Plymouth meeting only in the northern half of the county. Pettigrew lived in southern Washington County, and he presumed the move an effort "to prevent my friends from being present." Latham's tactics worked. At the Plymouth meeting, one unionist "approved of [Pettigrew's] speech" but supported Latham because "Pettigrew's two brothers were secessionists." The man reasoned that "Mr. William Pettigrew could not therefore be sound."[31]

· **V** ·

William Pettigrew, however, did not give up. Too much was at stake. He returned home Wednesday, February 19, to prepare himself. He and Latham would meet to debate at Plymouth on Friday, Long Ridge on Saturday, Lees Mill on Monday, and on Tuesday in Cool Spring, his home militia district (which included the Scuppernong and Newland neighborhoods). The election was scheduled for Thursday, February 28, 1861. For this round of debates, Pettigrew wrote an entirely new speech in which he returned to the themes that earlier had attracted yeoman farmers—protection of property and civil liberties—in addition to an appeal to common experience.

At Plymouth, Pettigrew expounded at some length on the past he and his listeners shared, "the memories of battles fought & victories won" in the American Revolution, "the memories of our heroes." The planter then shifted his focus to the crisis at hand. North Carolina must ensure "the security of her property & her honour," the main issues that lay before the proposed convention. He, however, declined to elaborate further. Instead, Pettigrew laid the blame for this "threat" upon the Republican party which, he argued, still could concede certain "southern rights" that would prevent North Carolina's secession. But if those "rights" could not be secured, then the state must leave the Union. The planter ended as he began. He talked at length about the past that all Washington County residents shared. "I have lived among you" he told his audience, "for more than 40 years, with but little interval. I have grown gray among you. I have aspired to no office, to no honours. I have lived among you as quietly & as unobtrusively as the humblest citizen. I have wronged no man. I have despised no man."[32]

Afterwards, Latham gave a speech in which he declared himself a Union man and publicly blasted Pettigrew for representing only the views of large planters. As evidence, he pointed out that the "respectability" or "slaveholders" at the party caucus in Plymouth "all voted for Pettigrew." But Latham reserved his most sensational charges for private discussions among the county's small farmers and laborers. To them, he argued that the planter, if elected, would, "in a few days time, hurry the state out of the union." To lend credence to his characterization of Pettigrew, Latham contended that the planter, in fact, had received a telegram from his brother James Johnston Pettigrew, then in South Carolina, urging William "to go to the Convention & hurry the state immediately out, without giving her time to breathe." Less credibly, Latham charged that Pettigrew intended to seek revenge for unionist opposition to his candidacy. While he reportedly "shed tears," Latham told his fellow unionists that Pettigrew intended to "cause all his poor children & wife to be put to death, as well as the children of all who heard him." Finally, Latham declared himself the "poor man's candidate."[33]

In the end, Latham succeeded in turning the county's yeoman farmers against William Pettigrew. By election day, unionists near Plymouth had worked themselves into a "furious agrarian spirit." Latham's friends in the town walked the streets "with their coats off anxious to fight any who might think differently from them." Not surprisingly, Washington County's unionists dominated at the polls. In Skinnersville, Latham received 76 votes to Pettigrew's 33; in Lees Mill, the count was 87 to 13; and in Plymouth, 219 to 83. Pettigrew triumphed only in Cool Spring, where he got 147 votes to Latham's 14. Overall, Latham defeated Pettigrew 392 votes to 276. The yeoman farmer's efforts also mobilized the county's voters against the constitutional convention itself. By margins similar to the delegate vote, farmers in Plymouth, Lees Mill, and Skinnersville defeated the proposal. Only in Cool Spring did voters favor the convention.[34]

Statewide, secessionist Democrats suffered a crushing defeat. North Carolinians turned down the convention proposal by roughly a two-thirds majority. Similarly, about two-thirds of the delegates elected came from the Whig party. Whiggery and the cause of constitutional unionism had triumphed, especially around the Albemarle Sound.[35]

The Whig victory, however, concealed as much as it revealed. In Washington County, the campaign had severed a large yeoman constituency from planter leadership. Yet, Charles Latham and his unionist supporters had wrought nothing permanent. They had attracted some small farmers and laborers to the Whig party with vague statements about the Union. But nationalism carried little weight in this distinctly local society. The Union remained an issue, not an enduring interest, as property claims had been. Latham admitted as much when he ran a purely negative campaign; he attacked Pettigrew because he had nothing substantive to offer small farmers and laborers. Therefore, little stood in the way should secessionists attempt to restore their power by rebuilding a local coalition of interests in land. Washington County planters required only some threat to the state government that guaranteed farmers their "rights" in property.

· **VI** ·

On March 4, 1861, Abraham Lincoln rode with President James Buchanan in a carriage up Pennsylvania Avenue to the Capitol. In short order, Lincoln was sworn in and began to address the audience. He confronted the South directly and boldly, warning Southern leaders that the Union had been formed in perpetuity years before the authors of the Constitution put pen to paper. In so saying, the president implied that the Union superseded any constitutional compromise over slavery. Therefore, an effort to void the Union in order to preserve slavery would be considered "revolutionary or insurrectionary, according to circumstances." The test, he went on, would focus on federal property and revenues. He warned that "the power confided in me will be used to hold, occupy and possess the property and places belonging to the Government, and to collect the duties or imposts."[36]

Initially, Lincoln's address neither satisfied nor offended North Carolina Whigs. Whig leaders criticized Lincoln's determination to protect federal property. They argued that any such effort would lead to a confrontation between the Northern government and Southern state troops. Moreover, Southern Whigs began to indulge themselves in thinking that Lincoln would refrain from acting on his own words. Many Washington County planters also held this hopeful interpretation of the political situation: "The Washington administ[ration]," one planter thought, "will find it farther to their interest to abandon the coercive policy altogether" and let the Southern states secede peacefully. For the moment, an uneasy peace settled over North Carolina and the Albemarle region. All awaited a confrontation, the first sign of federal "coercion."[37]

"Coercion" came at Fort Sumter in Charleston harbor, South Carolina. The government in Washington refused to vacate the installation on the grounds that it remained federal property even after South Carolina's secession. On April 4, 1861, Lincoln sent a relief expedition to reinforce the fort's garrison. In doing so, he acted on the pledge made in his inaugural address, the very one North Carolina Whigs had persuaded themselves he would ignore. In response, on Friday, April 12, South Carolina troops fired on the fort, forced its surrender, and thus, civil war began.[38]

News of the battle did not reach Washington County until several days later. On Tuesday evening, April 16, secessionists on the north side of the Albemarle Sound celebrated by firing their guns late into the night. Slaves at the Lake Phelps plantations listened closely to the echoes. The next day they reported the commotion to their masters, perhaps in hopes of learning its meaning from the white folks. On Wednesday morning, the news finally reached Plymouth, where secessionists also celebrated. The noise could be heard clearly at Magnolia plantation twelve miles from town.[39]

Within a week, Washington County's leaders, both planters and yeomen, had papered over their differences. In Plymouth, Whigs held an emergency meeting where all "pledged to forget the past & unite for the present & the future." As one man put it: "Mr. Lincoln seems determined to carry out his views, and so I see nothing left us but to secede lawful or not, and join the S. Confederacy. If any thing can restore peace I see at present nothing else to do it."[40]

At issue now lay only the question of who might be chosen to represent the county in a new secession convention. In response to Fort Sumter and Lincoln's call for seventy-five thousand troops,

Governor John Ellis had issued a proclamation summoning a special session of the General Assembly to meet on May 1. Its sole purpose was to authorize the election of delegates to a secession convention.[41] Charles Latham, the county's representative, agreed to support the convention bill, and he suggested William Pettigrew as a candidate for the convention seat. Latham now seemed "desirous of presenting such a candidate as would effectually allay all old party feelings." He urged that "all differences" between he and Pettigrew "be forgotten."[42]

William Pettigrew agreed to run. He faced no opposition but campaigned anyway, hoping to unify for the war effort all elements of Washington County society. On April 26, Pettigrew spoke in Cool Spring. "The day has arrived," he argued, "when every man among us, let him be whom he may, rich or poor, strong or weak, peaceful or contentious, saint or sinner, must take his stand by the side of his country or against it." There would be no middle ground, no compromise, most importantly, no unionists among secessionists. All must submerge the various political and economic interests that divided Washington County residents.

Pettigrew then attempted to justify the formation of a new nation. He argued that "a southern confederacy now constituted an accomplished fact." Those states had established themselves as a nation in a perfectly legitimate manner—legitimate because the safety of all Southerners required separation from a Union controlled by Republicans who had demonstrated "undying hatred to the South, hatred to her soil, to her people, to her institutions." Pettigrew also attempted to undermine the legitimacy of the federal government. Republicans had rejected all attempts over the past decade, he claimed, to compromise differences between North and South. They clearly did not want any government in which Southern interests might be represented fairly. Pettigrew pointed to Lincoln's call for seventy-five thousand troops, which he took as proof of the Republicans' desire to rule the country by force and without popular support. Pettigrew believed the Union now destroyed. His listeners must choose to support either family and community or a Northern despotism.[43]

Given such a choice, what could Washington County residents do? Little it would seem, except to urge North Carolina's immediate secession. Yet, political matters had not become as sharply defined as Pettigrew portrayed them. The candidate admitted as much himself when he begged his listeners: "Think not of preserving the Union." "Talk not of peace." For many people in the county, union and peace remained possibilities. To counter such sentiments, Pettigrew shifted his emphasis in a later speech from choices to obligations. When the planter spoke at Columbia in Tyrrell County on May 4, he stressed the reciprocal duties of a nation and its citizens. "Your country owes you protection; she owes you wise, just & wholesome laws. You owe her obedience; you owe her, if required for the defense of her soil, the service of your strong right arm; the service of a brave heart; and, if it must be so, you should be willing to lay down without a murmur even your life on the Altar of your country," that country now being the Confederacy.[44]

In the end, Washington County voters elected Pettigrew almost unanimously. He received three hundred votes, but this constituted a very small turnout compared to the 662 votes cast in the previous convention campaign.[45] The election, in fact, had become a dead letter. The state would secede whether Washington County voters approved Pettigrew's nomination or not. But the vote did have a distinctly local meaning of some consequence. It was the first measure of public opinion taken after the breakup of the local Whig party's coalition of planters and yeomen based on a common interest in property. In making that vote unanimous, planters demonstrated that they could mobilize their dependents in the county and prevent others from wielding power. Local planters could count on roughly three hundred men to support the Confederacy, about the number from Washington County who would join the Confederate army over the next four years. But what of those who chose not to vote? The documents are silent on this point, but it is fair to assume that they were unionists. They numbered perhaps 350 men, roughly the number who would join the Union army during the war.

In April 1861, William Pettigrew and his friends succeeded in rallying planters and their dependents to the Confederate cause. But they did not rebuild the coalition of planters and yeoman farmers that had constituted the local Whig party for decades. Pettigrew failed to provide small landowners with any compelling reason—such as protection of property—to support planter politicians. He made it clear that the Confederacy had little to offer yeomen beyond bellicose nationalist rhetoric. At the same time, Pettigrew revealed the limits of his own commitment to majority rule. The planter did so as he elaborated on the duties local men owed the new Southern government which they had not approved.

When yeoman farmers failed to give secession a vote of confidence, local planters might have taken the hint. The time was ripe for a new round of hard bargaining between the two parties. Instead, planters attempted to militarize the disaffected, having failed to mobilize many small farmers and laborers by political means. In doing so, secessionists hoped to subsume the interests of unionists to those of the new Southern nation.

· **VII** ·

In April 1861, the work of organizing local troops fell to H. G. Spruill, a planter and mayor of Plymouth who had been appointed in 1832 as general of the militia around the Albemarle Sound. Spruill responded to a general order issued on April 20 by Robert F. Hoke, the adjutant general of North Carolina, which called for thirty thousand men to be mustered and equipped by themselves and their friends. When the troops arrived in Raleigh, they would be commissioned and armed. "We are organizing for home defence," Spruill told his fellow planters. "Every man must face the music. The people should immediately organize with the best & boldest officers. & strict vigilance is necessary."[46]

In Washington County, planters formed three bodies of North Carolina volunteers destined for state service. Henry A. Gilliam, the attorney, organized the first company composed of men from Plymouth. D. G. Cowand, the merchant, recruited a second Plymouth company and became its captain. In late May, both companies received orders to sail to Ocracoke Inlet on the Outer Banks. Finally, Charles Pettigrew organized a company of ninety volunteers from Washington and Tyrrell counties, although he did not volunteer for service himself. The company elected E. C. Brabble as its captain but did not receive marching orders immediately.[47]

Yet, local volunteers did not flock to the Confederate cause. They had to be cajoled. Like small farmers and laborers in many parts of the South, they found this a rich man's war and a poor man's fight and believed that the purpose in fighting was to secure the property of slaveholders. In this, many yeoman farmers and white wage laborers had no interest. To counter such logic, Richard H. Wills, a local Methodist minister, instructed planters in his sermons to focus not on slaveholding but on the institution of slavery. He conceded that "a large majority of the population own[s] no negroes." But he went on to argue that all have a faith in the institution. The "whole South, as a section, as a body, (some exceptions maybe) believe that slavery is right." Therefore, while farmers and laborers might not have a direct material interest in slaves, they might be persuaded to consider slavery a part of their community's social fabric.[48]

There also remained the problem for planters of how to militarize those men who refused to volunteer for the Confederate army or those men too old for state and national service. Local planters turned to the county's militia for a solution. But no one knew if a militia could be organized. For ten years, Washington County had seen no muster of local troops; General Spruill had received no returns from his captains, and in turn, Spruill had made no report to the adjutant general. The general, in fact, believed that "all the militia offices" had become "obsolete." Others, however, disagreed. In late April, Colonel E. W. Jones, a unionist acting on an antebellum commission, held elections for officers in the Washington County militia. But at the same time, the North Carolina legislature repealed all former laws governing the formation and conduct of local troops. Therefore, all militia offices in North Carolina became vacant. No one in Washington County had the authority to organize a home guard.[49]

Spruill's difficulties in mustering a home guard, however, may have proved a blessing in disguise. With the secessionist volunteers stationed outside the county, most of those who remained in the Albemarle region favored the Union. Richard Wills noted that "there seem to be a good many [in the county] that are not willing to enter in to the defense of their country."[50] Washington County planters had girded local secessionists for a defense of the Southern nation and the Albemarle Sound region. But planters had failed to militarize the entire local population. A large number of farmers and laborers declined to serve the Confederacy and remained at home. They now constituted the only men available for defense of the county.

The ever cautious William Pettigrew responded by ordering from Baltimore one thousand cartridges and one thousand percussion caps for a carbine, one thousand cartridges for a Smith and Wesson repeating pistol, an additional pistol plus ammunition, a bowie knife, and a musket or rifle with appropriate ammunition. "Perhaps, ere long," Pettigrew thought, "it will be next to impossible to procure weapons; it is therefore but a prudent forecast to be prepared immediately for any emergency."[51]

· VIII ·

In the spring of 1861, the crisis of the Union jeopardized planters' local political power and, hence, their interests in land and slaves. They, therefore, found it needful to submerge their lesser differences and unite around fundamental interests. Yet, they found it impossible to persuade yeoman farmers to join in common cause against the Union. Why this was so remains a mystery in the absence of direct testimony from yeoman farmers. We may speculate, however, that yeomen correctly perceived that they had little to fear from a federal invasion. The threat to property that so exercised planters, in fact, applied mainly to a certain species of property—slaves. Besides, the Republican party had its origins in the efforts of small landholders to secure their interests. Landowning formed a part of the Republican creed—free soil, free labor, free men—and yeoman farmers might rule the county in their exclusive interests if federal troops occupied the area.

In the secession crisis, planters and yeoman farmers, united in the Whig party before the war, had begun to compete for a constituency among the county's poor farmers and laborers. Those men split among themselves, some perhaps hoping to remain in the employ of planters or to lease land and timberlands, others seeking in this war an opportunity to seize the resources which might make them yeoman farmers too. Hence, the county divided, but not strictly along class lines. This would be a rich man's war and a poor man's fight, but it would not be a war between the rich and poor. In Washington County, that would come after 1865.

Washington County planters understood this reasoning. Hence, their representative in the Constitutional Convention quickly abandoned all pretense of government by a majority of voters. Thereafter, they sought undemocratic means by which to rule. They demanded troops to garrison the region. Failing that, they attempted to organize local militia groups so as to secure planters' interests from the disaffected. Such efforts did not pass unnoticed by the planters' opponents. In the next few months, unionists developed a plan and the means to enforce their will against local planters and their clients.

2

The Yeoman Challenge

· **I** ·

On Sunday, June 23, 1861, Ellsberry Ambrose attended services at Concord Church in the Newland neighborhood in south-eastern Washington County. Afterwards, Ambrose stood in a crowd of his friends and relatives and neighbors chatting about crops, weather, livestock, and all manner of country concerns. Then, the talk turned to politics. A farmer named Durham Oliver told Ambrose that he would go with him and "carry the pole" if Ambrose would "bring it." Andrew Bateman, standing nearby, inferred from the drift of the conversation that Oliver meant to display the "Old Union Flag." Ambrose concurred in Oliver's plan. Moreover, the two unionists declared that they would raise the federal flag on Bateman's farm on July 4. Bateman did not object to this. Ambrose boasted that, if the other unionists did not act, he would "go by [him]self and [therefore] have a better chance." But Ambrose believed that there were "a good many" who would help him.

At that point, Durham Oliver began to have second thoughts. He warned Ambrose that "if he did not mind" what he said, at least publicly, he would get himself "into trouble." "They," presumably meaning the county's magistrates, "would order out the militia and take him." But Ambrose answered, "No they won't." Oliver then demanded to know, "How are you going to help it?"

After all, "You have got no powder and shot." Ambrose replied, "Yes, I have got plenty of it." And besides, Ambrose asserted, he lived "in a free country," and he "be damned" if he did not do as he pleased.

Ellsberry Ambrose then launched into a lengthy attack on local planters and their support for secession. He declared that the Union was "not destroyed." It was "as good as it ever was." Ambrose went on to use much other "violent language" about North Carolina and the part it was playing in the secession crisis. Moreover, Ellsberry Ambrose warned that in the coming war "the rich people were going to make the poor people do all the fighting." But another man pointed out that "the rich had volunteered as well as the poor." In reply, Ambrose claimed, "The rich people only pretend to go" into the army. And they did so just "to get the poor ones off." In this fight on behalf of the wealthy, Ambrose was determined to take no part. He told his fellow churchgoers that he would "never muster under a secession Flag." According to one report, he "threatened violence" to any person who should "attempt to compel him to muster." This was no idle conversation. Durham Oliver testified that Ambrose appeared "perfectly sober," and Oliver judged Ambrose to be "by no means an ignorant man."[1]

Had Ellsberry Ambrose spoken for himself, his remarks might have drawn little notice from the county's planters. But Ambrose was a substantial citizen in the Newland community. In 1860, he cultivated 206 acres on a farm valued at $1492—two-thirds in land and one-third in livestock.[2] Ambrose was also well connected with his neighbors. His compatriots, Durham Oliver and Andrew Bateman, poor men themselves, lived within a mile or two of Ambrose's farm, besides attending the same community church.[3] And six other Ambrose families lived in Newland. All operated farms smaller than eighty acres. Some apparently farmed on rented land or for shares.[4]

Three days after Ellsberry Ambrose had spoken his mind, Josiah Collins and Henderson B. Phelps, two of the county's largest planters, met as magistrates at Phelps's house in the Newland community. They convened a court of inquiry to act upon a complaint lodged by Durham Oliver alleging a disturbance of the peace by Ellsberry Ambrose. The complaint gave an account of Ambrose's remarks. Then it reported Oliver's "fear" that Ambrose's statements might "be repeated, and so result [in violence and bloodshed] if persisted in and not checked." But the complaint failed to identify the man who first spoke of raising a Union flag at Bateman's farm—Durham Oliver himself. Very likely then, Oliver testified against Ambrose in exchange for immunity from prosecution for his own role in disturbing the planters' peace.[5]

Whatever the case, Josiah Collins and Henderson Phelps wasted little time in arresting their man. Within hours, the local constable found Ambrose and hauled him before the two magistrates still at Phelps's house. After an examination of witnesses, Ellsberry Ambrose was bound over to the September term of the Washington County Superior Court. The two justices set Ambrose's bond at $2,000, though the usual bond for such an offense was only $150. The bond required Ambrose "to keep the peace and be of good behavior towards the citizens of the State of North Carolina and not to offend again in like manner in substance or in tenor, or in matters having like tendency." Should Ambrose fail to keep the peace, he could be "committed to jail until discharged" by the Superior Court. In such a case, Ambrose would have no choice but to remain in the county prison until the court convened in September 1861. Finally, the magistrates charged Ambrose "for all the costs of these proceedings."[6]

Ellsberry Ambrose experienced no difficulty in raising the excessive bond, pledging on the next day some of his own property to help secure the obligation. But several friends and neighbors also volunteered to spread the risk among themselves. These men included T. S. Hassell, Isaac M. Bateman, Zepheneah D. Spruill, Jordan H. Phelps, and Ashby Phelps. Each lived within a mile or so of Ambrose's farm, probably along Ambrose Road, on the northern edge of Newland. They all grew grain and tended livestock mainly for their own subsistence, much like Ellsberry Ambrose himself.[7]

Thereafter, Ellsberry Ambrose remained silent. But in his place others spoke out as he had earlier. Unionists in the Newland community, for example, threatened to shoot through a certain Confederate flag flying in the neighborhood. William Pettigrew had made a gift of the flag to a man named Levi W. Ambrose. Similarly, a group in Plymouth led by (C. H.?) Willis, Woodhouse, and

Bennett opposed secession vigorously and publicly in late June.[8] At about the same time, Henderson B. Phelps, the planter and also militia captain for Cool Spring, was "informed on good authority" that the district's yeoman farmers "won't muster under the flag of the Southern Confederacy." Worse still from Phelps's viewpoint, local farmers proposed "to get up a company to muster under the Yankee Stripes."[9]

In response, local secessionists implored William Pettigrew, by then at the secession convention in Raleigh, to seek the immediate appointment of a secessionist militia colonel for the county. Henderson Phelps argued the necessity of quick action "so the officers of the county can have authority" to organize and discipline local farmers. William A. Littlejohn, a militia major residing in Plymouth, urged the same and hinted of disloyalty not only among the county's common men but also among local militia officers. He urged Pettigrew to persuade the governor to appoint a man other than Colonel E. W. Jones, then current militia commander for Washington County and an avowed unionist. "We must have someone," wrote Littlejohn, "who will not only reorganize but keep the militia on an effective footing, and that is more than Col. Jones can do." Littlejohn offered himself as a likely candidate for the commander's position.[10]

Local unionist leaders, meanwhile, divided among themselves. Charles Latham, the county's representative in the General Assembly, attempted to preserve what remained of an alliance between planters and yeoman farmers in the Whig party. He "apologized" to planters "for some of his friends who [had] openly declared that 'Lincoln had done nothing wrong, nothing unconstitutional, nothing but what his oath of office constrained him to do.' " By contrast, Colonel Jones broke with the planters completely and attempted to build a class-based constituency for the local Whig party. He "openly proclaim[ed] in the public streets, in the presence of poor men," that, in the colonel's own words, "this present war will at the South make the poor man poorer and the rich man richer, while at the North the rich man will become poorer and the poor man will become richer."[11]

Other poor men, however, did not wait to be organized by Jones and other leading unionists. By the first week in August, farmers and laborers living near the Long Acre Road in southwestern Washington County had formed a mutual aid society. Its members pledged to support each other in the event of a "draft for the war." And they vowed to oppose "any arrest that may be made" and to compensate members for "damages sustained by reason of their opinions or conduct." The unionists also organized themselves into a private militia and elected officers "from the captain downward." At first, they observed a rule of secrecy to prevent harassment by planters. As one observer wrote, they "refus[d] to communicate any information" concerning the organization. But in mid-August, these same unionists held an open meeting during which they approved several unionist resolutions, declaring among other things that they would neither muster for the county militia nor pay taxes to support the Confederate war effort.[12]

By mid-summer 1861, Washington County's yeoman farmers had articulated a unionist position and gained a constituency among some farmhands and shinglers. And planters had succeeded in silencing one unionist leader, Ellsberry Ambrose, only to see others rise to take his place. Yet, all was not lost in the planters' view. They continued to control local courts and the militia. Hence, Washington County's political affairs might yet be managed to the Confederacy's benefit, unless some greater force intervened.

· **II** ·

At ten a.m. on August 28, 1861, a federal fleet pulled alongside the Confederate Forts Clark and Hatteras located at Hatteras Inlet. The inlet formed a break in North Carolina's Outer Banks about eighty miles southeast of Washington County, and it provided the only deep-water passage between the Albemarle Sound and the Atlantic Ocean.[13] The fleet had departed from Fortress Monroe, opposite Norfolk, Virginia, two days earlier. On August 28, federal warships began bombarding the forts at Hatteras. Meanwhile, several troop ships made their way to a beach three miles north of the inlet. These ships carried the 9th New York Volunteers commanded by Colonel Rush C. Hawkins. The New York soldiers, many of whom later would occupy Plymouth, made two attempts to land but turned back after several of their boats broke up in the surf. The next day, they made another attempt at about eight in the morning, landed successfully, and quickly stormed Fort Hatteras.[14]

In all, the federal forces, commanded by General Benjamin F. Butler, captured 750 Confederate soldiers, 1,000 guns, 75 kegs of powder, 31 cannons, and 3 boats in addition to the forts. The men captured at Hatteras included all the secessionist volunteers from Washington County; on August 29, two companies (roughly 120 volunteers) surrendered to federal officers.[15] Captain Henry A. Gilliam, the Plymouth attorney, lay injured after the battle. A few of his men managed to escape to New Bern on a small steamer. "One or two" reportedly "died on the way."[16] But most of the Washington County soldiers gave up voluntarily and were transported by ship to a federal prison on Governor's Island in New York harbor.[17]

Shortly after news of the Confederate defeat reached Plymouth, many planters and their families fled the county for places further inland. Although they had no way of knowing federal plans, it seemed safe to bet that the federal army would use Hatteras as a base from which to push inland.[18] To calm their fellow planters, William Pettigrew and his friends organized a secessionist rally in Plymouth on September 10, where Pettigrew actually repeated a speech he had delivered at Cool Spring on July 4. In their confusion, local planters could find no way even to think about the specific threat federal forces posed to their lives and property.[19] Other Washington County planters occupied themselves in scarcely more constructive activities. They searched high and low for a scapegoat and found one close at hand in C.S.A. Brigadier General Walter Gwynn who had supervised the defense of the Albemarle Sound.[20] In the reorganization that followed, Brigadier General D. H. Hill, a North Carolina native in Confederate service, was appointed to succeed Gwynn.[21]

Later however, secessionists rallied to defend their interests in the region.[22] During the first week in October, two "intelligent and worthy citizens from Washington County" pleaded their cases before Asa Biggs, a resident of Martin County (located across the river from Plymouth), a judge in the Confederate court, and a prominent secessionist Democrat. "In consequence of the volunteers being taken away" from Washington County, the two doubted "whether there is a reliable majority of the people in case of invasion." They admitted that few unionists spoke publicly in favor of Lincoln's government. Still, "there is that indifference which excites distrust." Moreover, the planters argued that unionists, those men who earlier had organized themselves secretly, especially infested the southwest portion of the county near the Pamlico River. Should Confederate forces hold Roanoke Island and block entry by water to the Albemarle Sound, an invading army could pass easily with unionist help through that portion of the county on its way inland.

Other Washington County planters, meanwhile, appealed directly to the Confederate government. During the last week of September 1861, William Pettigrew and two others traveled to Richmond, in Pettigrew's words, as a "self-constituted committee to the government."[23] In a personal interview with Jefferson Davis, the planters complained of an "unsound feeling [that was] beginning to manifest itself" around the Albemarle Sound. "The subject of who will & who will not take the oath to Lincoln's government," William Pettigrew noted, was "frequently spoken of" among those people "more attached to the old Union than the new government." Worse, Pettigrew told the secretary of war, "rumor says that a man of some wealth & influence in one of our towns who was an early secessionist publicly declared that he would take the [Federal] oath." The same planter vowed to "advise his friends to do the same" and to invite the federals to drink with him.[24]

In response, the Confederate adjutant general told the Washington County delegation that "the government [was] well aware of the importance of North Carolina & that [it] would make every effort to defend the state." The secretary of war, however, replied with more caution, saying that he would "take the matter under advisement."[25] In the end, the War Department authorized a transfer of a small number of Confederate troops from Virginia to eastern North Carolina. Another company of Washington County volunteers, commanded by D. G. Cowand, were among those soldiers assigned to Roanoke Island.[26] The government in Raleigh, for its part, dispatched five thousand troops to the coast, but none occupied Washington County. To compensate, the local militia general, H. G. Spruill, ordered guards posted along the Sound's shores and on the Roanoke River.[27]

Unlike panicky planters, unionists around the Albemarle Sound did not seek outside intervention, but they did act in the knowledge that federal authorities intended to encourage their efforts. General Burnside and his officers had been heartened by the unionist sentiment they found on the Outer Banks and in Hyde County. And Colonel Rush C. Hawkins, commander of the 9th New York Volunteers which had occupied Hatteras, issued a proclamation to unionists that circulated throughout eastern North Carolina. In it, he assured area residents: "We come not to destroy, but to secure place and uphold the laws of the United States. The rights of property and persons will be respected and protected."[28]

Unionists, therefore, took the fall of Hatteras as an opportunity to organize themselves and to develop an alternative vision of local society. By early September 1861, they had begun to understand the Great Rebellion as a "property war." Many of those who lived "on the edge of the swamps" thought that "if the Yankees succeeded, the rich men *wld* be forced to divide with them & all share alike." Even visitors noticed how boldly local poor men asserted their claims. A certain Judge Dick, a Superior Court justice from western North Carolina, commented on what he saw and heard in Columbia, the seat of Tyrrell County, located just four miles from Scuppernong. There he listened to the conversation of a few men, probably swampers and laborers, whom he called a "low drunken set." They spoke openly enough in favor of the Union so that Dick had no trouble identifying them as "unsound." Moreover, they revealed that yeoman farmers and swampers had organized themselves around a certain neighborhood leader, "one bad man," as the judge put it. In short, unionists around the Sound had been transformed by the events at Hatteras into the "most thorough agrarians."[29]

· **III** ·

Washington County planters attempted to head off trouble with local unionists by scheming to keep their leader, Ellsberry Ambrose, at bay. On September 10, Washington County's Superior Court met in Plymouth, Judge Dick presiding, and it considered a charge of treason against Ambrose in place of the earlier charge of disturbing the peace. The grand jury chosen for that session included William Pettigrew. The other large planters from the Scuppernong neighborhood, Josiah Collins and Henderson Phelps, would act as plaintiffs in the case. Pettigrew anticipated no opposition to their position, but Colonel E. W. Jones, an attorney and the county solicitor, had other plans. He sympathized with local unionists and hoped to remain commander of the county militia with their support, which he sought to gain by keeping Ellsberry Ambrose out of jail.[30]

While the grand jury remained in session that morning, Jones sent Pettigrew a note. It requested that the planter confer with Jones "on a subject of importance." When the two met shortly afterwards, the solicitor told Pettigrew that he wanted to know whether the foreman intended to bring the Ambrose case before the grand jury. At that point, Jones placed a pile of papers connected with the case in Pettigrew's hands. But the solicitor did not hint that they contained anything other than the testimony taken down by Phelps and Collins. Pettigrew then made a grievous error; he failed to read the documents. The papers, in fact, included a recommendation to dismiss the case, which Pettigrew implicitly approved by his failure to object.[31]

Meanwhile, William Pettigrew guilelessly explained his position in the Ambrose case. The planter told Jones that he feared the difficulty "of convicting a person of treason." The problem, simply put, was that the law required an act endangering the safety of the state, not merely harsh words such as Ambrose had spoken. Pettigrew, therefore, felt apprehensive "that if the case were tested in Court," the planters "would fail to convict him." Should that occur, Pettigrew told Jones, the outcome "would render the cause of the south weaker and disloyalty stronger among our people." To all this, Jones supposedly "expressed his approbation." Then, according to Pettigrew's report, Jones told the planter: "If [you] did not think proper to take the case up at this time, it might be deferred until another Court." But Pettigrew later could not remember clearly whether he or Jones had originated the sentence.[32]

What did Jones (or perhaps Pettigrew) mean by "deferred"? In fact, the term could refer to several different courses of action. Pettigrew claimed later that he told Jones, "Let it [the court's decision] be suspended over him; it will be a restraint on him, and should any subsequent Court think proper to act in the case, they may do so." By using the word "suspended" Pettigrew apparently intended that the solicitor enter a plea of nolle prosequi which would have halted prosecution of Ambrose. In such a case, the accusation of treason would remain on the books and local magistrates could require Ambrose to post bond indefinitely. Then in the future, should Ambrose cause serious trouble, his case could be brought before a grand jury for indictment at any time. But Jones did not interpret "deferred" to mean that he should seek a continuation of the case. Instead, the solicitor moved to dismiss the charges. Judge Dick, being an outsider and ignorant of the political implications in the case, made no objection to the motion. Neither did William Pettigrew. He had left town about noon, before the court came to order. Therefore, Ellsberry Ambrose went free after paying court costs.[33]

· **IV** ·

In the case against Ambrose, secessionists struggled not only to silence an articulate unionist but also to discourage a leading candidate for the position of militia captain in the Cool Spring district. The district was crucial because it encompassed most of Washington County's largest plantations in the Scuppernong and Newland neighborhoods. Josiah Collins lived there—so, too, did William Pettigrew, his brother Charles, their friend Henderson B. Phelps, and others. Whoever commanded the local militia would determine during the war all claims to property, including slaves.

Control of the local militia, moreover, had become increasingly problematic as a result of a new state-militia law approved by the North Carolina General Assembly on August 20. Among the new law's many provisions, section ninety-two required that all current officers must be registered immediately by the local commander, usually a colonel, with the adjutant general's office in Raleigh. This provision was intended to allow militia commanders quietly to dismiss incompetent officers who had received appointments as an honor before the war and to rid themselves of unionists in the ranks. Local commanders could simply fail to forward certain names to the state government. But in the case of Washington County, Colonel Jones turned this law to the unionists' advantage. In late September, he composed a very select list indeed for the adjutant general that failed to record the names of any Washington County secessionists. Among those neglected was Henderson B. Phelps. Phelps had been elected captain of the Cool Spring militia in May, 1861.[34]

To fill the several captain's positions that Jones had reported vacant, the colonel called for militia elections to be held on October 24, 1861. In the Cool Spring district, three candidates openly campaigned for the captaincy—Henderson Phelps as a secessionist; a second secessionist whose name has been lost; and Henry Ambrose, a unionist and small subsistence farmer from the Newland community. Henry Ambrose (perhaps related to Ellsberry Ambrose) farmed strictly for his own subsistence on fifty acres of land—half improved and half unimproved. In 1860, he owned a horse, a milk cow, two beef cattle, and six hogs. Henry Ambrose lived modestly, within his means, and, very likely, without recourse to commodities markets or credit. He could afford to oppose local planters.[35]

We do not know how the two secessionists campaigned. Some of those who listened to Henry Ambrose, however, left a record of his remarks. For example, Joseph B. Davenport—a substantial planter, a local constable, and Henderson Phelps's neighbor—questioned Ambrose closely at a public gathering held the third week in October. He was accompanied by another man, L. B. Davis, who also vigorously queried the unionist. This was perhaps a part of an organized campaign to harass Ambrose; Davis had been elected the previous May as Henderson Phelps's first lieutenant in the Cool Spring militia.[36]

At that meeting, Henry Ambrose declared himself a "Union man." But Davenport rose and demanded to know what Ambrose meant by that. Do "you mean a union man is a Lincoln man, or not?" Ambrose answered: "I am a Lincoln man." There was no hesitation; no equivocation. Davenport then posed a string of similar questions to Ambrose. In every answer "all his conversation was in favor of Lincoln." "I am a Lincoln man," he repeated, "&

I do not care who knows it." "I am in favor of Lincoln & opposed to the Southern Confederacy."

Henry Ambrose then clarified his opposition to secession. He contended that, in fact, North Carolina had never legally left the Union, presumably because the secession convention appointed by the legislature lacked authority. It, after all, met without the approval of North Carolina's voters and never submitted the articles of secession to a plebiscite. Ambrose then blasted William Pettigrew for his role in these undemocratic proceedings. "I never voted for Pettigrew," he cried. And turning to L. B. Davis he declared: "Any one who voted for Pettigrew was a damned fool." "God damn [Pettigrew] to vote North Carolina out [of the Union]." The yeoman further vowed he would "be damned if any one [who] voted for Jeff[erson Davis] ought not to be hanged—or any Secessionist" for that matter. Finally, Henry Ambrose threw down the gauntlet to all Confederates present, predicting that "there will be more secessionists hung than union men."[37]

When Henderson Phelps heard reports of Ambrose's campaigning, he became desperate. Local public opinion had begun to shift toward the Union. Phelps had to stop Henry Ambrose. But how? As a magistrate he could order Ambrose's arrest on a charge of treason. But he hesitated. The arrest of Henry Ambrose would transform the farmer into a political martyr. What could he do?[38]

On Sunday morning, October 20, Henderson Phelps sent a note to William Pettigrew in which he begged, "I am a J.P.; I am aware you are not [and hence ordinarily do not give legal opinions]; but I want your advice." Phelps told Pettigrew that Joseph B. Davenport and L. B. Davis had come to him the night before with reports of Henry Ambrose's unionist talk. Phelps forwarded a copy of the evidence to Pettigrew and requested that the planter examine the papers "and give me your opinion whether you think the testimony sufficient to convict Ambrose or not." Should Pettigrew think a conviction likely, Phelps further sought the planter's aid "about writing the warrant." Phelps sent the message by a slave and requested that Pettigrew immediately "answer by the boy."[39]

In his reply, Pettigrew argued that Henry Ambrose should not be arrested. Besides the political consequences, there remained the fact that Ambrose had committed no treasonous act. Hence, the unionist could never be convicted, even if charged. Pettigrew, therefore, advised Phelps to apply for military intervention. "I would suggest," wrote Pettigrew, "the propriety of your addressing a letter to Gen. Hill," commander of the military district in northeastern North Carolina, "enclosing a copy of the Oaths made to you last night by the two witnesses." But what could Hill do that Phelps could not? Pettigrew pointed out that the general "knows what is actionable and what is not; where the Civil Power ceases, and where the Military should commence." In a word, the general could try the case before a military tribunal. And if Hill chose to do so, he need not empanel a jury of Ambrose's peers (all unionists by then) to try the case.[40]

William Pettigrew, however, did not trust his neighbor to act decisively. Phelps was frightened and cowed. Therefore, Pettigrew took it upon himself to address General Hill. "There will be an effort made on Thursday next to elect a Union, or Lincoln, man captain of the Company in this District—Cool Spring," the planter wrote. Worse, Pettigrew had learned that a unionist triumph was almost certain. "It is deeply humiliating that there should be such instances of disloyalty among our people." "Yet, humiliating as it is, I hear from various sources that it is true." Pettigrew then hinted that the army should stop the election. He expressed his "gratification" for Hill's "military control of north eastern North Carolina." And he wished the general "success." Pettigrew and his friends, however, had acted too late. Phelps failed to arrest Henry Ambrose. And Hill did not respond until some days later.[41]

Unionists in the Skinnersville district, meanwhile, waged a similar campaign. They were led by a farmer named James Cahoon, a poor man indeed. He cultivated just one acre of land and grazed his livestock, four hogs worth twelve dollars, on ten acres of unimproved land. He judged his farm worth a total of $125.[42] Perhaps Cahoon's poverty, and that of men like him, accounted for the different character of the militia campaign in Skinnersville.

James Cahoon, of course, repeated the standard unionist position that prosperous yeomen expected to hear. In a conversation with Asa Steely, a moderately well-to-do farmer, Cahoon called himself "a Union man," and told Steely that he "stood up for the Constitution [and] would not fight for the South." He further asserted that "if [he did] any fighting, he would fight at home, and then he would be good for two or three of them [meaning secessionists]." To a different man, Cahoon said, "I am a Black Republican and let them take me up." Other unionists, however, threatened a more fundamental change in the local social order. Some in Skinnersville "avowed themselves in favour of John Brown's raid," wrote one planter, "& expressed a determination to institute it in their own county." In addition, the unionists threatened to "organize a company in opposition to the regular Company headed by Capt. [Henderson] Phelps."[43]

During the last week in October, militia elections were held as scheduled throughout the county. Unionists won all four officers' posts in Cool Spring by large margins. But at the last moment, Henry Ambrose withdrew. In his place, Ellsberry Ambrose ran for the office. The two evidently had struck a deal. Henry would campaign publicly while Ellsberry spoke in secret to his friends and neighbors. Meanwhile, unionists in Skinnersville experienced similar victories. There, voters elected unionists to the posts of captain, first lieutenant, and second lieutenant. A secessionist was elected third lieutenant. The voting in every case turned "only on the ground of the loyalty of the one & the disloyalty of the other."[44]

· **V** ·

Having lost the militia campaign, planters now sought to invalidate the results. While still at the Cool Spring militia grounds, William Pettigrew drafted a petition to Governor Henry Clark. In it, Pettigrew recounted recent events and argued that the unionists planned to rule the county, impose their "Northern views" on local secessionists, and give the county up to the Yankees when they invaded. Pettigrew's fears were probably well-founded. Wilson Hatfield, a unionist and second lieutenant–elect in the Skinnersville district, boasted after the election: "Now we have our own officers elected. [Therefore,] we intend to go back to the old United States' laws." He went on to say that there was "no law but the United States law." "No other law will we obey," he concluded and swore that he would never "take an oath to support the Southern Confederacy." From this and similar statements made at Cool Spring, William Pettigrew concluded that "the election of Ambrose in the Cool Spring District is but a part of an organized plan to transfer the allegiance of the County of Washington to Black Republicanism."[45]

When he put down his pen, William Pettigrew sought out secessionists remaining at the militia grounds to sign his petition. Many had left "in consequence of the day being far advanced," but twenty-eight men affixed their signatures to the paper. The list included Cool Spring's leading planters, of course.[46] But most of those who agreed with William Pettigrew were not wealthy. Among the signers were small planters who required access through large planters to markets and credit outside the county.[47] Other men had forged different dependent connections with the district's largest planters. Josiah Collins's sons, the two ministers he supported, the schoolteacher who lived at Somerset Place, and the medical doctor who treated his many slaves all signed. Then, there was a large group of landless men (who do not appear in the agricultural census), probably laborers employed by Collins and his friends.[48]

On October 28, William Pettigrew traveled to Raleigh bearing his petition. In a meeting with Governor Henry Clark, Pettigrew presented "the memorial," as he called it and "various other papers & certificates having reference to the disloyalty existing in the County of Washington."[49] But in the end, the governor decided to wait for General Hill's response to Pettigrew's earlier call for intervention.[50]

D. H. Hill did not disappoint them. On October 31, the general dispatched to Washington County a squad of twenty-one Confederate cavalrymen. The troops traveled under sealed orders and reached Cool Spring sometime Friday night. Up before dawn, the troopers appeared at Ellsberry Ambrose's house in the Newland community at five o'clock "in the midst of a storm of wind and rain." When Ambrose in his nightshirt answered a knock at his door, he was confronted by seven soldiers, one of whom pointed a cocked pistol at him. They told him to "put on his clothes & come instantly," but nothing more. Evidently, there was no arrest warrant. Ambrose had no way of knowing with what he might be charged or by whom. And the men did not tell him. Ambrose put up no fight, but he did plead for his life, arguing that he had not caused the conflict now underway in Washington County. He declared that "the leaders," evidently meaning planters, "were to blame."[51]

For the moment, Ambrose's arrest had the desired effect. As the unionist's captors traveled along the road to Plymouth, the procession "excited the greatest consternation." Unionists had every reason to fear the rebel troops. One of the soldiers "had a large rope around his horse." And according to a secessionist report, "every man who felt he had acted suspiciously trembled for his neck." "There was," one planter reported, "the greatest panic" among the unionists. Just "a day or two" later, secessionists found it "impossible to find a Lincolnite" in the county. Ten days after Ambrose's arrest, the Confederate presidential election was held, and by one planter report, "Cool Spring turned out to a man—a larger vote was polled than has been known for years." "Never," thought another planter, "did any tree bear such quick fruit."[52]

Perhaps. But William Pettigrew anticipated renewed opposition from yeoman farmers and their more radical constituents eventually. He thought it "probable" that "in the course of the next fortnight . . . the arresting of Ambrose may produce some decided effect on the minds of the disloyal." The planter, therefore, wrote to Governor Clark again, begging that Confederate troops be sent to the county to control the local militia companies. In the end, Clark dispatched three Confederate companies—one composed of men recently recruited from the Plymouth area and commanded by Captain McRea and two others from outside the county. Pettigrew applauded the action. But he argued that some of the troops came from too close by. The Scuppernong Grays from adjacent Tyrrell County had been recruited from around Columbia near the Newland community. He explained that the "efficiency" of such troops "might be marred by the fact of their relationship or acquaintance with the people." These men very likely would refuse to shoot their unionist neighbors and kin.[53]

William Pettigrew also proposed a thorough reorganization of the local militia. But how? New elections would produce more unionist officers. That was unacceptable. The solution lay in abandoning democratic procedures altogether. Pettigrew urged the governor to ignore the recent militia election results and to commission illegally all the officers elected previously in May. "This, I am aware," he wrote to Clark, "would be in contravention to the 92nd sec. of the Militia Law." "But," the planter argued, "the exigency of the case appears to justify and ever to require some assumption of power by the Executive." Such a plan, however, could undermine the legitimacy of the new statewide militia organization, largely because unilateral and illegal action had no constituency except among a handful of planters in eastern North Carolina. To ease the political difficulty, Pettigrew offered to push an ordinance through the Constitutional Convention later in November that would "sustain the action of the executive and authoriz[e] it in similar cases during the continuance of the War." By these measures, Pettigrew and his planter friends "look[ed] forward to having the spirit of disaffection promptly crushed."[54]

· **VI** ·

Washington County secessionists, meanwhile, sought ways closer to home with which to "crush" unionists. Acting as magistrates, local planters arranged to "elicit" an "array of testimony" from unionists that would convict them of sedition and treason. A few exemplary individuals hanged or imprisoned would serve to inhibit local unionists in their words and actions. D. G. Cowand, who before the war had acted as Josiah Collins's personal secretary, put it this way: "I think [Ellsberry] Ambrose and the other Captain [Cahoon] should be arrested, tried, found guilty, & shot. This is the only way to treat them." Such action, he continued, would "show the rest that they will face the same and soon you will have none to say they aid or sympathize with Old Abe."

Planters had good reason to believe that such tactics would work. The arrest of Ellsberry Ambrose, wrote William Pettigrew, already "has had the salutary effect of causing the disloyalists around us to vote largely for Davis & Stephens." "This apparent repentance," the planter went on, "is the result of fear of the strong arm of military power rather than any change of sentiment." There was no mistaking the effectiveness of brute force. Washington County's magistrates began their campaign of judicial repression immediately.[55]

Uriah Swanner, a former Whig politician and ex-county sheriff now acting as a magistrate, ran the planters' inquisition. In choosing Swanner, a substantial yeoman farmer and also a slaveholder, secessionists executed a deft political maneuver. Swanner had represented the interests of small property holders for years, and he possessed a reputation for standing up to the county's planters. He was, after all, the man who had allied with Colonel Jones to oppose Pettigrew for the secession convention seat. Therefore, Swanner had connections and credibility among yeoman farmers. If anyone could gather information on unionists, Swanner could. But why should he? Although Swanner left no record of his reasoning, it is likely that he reacted to the shifting composition of Washington County's unionist coalition. Swanner could accept property holders who espoused the benefits of free soil as many yeoman farmers then did, but he could not bring himself to associate with propertyless laborers who spoke of John Brown law, who defined the local struggle as a "property war" and who urged the use of violence against planters. The opposition against planter rule had gone sour for Swanner. Now he sought to make his political amends.[56]

On November 8, 1861, Uriah Swanner began taking testimony. Some statements simply repeated unionist sentiments uttered earlier. After the militia election in Skinnersville, the captain-elect there, James Cahoon, declared himself a "union man." In the election, he had "stood up for the old constitution" and called himself a Republican in public. Moreover, Cahoon told his listeners that he would "not fight for the South." If there was any fighting, he vowed to "fight at home." Calvin Chambers, a bit more enthusiastically, cried out in public: "Hurra for the man that takes the South dead or alive." Similarly, when asked if he opposed the Southern Confederacy, Henderson Spruill answered: "Yes I do say I am apposed to it." After the election, however, some unionists took a more menacing tack. Wilson A. Lamb "wished that all the seceders were in a bag over the Gulf [Albemarle Sound?], and he, Lamb, with his cutlass to cut them down." When cautioned by a secessionist for using such language, Lamb rebuffed the man. Lamb concluded, "I will not be a seceder."[57]

Men such as Lamb interpreted the war as more than a battle between secessionists and anti-secessionists. Some viewed it as a fight between rich and poor, the issue between them being the control of land and labor. According to one planter's account, the unionists "assert [that] they are the poor man's friends & wold only take from the rich." Moreover, "some have gone so far as to declare [that they] wld take the property from the rich men & divide it among the poor men." In the opinion of Caroline Pettigrew (Charles Pettigrew's wife), "After the [militia] elections these agrarians, for such they really are, threw off the mask." "Their success transported them," she reported, "beyond caution & [therefore] many threats against the worthy and respectable citizens of the county were uttered."[58]

Obadiah Chambers, for example, was a swamper, probably a day laborer or shingler, who, perhaps, poached timber as well to make ends meet. He farmed no land and had no identifiable connections to planters in Washington County. Sometime after the fall of Hatteras, Chambers carried on a casual conversation with L. Harry Spruill, a secessionist. Chambers inquired of Spruill, "What's the news?" Spruill replied, "Not much of any importance." Chambers went on, "Hav[e] you heard those guns[;] do you know what it means?" But Spruill did not know. Chambers commented almost to himself: "I am anctious to here." "So am i," Spruill added: "I am in hopes our men at Roanoke has retaken Hatteras." Chambers replied with surprise: "I be damb if I do." Spruill then repeated his wish and added that he hoped "every other Yankee on the Southern Coast" would be driven off. Chambers now took offense. He asked Spruill, "What do you suppose we poor men would do if it ware the case?" Well, thought Spruill, "We will do better when we gain our independence than we ever have done [in the Union.]" Now Chambers was incredulous. "Do you think," he queried Spruill, "they will ever be a southern government established?" Spruill replied, "I do." Chambers then said, I'll "be dambed if I dont hope my head and all my limbs [?] may be cut off before there ever is a southern government established in the southern states."[59]

Obadiah Chambers was not through. Joseph P. Patrick, a slave-owner, testified that he had asked Chambers if he "would cast a voat to take away my negro." Chambers replied, "I will be god damb if I wouldent." Evidently aghast, Patrick then accused Chambers of being an abolitionist, but Chambers denied it and called Patrick "a damb liar." Then, confused, Patrick demanded to know "what kind of a man you are." "I am a John Brown man," Chambers declared, "and damb my sole if i dont carry out John Brown law."

Chambers and his fellow swampers proposed to destroy slavery in Washington County and with it the slaveowners whom he believed kept poor whites impoverished. Chambers, thereby, hoped to create at one stroke a constituency of blacks and swampers that would support yeoman-farmer rule. He would not settle for speaking idle words and printing ineffectual tracts as the abolitionists had done. Like John Brown, he committed himself to violence against the rich on behalf of the poor, both black and white. To all this, Patrick expressed defiance. But Obadiah Chambers had the last word. He told Patrick that he "should be whiped" along with his "damb party," and "damb bad whiped" too.[60]

To carry out their revolt, some Washington County unionists proposed to enlist the area's slaves in their cause. They may have begun their campaign as early as the second week in May 1861. At that time, Josiah Collins found a note addressed to his slaves "exciting the negroes to *rise—calling* upon the *boys,* as it termed them at [Lake Phelps where Collins's plantation was located] to be in readiness." The note went on to say that "the volunteers," meaning the local troops now destined for Confederate service, "would soon be out of the county, & the whites would be defenseless, & then would be [the slaves'] time." According to one account, the note was "evidently written by an educated person—about the time Parsons left—so no doubt he was the very scamp dropping it." It is not clear, however, that this note represented a genuine attempt to encourage a slave rebellion. The fact that it had been "dropped" on the plantation suggests that its author composed the note simply to threaten and agitate Collins. Whatever the case, it did not persuade Collins's slaves to oppose his rule, if they ever saw the note. The "servants" at Somerset Place remained "well behaved."[61]

Later, however, some unionists began actively to recruit slaves in their attempt to harass Washington County planters. A certain Isaac Ambrose, for example, testified that John T. Phelps, a prosperous yeoman farmer living next door to William Pettigrew in the northern end of the Scuppernong neighborhood, came to his farm and spoke to his slaves of the prospects for emancipation. In 1860, he farmed 200 acres of improved land and 134 of unimproved and owned a few slaves. After the militia elections, Ambrose heard Phelps "say in the presence of several negro slaves, that the object of the Yankees was to free the negroes and place them on an equality with the white men." Phelps went on to say that he was willing to give up his own slaves and that "he would be damned if he did not join the Yankees when they came." Perhaps as an act of good faith towards the slaves whom he hoped would join the unionists, Phelps returned to Isaac Ambrose's farm later. There, he spent two days "with the negroes engaged in teaching [them] to spell and read."[62]

By late summer, the planters' campaign of judicial repression had failed. Worse, it offered local unionists a public forum in which to air their views and from which to build a political constituency behind their position. Chambers's few words and Phelps's actions posed a challenge to local political arrangements that planters understood as fundamental. A week after Uriah Swanner took testimony, Caroline Pettigrew wrote, "One monster had said after the militia election, 'Now we shall have John Brown law, now *we* will show *them!!'* " Doubtless to emphasize the importance of a biracial alliance in this poor people's war, the "monster" also "named some negro who *shld* go arm in arm [with] the daughters of a respectable citizen." Caroline Pettigrew knew then what must be done. "You see the wretches need strong hand upon them."[63]

Washington County planters did not hesitate to wield that strong hand. After the militia elections in October, the North Carolina governor, following William Pettigrew's advice, refused to commission the county's new unionist officers. Afterwards, a "reaction," as Pettigrew called it, took place. Planters reorganized themselves and their dependents—friends, relatives, and neighbors. They sent William Pettigrew back to Raleigh to seek an ordinance from the Constitutional Convention that would ratify the governor's action, and they scheduled new illegal militia elections. How they did so remains unclear. E. W. Jones could have called for new elections because the officers elected in October remained uncommissioned. But no evidence survives to indicate that Jones assented to such a plan.[64]

On November 18, militia elections again took place in the Cool

Spring district. Henderson B. Phelps ran against yet another of the Ambrose clan, Warren Ambrose. In the course of the morning's voting, only a very few men actually came to the polls. The county's secessionist volunteers remained out of the county, and most unionists refused to commit themselves publicly for fear of being arrested like Ellsberry Ambrose. But John Giles and two friends, plus "perhaps one of Ellsberry Ambrose's sons," made an appearance. They voted for Warren Ambrose, thus encouraging other unionists to do the same.[65]

Hence, about noon, Josiah Collins, acting as an election official, "discovered" an "informality" "in the manner of holding the election." Collins voided all the ballots cast to that point, including those turned in by Giles and his compatriots. Afterwards, Josiah Collins took Warren Ambrose aside for a private chat. "Some conversation" passed between them during which the planter gave the farmer "some good advice." What that included, the records do not say. We do know, however, that Collins's words left a strong impression on Ambrose. The farmer "in consequence" immediately "withdrew his name as candidate." Moreover, Ambrose allegedly declared that he did not "wish to cause a division among the people," and he supposedly professed "the strongest southern principles." Shortly thereafter, Collins reopened the polls. Now Henderson Phelps faced no opposition, not even from John Giles and company, who with several other unionists had left before noon, doubtless thinking their votes already counted. In the end, Phelps received the "unanimous" approval of "90 to 100" voters.[66] The next day, Josiah Collins traveled to Skinnersville district where he supervised a second militia election. But local unionists had learned their lesson at Cool Spring—their votes meant nothing. Secessionists ran unopposed for the three posts open there.[67]

Washington County planters rejoiced. Hardy Hardison, a local physician, summed up the feeling this way: "These elections show an improved condition among our people." Yet, he warned, planter rule rested on a very small and precarious base. Of the county's 700 eligible voters, 370 remained stationed elsewhere. And of the remaining 330, only about 100 could be counted on to support the secessionist cause. That left at least 230 unionists in the county. Hardison argued that "this gives to us who remain a more anxious charge with regard to those who may be unsound." Moreover, the small number of secessionists "makes it the more necessary that we may act promptly and summarily" against unionists.[68]

· **VII** ·

Having won the several contests for militia captaincies, Washington County planters sought to replace Colonel E. W. Jones with a secessionist. William Pettigrew approached the state adjutant general, requesting permission to hold the election immediately. The adjutant general agreed to do this, but only after he had received the official returns of Washington County's district-level elections. He then could commission the officers-elect, and they, in turn, could select a colonel. Two men jockeyed for the position—the current colonel, Jones, a unionist; and William A. Littlejohn, a major in the militia, a Plymouth merchant, and a secessionist.[69]

E. W. Jones was determined to control the local militia despite recent setbacks. When the election returns reached him, Jones sat on them for nearly three weeks. Then on November 20, he mailed the papers to General H. G. Spruill, the militia commander for the Albemarle Sound region and a resident of Plymouth. Spruill, however, as Jones well knew, had just left for a tour of his militia troops in Hyde County, taking with him Major Littlejohn. Therefore, when Spruill returned, he could hardly believe that the election results now rested in his hands. He had assumed that Jones would send them to Raleigh. "Why the report was not made directly to the Adj Genl," he wrote, "I cannot conceive"—but Littlejohn could. "By directing the returns to Gen H. G. Spruill," the major wrote, "nearly a week is gained"—for political maneuvering by Jones. Littlejohn noted that "the strict letter of the law may require this—but it was not done in the election before."[70]

In the time gained, Jones worked doggedly to assure his reelection. First, he traveled to Raleigh. What exactly he sought and to whom he spoke, we do not know. Very likely, he lobbied his friends in the state government, perhaps hoping that they could persuade the adjutant general to delay further the colonelcy election. Then, Jones returned home, where he issued an order calling for a general muster on November 30 in Plymouth of all the county's militia companies. With the troops assembled, the colonel hoped to have two companies, one from Plymouth and the other from Cool Spring, vote to divide themselves each into two new companies. That would create eight additional officers, most of them unionists. In the meantime, there was "much electioneering going on" in the county. Around Scuppernong, farmers from the Newland community spread a rumor saying that William Pettigrew's slaves at Belgrade had run their overseer, Malachi White, off the plantation. White denied the report. "Tha[t] is a fals-[hood]," he wrote to Pettigrew, "for I have not seen nothing like it." Doubtless, the unionists hoped to panic the planter into abandoning his seat at the convention and his efforts to get the county's secessionist militia officers quickly commissioned.[71]

On the appointed day, the county's militia met in Plymouth. There, Warren Ambrose "& others of that ilk," as one secessionist put it, presented a petition requesting that the Cool Spring district be divided into two parts. Evidently, the petition proposed that the line run along Newland Road. Such a division would have placed the Newland community and the area north of Concord Church in the same district. To the south, the plantations belonging to Charles Pettigrew and Josiah Collins, plus a handful of smaller farms, would form a second district. Unionists liked this plan for two reasons. First, it would create a district north of the road in which the unionist residents of Newland (including all the Ambrose clan) would dominate. Henderson Phelps, a Newland resident and militia captain for the neighborhood, surely would be defeated if he were forced to stand for another election, which Colonel Jones almost certainly would call if the division succeeded. Second, the new southern district, dominated as it was by planters and populated mainly by slaves, would have virtually no soldiers available for duty. Josiah Collins and Charles Pettigrew would become leaders without a following.[72]

Henderson Phelps and his secessionist friends countered by proposing to divide the district along the Scuppernong River. Both the Newland community and the Lake Phelps plantations lay south of the river. Therefore, planters might retain their influence and Henderson Phelps his post without the formality of a new election. North of the river lay William Pettigrew's plantation, Belgrade. Perhaps Phelps thought that Pettigrew, his friends, and his clients would dominate the new district. Or, perhaps Phelps simply hoped the colonelcy election could be held before unionists north of the river found time to organize an election for officers. In the end, the secessionists prevailed, and Phelps and his subordinates retained their posts while the new district had no officers for the moment.[73]

Colonel Jones, therefore, shifted his attention to the Plymouth district. He and his unionist friends originally had hoped to divide Plymouth into two parts also. But after Phelps maneuvered to dominate Cool Spring, the unionists proposed to divide Plymouth into three districts. This necessitated some slight bending of the militia law. The ordinance required that a certain number of soldiers be enrolled in each new district. Therefore, Jones was forced to use a muster roll that included men exempted from service for various reasons, such as age or infirmity. According to Littlejohn, the unionists "expected by those means certainly to obtain enough votes to defeat me." Jones and his unionist friends "expected" correctly. When the counting ceased, the unionists had produced a majority of the votes. The district was divided into three parts.[74]

Earlier, however, H. G. Spruill had written to the state adjutant general in Raleigh urging him to act immediately on the pending captain's commissions. On Friday night, November 29, Spruill received a reply. The letter commissioned some of the officers elected in late October and those chosen in the second elections in Cool Spring and Skinnersville in November, and it instructed Spruill to hold elections for a colonel at once. Spruill, presumably at the general muster on Saturday, therefore notified all the newly commissioned officers to be in Plymouth on Monday, December 2. On that day, seventeen officers voted—twelve for Littlejohn and five for Jones. The officers from Lees Mill (between Skinnersville and Plymouth) voted for Jones, as did the county's lieutenant colonel, a man named Johnston. That came as a surprise to local planters, for they had thought Lees Mill a secessionist district. But the vote had taken place before Washington County unionists could organize elections for officers in the two new Plymouth districts. Had they been elected and commissioned, the eight additional officers would have ensured Jones's election—thirteen to twelve.[75]

· VIII ·

Having secured the county's highest militia post, Washington County secessionists now hoped to purge their remaining unionist opponents. But this was no small task. The unionist officers had been elected legally, and they enjoyed great popular support in the county. Washington County planters, therefore, sought other means to dislodge the "Lincoln men." In November, they settled on a plan to charge each unionist leader with sedition based on the testimony Uriah Swanner had gathered earlier. There was only one hitch. North Carolina had no law against sedition. Consequently, local planters urged William Pettigrew to push an ordinance through the Constitutional Convention that would prohibit all speech, writing, and acts that expressed any opposition to the Confederacy, its officers, or its policies—never mind that Washington County's planters proposed to use evidence gathered before sedition ever became a crime.

Pettigrew, however, came away from the Constitutional Convention empty-handed. Both his ordinances were defeated at the hands of a majority composed of hostile Democrats and lukewarm Whigs.[76] Henceforth, local planters would have to rely on their own guile and the state's existing laws to ensure their rule. This they did. First, local planters again requested that the governor illegally refuse to commission "disloyal officers" recently elected. The petition presumably referred to the militia officers in Lees Mill who had voted for E. W. Jones in the colonelcy election. Second, they maneuvered to elect George Collins, Josiah Collins's son, to the captaincy of the militia district in Cool Spring. Finally, William Littlejohn, the new secessionist militia colonel, organized a movement to oust H. G. Spruill from his position as general of the militia around the Albemarle Sound. Littlejohn argued that Spruill paid far too much attention to the wishes of Washington County's voters. The general had displayed "a contemptible timidity of popular disapprobation."[77]

These measures, however, did not stop local unionists from harassing secessionists. In late December 1861, unionists focused their efforts on James H. Smith, Littlejohn's first lieutenant and a strong secessionist, who ran for the post in Plymouth vacated by Littlejohn. Charles Latham, E. W. Jones, C. H. Willis, and

Daniel Whitehurst organized an opposition against Smith, in the planters' view because he was "a true southern man and did not vote for Jones" in the colonelcy election. Moreover, local unionists complained that Smith had drilled his troops too long on the days they mustered in November—two hours at a time. But in fact Jones himself gave the order to drill long hours, a bit of information the former colonel had failed to reveal to his fellow unionists. In the end, the militia troops elected a secessionist captain. But local unionists had exacted their revenge for Smith's past opposition.[78]

In response to continued unionist activity, Washington County planters attempted one last time to intimidate unionist leaders. On November 27, Confederate troops captured Henry Ambrose and transported him to Raleigh to stand trial for treason. Local planters already had attempted and failed once to bring an Ambrose to trial on that charge. Now, evidently the military fared no better. By December 1861, Ambrose had returned to Washington County as a free man. In the end, local planters silenced Henry Ambrose as they had Ellsberry Ambrose earlier. In January 1862, Henderson B. Phelps and Josiah Collins, acting as magistrates, charged Ambrose with disturbing the peace and bound his case over to the spring term of the Washington County Superior Court. Phelps and Collins set Ambrose's bond at $2,000.[79]

· **IX** ·

After Henry Ambrose's arrest, Washington County planters rejoiced in the knowledge that "the agrarians, that movement is completely crushed." In December, a certain quietude settled over the county. Charles Pettigrew wrote to his brother William: "There is no news in the country. The people all talk strong for the Confederacy, I hope they may be honest."[80]

Washington County planters believed that they had survived their most serious political crisis since the mid-1830s. Unionists had mounted a strong challenge for control of the local militia. And secessionists had responded with force drawn from the state government. On the surface, planter power remained intact. But in reality, Washington County planters did not succeed in restoring the antebellum political order. They created a new and unstable political economy that relied solely on outside force to ensure their control of land and labor. No longer could they confidently expect deference from laborers and shingle makers who had worked for planters in the past. Some remained clients, some also serving in the Confederate army. But others now chose to ally themselves with the Union cause and to use that new power as a stick with which to beat their former superiors.

Unionist leaders, meanwhile, had forged a new political alliance among small-scale farmers and white wage laborers. (There is no evidence to suggest that any slaves responded to unionist overtures.) They set an entirely novel political agenda for themselves and their allies and defined the war as a battle between rich and poor. Specifically, they made the overthrow of Washington County's planters and the division of plantation lands among poor people the object of their struggle. To achieve this, they proposed to use violence, to organize themselves into militia companies, and to call upon the federal government to aid their cause. No longer did the county's political alliance center on protecting the interests of property holders, large and small. In its place, a coalition of poor people arose that focused on the distribution of property and the control of one's own labor.

In December 1861, Washington County's unionists lacked only an armed force equal to the North Carolina state troops operating intermittently in Washington County. In January, as the Burnside expedition approached North Carolina's Outer Banks, that was about to change.

Removal: The First Crisis in Paternalism

· I ·

In September 1861, after the fall to federal forces of Hatteras Island on North Carolina's Outer Banks, Major General John Wool, commander of the island, reported that "negro slaves" were "almost daily arriving at this post from the interior." They came in small groups, many traveling over one hundred miles from the counties bordering the Albemarle Sound.[1] At Columbia, Tyrrell County, about eighty miles inland, a certain planter brought his slaves to town, presumably for safekeeping. The militia had mustered there, and the town had a jail if he needed it. But shortly after their arrival, thirteen of the man's slaves quietly stole a boat and sailed for Hatteras, setting in motion a chain of events that quickly spread through counties all along the Albemarle Sound. Referring to the Tyrrell County slaves, one planter complained, "Other negroes know" about the successful escape. Therefore, the planter reasoned, "we may look for others to leave soon."[2]

In January 1862, U.S. General Ambrose Burnside led an expedition from Fort Monroe, Virginia, to North Carolina's coast that succeeded in capturing, among other places, Roanoke Island, strategically located at the mouth of the Albemarle Sound. That island soon served as a base from which the federal navy launched patrols far into eastern North Carolina. It also became a destination for thousands of slaves who escaped from plantations located alongside the Roanoke River as far away as 150 miles inland. For planters around the Sound, the proximity of federal forces posed a fundamental challenge to mastery over the remaining slaves. Shortly after the federal victory, many slaveholders removed their chattel property to counties in the North Carolina upcountry, hoping to preserve both their financial assets and their social power, in short, to reestablish their roles as patriarchs. For slaves, by contrast, Union troops provided hope and opportunity— hope that slavery might be abolished entirely and an opportunity in the meantime to secure some freedom piecemeal by small daily struggles.[3]

In those struggles, relations between planters and slaves would become strained as each sought to preserve their rights and privileges within a paternalistic framework, the rules of which had been worked out on a local and personal basis over decades. In those struggles, each side would expose to public scrutiny the social bases of the slaveholders' power—obscured to planters by their own ideology but obvious to slaves who had endured that personal despotism for decades.[4]

· **II** ·

In the spring of 1862, Charles Pettigrew arranged to move a few of "the people," as the slaves at Bonarva preferred to call themselves, to Cherry Hill plantation near Badwell, South Carolina, close to the home of his in-laws. In the third week of March, Charles Pettigrew directed Jackson, the head plowman at Bonarva, to lead a small expedition upcountry. Jackson outfitted himself with a wagon and several horses to haul supplies. The planter selected "five or 6 men & boys" to accompany Jackson. Pettigrew instructed his slaves to travel by way of Plymouth to Tarboro and then to Hillsboro in Orange County near the middle of North Carolina. There, Jackson and his companions were to rest a day or two before starting for Cherry Hill. Pettigrew hoped that the men might "be in time to accomplish something for their support" there.[5]

Jackson and his fellows complied cheerfully enough with their orders. Some of Pettigrew's other slaves at Bonarva, however, objected strenuously to the move upcountry. The trouble actually began in early March on brother William's Magnolia plantation nearby. The master there informed his slaves that he intended immediately to remove all of the men to the uncountry near Raleigh. But evidently after some consultation among themselves, the slaves at Magnolia plantation determined to resist. At any rate, neighboring planters believed the slaves' actions "to have been concerted." "They ran every man but two," reported Caroline Pettigrew, "when they rec'd their master's order."[6]

The slaves at Bonarva soon heard about events at Magnolia plantation, and they assumed that their master intended to act as his brother had. In fact, they were mistaken. In forwarding a few men to Cherry Hill, Charles Pettigrew simply attempted to cover all his bets. He had no desire or immediate plan to send more of his slaves upcountry. The planter thought the expense of moving them too great and the chance of growing crops at Cherry Hill sufficient to support them too small. But the slaves at Bonarva could not know plans that their master kept to himself. Therefore, when the news from Magnolia reached Bonarva, the slaves there "caught the infection & not knowing what they ran from took to the woods." The blacks followed two men, Prince and Jim, who appear to have been leaders in the slave community but who were somewhat younger than Jackson and the others who went willingly upcountry.[7]

Charles Pettigrew now faced his own private crisis in paternalism. He met it not with force but by dramatizing his role as the source of his dependents' livelihood. He immediately stopped the plantation mill at Bonarva from running. That prevented his slaves from grinding corn into meal, corn that they had grown on their own plots and stored in their own sheds. He also nailed shut the communal meat house in which the slaves stored hams and bacon that they had cured for themselves. Pettigrew took the added precaution of posting an armed guard at the meat house. Finally, the planter refused to issue any rations; "Not one ounce of provisions given out, women & children all without," reported Caroline Pettigrew cheerfully with a rhyme.[8]

The master of Bonarva had made his point. "You can imagine the consequences," wrote his wife. The next morning, all the men who had slept in the woods the previous night appeared ready to work. They evidently had decided to return as a group but not to submit under just any condition Pettigrew chose to impose. The group selected a "deputy" to negotiate with the planter. But the planter refused to speak with the man or with any of his slaves. The slaves then convinced Pettigrew's overseer, a white man named Jacob Spiers, to present their case. Again Pettigrew declined to listen. The planter simply ordered his slaves to work, and at last they submitted. He reported his slaves "humbled & subdued." "They went as quiet[ly] & orderly as possible," he told his wife.[9]

Charles Pettigrew had played the planter role perfectly. Using no physical force whatever, he had reestablished his position as the literal giver of life at Bonarva. The planter first showed by his actions that he could in good conscience starve his slaves before he gave up any power over them. He, thereby, demonstrated his own firm belief in the primacy of patriarchal power above all other considerations, humanitarian or otherwise. Second, he forced his slaves to confirm for themselves the peculiar nature of that power. This power proceeded from the planter downwards and admitted of no compromise or negotiation. Moreover, it required no agreement; patriarchal power implied no process of bargaining among equals. Finally, Pettigrew cleverly left two things undone in this little drama. The planter suspended judgment over his slaves, showing that he possessed the grace and goodwill of a proper master—in other words, he legitimated his own position. Then, he created a certain tension in leaving unresolved the question of punishments. That tension would serve to keep fresh in his slaves' minds the continuous surveillance over their every word and deed that a true patriarch always maintained.

Pettigrew, however, did not act with malice. He, in fact, sympathized with his slaves. He believed that their "aversion to leaving" resulted from the fact that "their families were to be left" behind. That may have been true, although the slaves' fears may have been more fundamentally at odds with the planter's interests than Pettigrew thought. They probably did not want to give up an opportunity to be freed when federal troops entered the county, as those soldiers almost certainly would eventually. But Pettigrew did not regret his harsh response to the slaves' actions. They, after all, had denied his authority both in lying out and in efforts to negotiate a settlement between planter and slaves. In the planter's view, his slaves' mistake resulted from failing to "ask their master" and to find out "more than they did" about his plans. Instead, "they followed evil counsel & thought they wold take matters in their own hands." Therefore, they must be punished. After "matters became more settled," Pettigrew planned "to sell the ringleaders," presumably Prince and Jim. The planter's power had been restored at Bonarva. But Prince and Jim had shown both the ability and disposition to conceive of things otherwise. Even if they submitted, the two slaves remained a danger to their master's rule.[10]

Charles's brother, however, possessed less confidence in his ability to manipulate his slaves. In early March, after William Pettigrew's slaves had lain out for several days, they returned to their homes. Then, the planter arranged for twenty-five Confederate cavalrymen to descend upon Magnolia plantation. The move took the slaves by complete surprise, and all were captured. That day, March 4, men, women, and children were loaded onto wagons guarded by armed troopers and transported upcountry. Charles Pettigrew "totally disapproved" of all this. He had good reason. William's actions implied that his slaves now had gone completely out of his control, and his obvious loss of confidence proved contagious among secessionist planters and farmers in the county.[11]

Jacob Spiers, Charles Pettigrew's overseer, succumbed to such fears one day in late March while his employer was away. In conversation with his friends, the overseer intimated that Pettigrew's remaining slaves had begun to organize an insurrection. This belief had no foundation in truth, but Spiers's friends understood his opinion to be a statement of fact. One man, a neighbor who lived close by, began to spread "wild reports" through the neighborhood of an "open insurrection" underway at Bonarva. A short time later, "a number of armed men" rode onto the plantation, roused the slaves out of their homes, and arrested those they could corner. Some of the men panicked and ran into the woods, among them Prince, who only "narrowly escaped being shot, just did miss him." The slaves in fact had been engaged that day in no activity at all, insurrectionary or otherwise. It had rained since early morning, and they, therefore, had stayed in their cabins. That fact notwithstanding, the vigilantes posted a guard of twelve men on the plantation with orders to await Charles Pettigrew's return.[12]

Pettigrew arrived at Bonarva about nine o'clock that night. "No sooner was it known that he had returned," reported Caroline Pettigrew, than all those who had fled into the woods reappeared on the plantation. They and the slaves who had been "arrested" now "rushed round their master, begged him 'never to leave them again.' " They told their master that "if he left" they would "go anywhere he said & at any moment." To the planter, his slaves "truely seemed rejoiced." "They really flocked about him as their friend & protector." In this, Pettigrew took considerable pleasure. The threat of armed intervention from slaveholding farmers renewed Pettigrew's role as the mediator between his slaves and the outside world.[13]

Yet, there was a danger in all this for Pettigrew. He had not anticipated the actions of Spiers and his friends. The planter failed to prevent an abuse of his slaves for the first time in memory. Hence, a new and even more troubling question may have arisen in the minds of the slaves at Bonarva. Could Pettigrew, in fact, protect them from the ravages of war? Might they do better if they could escape, even if the odds ran against them? Who could tell? To put such doubts to rest, Pettigrew resolved to remain indefinitely on the plantation. All arrangements upcountry now would be entrusted solely to his wife. He reasoned that "any more injudicious treatment might send a few to the Yankees." Then, he admitted, "the spell would be broken."[14]

A planter's control over his chattel property in Washington County proved to be a fragile thing. It required that planters maintain a monopoly over certain resources—access to stores and to the outside world. It thrived on isolation, a context in which slaves could do or say little that did not ultimately come to the master's attention. But force and violence undermined those conditions and, thereby, hindered the very operation of a planter's power. Hence, the presence of federal troops and the coming of war to the Albemarle area provoked a crisis in paternalism. The planters' power could only be preserved where few alternatives existed. Only in the southern upcountry could Washington County planters find a place congenial to their way of dominating black people.

· **III** ·

William Pettigrew grasped the crisis early on as well. Therefore, he resolved the first week in March to remove most of his slaves to central North Carolina.[15] On Thursday, March 4, "at breakfast time," Pettigrew and his slaves at Magnolia plantation, under the guard of twenty-five Confederate troopers, left for the upcountry. In twenty-five ox-drawn wagons and horse carts, the planter removed "all my negroes but a ½ dozen, [and] all my horses & mules consisting of about 40." The wagon train traveled slowly to Plymouth and then to Williamston in Martin County, where they rested a day. From Williamston, they marched to Hamilton, to Tarboro, to Rocky Mount, and finally to Wakefield, located in Wake County east of Raleigh. The planter and his slaves arrived at their destination on March 15, after a nine-day journey. Altogether, the move cost Pettigrew $367.64. One hundred dollars of that amount went to pay the Confederate troopers. The remainder purchased corn to feed Pettigrew's slaves and forage for his livestock. On the way, the planter deposited several bales of cotton at the Battle family's textile mill in Tarboro, presumably to finance the trip.[16]

On March 18, William Pettigrew began his search for a place to work his slaves for the duration of the war. He traveled to Haywood, a small crossroads community in eastern Chatham County about fifty miles west of Raleigh where he located a small farm for sale. There, the planter would make his home for about a year. But the farm could not support most of his slaves.[17] Therefore, William Pettigrew moved them again the last week in the month. He marched them in five days to a place about fifty miles west of Haywood, where the planter hired out all his slaves at once.[18]

Altogether, William Pettigrew leased eighty-seven slaves in nineteen groups to fifteen different planters. Nine of those groups represented families large and small. The planter appears deliberately to have kept families intact, perhaps in response to the slaves' objections voiced earlier during the lie out at Magnolia. Also, Pettigrew evidently assigned only young, single men to be hired out by themselves. There were six such men. But the planter broke up the community as a whole by spreading the families among several planters. Pettigrew probably had little choice in this matter; the local market for slave labor recently had become saturated. After the fall of New Bern on March 14, 1862, planters from around the Pamlico Sound area had flooded the upcountry with slaves for hire. For his efforts, Pettigrew received promissory notes due the following January amounting to $863 for seventy-six of the slaves.[19]

· **IV** ·

The exchange of slaves for promissory notes signified more than simply a purchase of labor. It included a broader transfer of power from one planter to another. For this reason, William Pettigrew insisted that persons who hired his slaves provide them with certain goods in the coming year. William Gilbert, for example, agreed to hire at $40 a certain young man named Stephen for the remainder of 1862. That contract required that Gilbert "promise to feed & to clothe" the slave with the "usual amount of clothing" to consist of "two suits of clothes—one for summer of cotton & the other for winter of wool, one thick blanket or quilt, one hat and two pair of shoes." Pettigrew might have provided the goods himself and factored the cost into his asking price—but he did not. Instead, he included in the contract detailed directions specifying what his slave should receive. In doing so, Pettigrew ensured that his slave's new master would become the sole source of goods crucial to Stephen's survival.[20]

Such contracts, however, did not settle all questions of a planter's dominance and a slave's submission in the upcountry, because such social relations did not result simply from legal restrictions or even displays of force. Planters and slaves created their own mutual expectations, in part by contesting as had been done for decades the rules by which they lived. In the past, this had not been a conflict among equals, as Charles Pettigrew dramatically demonstrated earlier; it resulted in no contract based on mutual benefit and unfettered consent. Instead, the struggle between planter and slave presumed an unequal resolution—the master would rule and the slave submit. In 1862, the relations between planters and slaves had changed dramatically, even in the upcountry. Many of the Pettigrew slaves worked for new masters who might or might not be skilled in managing human property. Would these men have the wherewithal to nail the meat-house door shut, call in the slave patrol, or face down a personal challenge? No one knew. But the slaves from Belgrade and Magnolia plantations determined to find out.

Mary Jane decided early to see just what kind of master she had been assigned. William Pettigrew had hired her out as a cook to a planter named George Foushee, along with a slave named Dick Lake, his wife Jenny, and their five children. Mary Jane complained "mostly of colick" during her first three weeks at Foushee's place. In that period, she rendered "very little service" in the planter's view. According to Foushee, "She don't seem to be very bad off, just sick enough to keep [her] from work." The planter further wondered if "a good deal of it is deception." To find out, Foushee asked Dick Lake about her. Lake's answer confirmed the planter's suspicions. According to the slave, Mary Jane had "never done much the year she was in a family way." Mary Jane had a history of probing the limits of her master's power. Similarly, Jenny took advantage of the change of masters to renew work rules she had known at Magnolia plantation. She had just borne a child and informed Foushee that she had "never [been] required to do any work until her child was eight weeks old." She also objected to Foushee's plan to put her to work in the fields. At Magnolia she always had labored as a cook and now complained that she "could not work out."[21]

Mary Jane, Jenny, and their fellow slaves did not wish simply to avoid work by refusing occasionally to labor for their masters. Most, in fact, worked steadily and with a will both for themselves and for their masters. In late March, William Campbell, who saw some of Pettigrew's slaves "most every Sunday" (presumably at church), reported them at work and "well satisfied" with their new circumstances. Therefore, the actions taken by Mary Jane and Jenny must be interpreted as having some more specific purpose. Mary Jane in the past had succeeded in making pregnancy a privileged status at Magnolia plantation. Here, she renewed the rule by making a public event of her refusal to work while "in a family way." Similarly, she served notice upon George Foushee that Pettigrew slaves could not be required to work when ill, no matter how slight the planter thought evidence of any malady appeared. Jenny, for her part, sought to reinforce two rules. The first would give women a special status when pregnant. The second would renew a long-standing division between housework and fieldwork at Magnolia plantation.[22]

George Foushee understood all of this on a practical level. Doubtless, he could never admit publicly, or perhaps even to himself, that Mary Jane and Jenny's actions constituted a challenge to the local rules of paternalism. But Foushee did have the presence of mind to remain calm. He reported the two slaves' failure to work diligently to William Pettigrew. But Foushee did not propose that either he or Pettigrew take any action. The planter concluded his account of Mary Jane's behavior by saying simply, "I hope she will be better hereafter."[23]

Mary Jane did become "better." After she had made her point, she returned to work as usual. Other planters, however, did not fully appreciate the give-and-take that an exercise of a master's power required. Or perhaps some sensed in small challenges larger issues.

A. E. Caveness is a case in point. Caveness hired one slave family from William Pettigrew—Jack, his pregnant wife, Venus, and their six children. The children must have been young because the entire family hired out for $25, less than the cost of hiring a single prime male field hand. But Caveness got a good deal more than he bargained for when he paid his pittance to William Pettigrew. Members of the slave family initiated the same contest. But Caveness could not comprehend their actions for what they were. In his view, the slaves attempted to "overrun" him. Finally, in a fit of ill-temper, the planter whipped the oldest child, a girl named Sarah, for what he considered her "laziness and disobedience."[24]

The girl's parents objected violently to this. They "made a great ado about it," according to one account, so much so that Caveness felt compelled to "take Venus in hand." At that point, Venus "started off" down the plantation road, and as she walked, turned to the planter and told him off. What exactly she uttered that day remained a matter of dispute. Caveness claimed that she shouted, I am "going to the Yankees." Doubtless, she had no such intention—if she spoke those words. Venus and her family had just made the nine-day trek afoot from the coast. She well knew that she needed food and clothing for such a journey, that eastern North Carolina lay blanketed by Confederate troops who would demand a pass from her, and that William Pettigrew would hire a slave catcher to find her long before she reached federal lines. Later, Venus's husband claimed that she had said no such thing. By the slave's account, Venus told Caveness that she intended to walk to William Campbell's plantation, presumably to lodge a complaint against her new master for his actions. Whatever the exact words, Venus had made her point in producing this small drama—publicly and loudly. She feared no man, planter or otherwise. And if she chose to oppose that man, she would make her claim a matter of public debate.[25]

Caveness "ordered her to come back," but Venus refused and continued walking down the road. The planter then got his whip and followed her. Some distance from the house, he finally caught up with her. Again, Caveness commanded Venus to return to the plantation. Once more, the slave refused and voiced her intention to leave. At that point, the planter lost all patience and good sense. Caveness began to whip Venus, at which time Jack, who evidently had followed the two, "got in between them." The planter then "fell to work on Jack, and drove both slaves back to the house."[26] But Venus had succeeded in her purpose, even as she and her husband bore the lashes of the planter's whip. Caveness complained that "the fuss might have been heard all over the neighborhood." If he hoped to exercise any power over Pettigrew's slaves, Caveness would have to submit to the scrutiny of his neighbors, both black and white. Each side in this conflict would mobilize its supporters. The battle between master and slave became a public controversy.[27]

The next day, Caveness traveled to William Campbell's plantation, where he hoped to make his case to the county's planters. To Campbell, he gave an account of the basic facts in the matter. But Caveness made no attempt to justify his actions. Instead, he simply announced a solution. He demanded that Campbell, who had been charged with managing William Pettigrew's interests in Chatham and Moore counties, write the slaves' owner seeking "permission to conquer them." If Pettigrew refused to grant him such authority, Caveness demanded that their master "take them away." By this ultimatum, Caveness cast the conflict in terms of fundamental issues—in this case, the interest of planters in dominating their slaves. Essentially, Caveness argued that all planters must stand with him, no matter what the specifics of this case, in order to preserve their power over slaves as a whole.[28]

Venus and Jack, however, also made their opinions known throughout the neighborhood. The couple communicated their interpretation of the conflict to slaves belonging to William Campbell who, in turn, approached their master after Caveness returned home. They told Campbell that Caveness had "not been good" to Pettigrew's slaves. They argued that Caveness was "a man of bad temper," and that he acted "very ill" to Jack and his family. In particular, Campbell's slaves charged that Caveness refused to give Jack and his family "enough to eat," even though he had "plenty of meat and bread" to sell to other persons in the neighborhood.[29]

During the next two weeks, Jack and Venus appealed directly to William Campbell. When Campbell visited the family, Jack accused Caveness of abusing them "without any just cause." To support the charge, the slave pointed out that recently Caveness had "knocked Edith [his youngest child] down with a handspike." The blow cut the little girl "severely on the head." And "since the first difficulty with Venus," Caveness had "knocked [her also] down with a chair." That piece of viciousness caused Venus to miscarry. On June 10, she was reported "very bad off." Moreover, after he struck Venus, Caveness "threatened to kill her if she did not get up and go to work," according to Jack's account. Jack, therefore, requested that Campbell write to William Pettigrew in order to give the planter Jack's version of events. In the letter, Jack argued that they had "worked harder" that spring than they had "ever worked in their lives," but Caveness could not be satisfied. Therefore, he implored William Pettigrew to remove them from Caveness's plantation. Jack declared his family "willing to live anywhere," even "on half feed," as long as they would "not be abused." We "did not want to put you to any trouble," Jack told his master, but we can "not stand it."[30]

In the end, Jack and his wife prevailed. Their story had a ring of truth that even Caveness himself made no attempt to deny. Moreover, Caveness's poor reputation in the area preceded his attempts to mobilize planter opinion in his cause. Campbell considered Caveness "very hard to please" and "a very passionate

man." Finally, Caveness did not help his own case when he admitted to Campbell that if he had carried his gun along, he would
have "killed some of them."

But all of this might have come to nothing if Venus had not
made the dispute a public event. By mobilizing local opinion, both
black and white, Jack and Venus forged a means by which Pettigrew's slaves could shape their own destiny. William Campbell
considered his slaves' version of events "only negro news" and,
therefore, "only [to] be used as such." Yet, he recommended to
William Pettigrew that Jack and his family be removed from
Caveness's plantation to a place where they would be "well cared
for." "If [Caveness] is not willing to keep them and treat them
humanely as other negroes are treated in this part of the country,"
wrote Campbell, "I should take them away."

In one sense, the customary rights of slaves acting within the
rules of paternalism had become renewed. Yet, there was more to
the story than a restoration of peaceable relations between master
and slaves. The abuse by Caveness of Venus and her child provided an unprecedented opportunity to challenge a slaveholder.
Caveness had made certain guarantees to Pettigrew—physical
safety and an adequate subsistence for the slaves—that he failed
to fulfill. And by insisting on Pettigrew's rights in his property,
Venus advanced her own claim as a human being. Indeed, she
used those double-edged claims to turn Caveness's own class
against him; she forced Pettigrew and others to recognize not only
her right to safety and a subsistence but also her right to be heard
and recognized as a person. In the next few months, another Pettigrew slave, Glasgow, would make even larger claims against his
new masters.[31]

· **V** ·

In mid-July 1862, Glasgow was hired out with his wife, Amy, and
four children to a Chatham County planter named Angus McLeod.
From March through June, the slaves apparently had worked
quietly.[32] Then in late July, McLeod's overseer, a Mr. McRae,
accused Glasgow's daughter, Clarky, of stealing a few eggs. McRae
went to Amy and informed her that she would be "corrected" for

her daughter's offense. At that point Glasgow intervened. He told McRae that he would not allow Amy to be "corrected." Furthermore, Glasgow said that he did not believe that Clarky had stolen any eggs. Then, Glasgow spoke "many other insulting words" to McRae.

At that moment, McLeod arrived on the scene. He told Glasgow that "if he said those words again," he would personally whip him. To this, Glasgow "drew himself in the attitude of a fight" and addressed the planter: If you lay a hand on me, you will "never lay a hand on another man." While the planter stood quietly, doubtless shocked, Glasgow continued his speech. Among his other remarks, Glasgow revealed that "he would not belong to anybody in a few days." The planter asked what he meant by that statement, but Glasgow declined to answer. Again, he defied the planter: "No man living should know that," the slave said. Thereupon, Glasgow grabbed his coat and walked away.[33]

Both planter and slave began to maneuver for advantage, each attempting to establish the legitimacy of their next action. After the confrontation with McRae and McLeod, Glasgow went into his own house and "talked very loud." The planter interpreted that action as an effort "to provoke me to do something in order that he mite have a little excuse to leave." But McLeod did not say a word to Glasgow. The next morning, the slave renewed his campaign. According to the planter's report, Glasgow "went to work talking loud and making threats." But again, McLeod said nothing to Glasgow. Instead, the planter wrote a letter to William Pettigrew, pleading for help in reconciling planter and slave. He implored Glasgow's owner to "come up and see what you can do with him." But in fact, McLeod already had decided on a punishment for Glasgow. He told Pettigrew, "I plan to whip him." Then, McLeod revealed the real purpose for his letter. "I want you present when I do it," he wrote to Pettigrew, so as to legitimate the punishment and his authority.[34]

Pettigrew did not choose to remove Glasgow and his family from McLeod's plantation. On July 26, Pettigrew received $31.20, paid in kind with pork, from McLeod, presumably a rental payment for the remainder of the year. Neither did Pettigrew sell Glasgow. The slave remained listed in Pettigrew's records throughout the war. But Glasgow had terrorized both planter and overseer. "I do not feel safe," wrote Angus McLeod, "when he will tell me to my face he will kill me if I lay my hand on him and that he is going to be a free man." Glasgow had challenged the right of his master to oversee, literally to see and know what the slave had done or might do. Glasgow did so when he disputed the planter's claim to know that Clarky had stolen some eggs—and again when he refused to say where and when he planned to escape. The surveillance essential to an exercise of the planter's power became a matter not of routine but of contention.

William Pettigrew, therefore, took an action unprecedented in his management of the slaves at Belgrade and Magnolia plantations. He ordered Glasgow jailed—and Jack, too, while he was about such business, for his role in disputing the authority of the planter named Caveness. Pettigrew wrote to the sheriff of Moore County explaining that the slaves' "impudent & threatening language" induced him "to think it unwise to permit them to go at large again until they have been made more submissive." The planter requested that Glasgow and Jack be housed in separate cells so they might "have, while in solitude, ample time to meditate on their misconduct." As an added punishment, Pettigrew directed that the two should receive no meat. This sentence was indefinite, to remain in force until the two manifested some sign of adhering to their master's will.

In the meantime, Glasgow and Jack were to be considered a danger. "I am informed," Pettigrew wrote, "that these men have both threatened to run away & go to the Yankees, particularly has Glasgow made this threat." In so threatening, the two promised not only to steal themselves but also to set an example for other slaves in the county. Should Glasgow or Jack escape, the act "would be attended with the most injurious consequences not only to my own negroes but to all others who may live within knowledge of the fact." The planter, therefore, could think "of no place so well suited for them as a jail where they can neither contaminate others nor put in execution any evil plans they may have in contemplation." And he urged the slaves' jailer to keep "an especial eye on them that they do not make their escape whilst in his charge."[35]

In this case, Glasgow challenged the very claim of his master to have a right to compel obedience. Glasgow threatened violence and denied his master the means to know his thoughts and actions.

Doubtless, Glasgow had done both in more subtle terms before, by running away and by various small subterfuges. But in July 1862, Glasgow made the disciplining of slaves a matter of public contention. He elevated a struggle between master and slave to a contest between classes—between all the slaveholders in his community and all the slaves. Elsewhere, this contest worked itself out in a very different manner.

· VI ·

In April 1862, Charles Pettigrew began moving most of his slaves upcountry. He managed to hire a few out to the North Carolina Railroad's repair facilities in Company Shops, not far from Hillsboro in Orange County. But most of his slaves were taken to South Carolina. On April 30, Jackson and several dozen slaves began their journey in Pennsylvania wagons from Hillsboro, North Carolina, to Cherry Hill plantation in South Carolina. The journey took seven days because the slaves were much delayed by rain and high water at several river crossings. As a result, they ran out of food, which Jackson then had to buy along the way. He left no debts, Jackson told his master, but he "spent six dollars of his own" money for which he expected to be reimbursed. Finally, the slaves reached Cherry Hill on Sunday night, May 4. Immediately, Jackson went to Badwell, where he reported to Caroline Pettigrew's sister. He said the slaves were "all well" and explained that they had been "detained by being water bound from time to time." They had suffered from over exertion and exposure. On Monday, they still lay "stretched off on the piazza looking fatigued."[36]

After they had rested a day or so, the slaves from Bonarva surveyed their situation. What they saw did not impress them. Jackson thought the piedmont hills "dreadful," and the prospects for producing a subsistence for the coming year even worse. It had rained constantly for several weeks at Cherry Hill, and that produced rust in the wheat that now stood ready for harvest, such as it was. The rain also prevented corn planting on the richest land at Cherry Hill plantation—the river bottoms. And there were no seed potatoes to be found for planting. An influx of planters and their slaves from the South Carolina low country also produced a scarcity of provisions for sale, especially of beef and corn. Therefore, although Caroline Pettigrew's sister attempted to buy food for the Bonarva slaves, she could find little, and that which she located commanded high prices. As a result, Charles Pettigrew's slaves found themselves on very short rations. The men protested that they could not live on one peck of corn meal and a pound of pickled pork per week. But Caroline Pettigrew's sister told them they "must try till better times."[37]

At this point, the slaves from Bonarva did not attempt actively to renew or redefine the limits of their master's authority, but they did gradually fill a void left by Charles Pettigrew's absence from Cherry Hill. The slaves continued to work diligently. Jackson and his brothers planted corn in the bottomland that had been flooded when they arrived. They assisted the slaves of Caroline's mother in hoeing weeds from their corn, and they "made salt very successfully." Yet, the Bonarva slaves' labor often fell short of the standard expected at home—no so much in substance as in style. "The people move indolently" in their hoeing, Caroline Pettigrew complained, "there is a certain slackness." "It is amazing," she thought, "how the servants lounge about." Charlotte, the cook, also completed her tasks. But at the same time, she lost a diffidence that had characterized her speech and action at Bonarva. She once walked from her work to the kitchen door in order to instruct her helpers outside. Now she shouted directions casually from wherever she happened to stand.[38]

The slaves from Bonarva had changed their manner. Why? Caroline Pettigrew explained the alteration as a paradox: There were "so many authorities on the place," yet she could see evidence of "no authority scarcely." In fact, these "authorities" were lesser masters, women and children, from whom the slaves ordinarily took only directions involving small or incidental tasks. Charles Pettigrew, with whom the Bonarva slaves had forged an understanding of the rules by which they must live, now remained in North Carolina, tending to his other business affairs. Therefore, the slaves saw little reason to keep up the deferential discourse that assured Pettigrew of their submission to his will. The gestures and language of paternalism could be dropped for the moment, even if the labor had to go on.[39]

The mistress of Bonarva saw a danger in this new manner. If

the language of paternalism could expire so easily, what small crisis might provoke a revolt against the practice as well? She, therefore, sought to hire an overseer. Caroline Pettigrew approached an old man, a German immigrant named Skister, who lived in the neighborhood. He had a reputation as a fine gardener and an excellent grower of fruit trees. But in interviewing him, Caroline Pettigrew learned that this man knew nothing whatever about managing slaves. Thereafter, Caroline Pettigrew attempted to do the job herself. In late June, she wrote: "My hands are very full, I am planter!! for the first time."[40] But in making her declaration, the planter's wife realized its absurdity. She was, after all, a woman. And she had no training or experience as a planter. Besides, her husband's slaves (being married, she legally owned nothing) would never accord her the status. In fact, she could only play the part. She conceded that she might "insist" upon being "very energetic" and "make an appearance of knowing more" than she really did. But she could never have any "ambition to be a manager." Caroline Pettigrew remained dependent on her husband, as the slaves did, but in different ways and through separate arrangements.[41]

Unlike William Pettigrew's slaves, the people from Bonarva experienced no transfer of power from one master to another. No rule had to be renewed—no limits discerned. But the mere lack of a planter close at hand caused the slaves' deferential habits to decline—not so much in substance, that is the amount of work performed, but in style, in the discourse of paternalism, the continual conversation of small words and manners between planters and their slaves. Among those slaves who remained in Washington County, however, this situation curiously reversed itself.

· VII ·

Charles Pettigrew remained at home in Washington County through most of the spring and summer of 1862. With perhaps a dozen older slaves, the planter directed his field hands to plant a few fields of corn; the slaves harvested a small wheat crop; but little else got done. Partly, the weather could be faulted. It rained heavily, causing the wheat to rust. Wheat became so scarce that the

little that was harvested was offered for sale as seed for the coming year. The rain also caused weeds to grow at an accelerated rate
among the corn stalks. The slaves at Bonarva hoed steadily but to
little effect. As a result of these conditions, Washington County
planters and slaves produced less than half an ordinary crop in
1862. Pettigrew feared a local famine. Even facing such a dire
prospect, however, the slaves at Bonarva did not bestir themselves
beyond a minimal effort on behalf of their master. "There seems
to be but little disposition to labor," Pettigrew reported of his
slaves.[42]

At Belgrade plantation, in contrast, the slaves undertook their
work with vigor. William Pettigrew had left Henry there to manage
a dozen or so field hands by himself. In a letter dictated by Henry,
the slaves reported themselves doing well and hard at work, plowing in order to plant corn later. In addition, they produced ninety-
seven gallons of molasses for themselves in May. At the same time,
three elderly slaves whom William Pettigrew had left at Magnolia
reported themselves satisfied with their new circumstances. "They
fare as well as they wish," one neighbor reported. When Charles
Pettigrew offered to move them to Bonarva plantation, the slaves
politely but firmly declined the planter's invitation.[43]

Why did slaves in the upcountry work only in the presence of
their master, while slaves in Washington County labor only in the
absence of a planter? The answer lay in the effect of federal troops
on the power of the master. In the upcountry, slaves had no choice
but to rely upon their masters to deal with the world off the plantation. To obtain the means for producing a subsistence—land,
tools, seed—they needed a planter present. But in Washington
County all those factors of production lay close at hand, free for
the taking, but only if the slaves' masters remained absent. The
presence of federal troops, then, did not produce any mystical
confidence among slaves in either themselves or the U.S. government. But it did force some planters to flee Washington County,
leaving blacks who remained at home free to labor for themselves.
Little wonder, then, that the slaves at Belgrade threw themselves
into their work; or that the elderly slaves at Magnolia turned down
Charles Pettigrew's effort to meet his obligation to his brother's
dependents; or that the slaves remaining at Bonarva worked without conviction, feeling imposed upon by their master's presence.

Paternalism, in its antebellum form, had reached an end for those planters and slaves who remained in Washington County. However much local slaveholders maneuvered to shore up their dominance over blacks, the "spell" that Charles Pettigrew feared might "be broken" in this war had shattered. By their actions, the slaves who remained at home demonstrated that they understood the fundamental workings and weaknesses of their masters' power. They also comprehended what they stood to gain in this war—not some abstract freedom, civil liberties promised to them by white men, but land and the means to produce for their own use a living and something more.

Washington County slaves living upcountry arrived at the same understanding but through a very different experience. They now sought to renew their customary rights within slavery as a minimal condition of their servitude. But they, too, saw that the routines of their masters' power lay in disarray. Whatever power planters wielded now relied on the use of physical force. William Pettigrew had worked his will by deploying armed men in secret by night. Charles Pettigrew had threatened starvation. Both had raised the price for defying a slaveowner to the ultimate sanction—death. The subtle language and practice of paternalism became ineffectual. As a result, a planter's means to know his slaves' thoughts and actions, the ability to survey and predict, failed. To planters, their slaves now seemed remote, almost cold and calculating. And in that perception, Washington County planters pierced the veil of pro-slavery ideology and glimpsed the actual workings of their power—but too late.

Paternalism had been exposed during the war as more than a personal application of force. It was a constantly recurring social drama, an idiom of unequal social relations acted out within a very particular context. That context consisted of a master's unchallenged control over certain life-sustaining resources, mainly food and clothing, and the means to obtain those items, money and access to markets outside a local community. Within these rules, however, masters found themselves subject to certain obligations, for example, customary divisions of work, rules to benefit pregnant women, a slave's prerogative in defining what constituted an illness, and protection of slaves from abuse at the hands of other whites. When planters failed to meet those obligations, slaves mobilized themselves, kin, friends, and sometimes whole communities not only to reestablish their rights and benefits, limited as they might be within slavery, but also to extend their liberties and to shift the struggle for freedom from a private to a public terrain. For planters, the irony of a war to preserve slavery lay in how it reduced slaveholders' power over their chattel property. The slaveholders' chief means of manipulating slaves, the power to survey their chattel property's thoughts and actions through close daily supervision, declined precipitously when they were forced to remove their bound laborers upcountry and then to hire them out to strangers.

How the decline of the power of slaveholders might be transformed into the abolition of slavery remained uncertain in 1862. A long struggle among whites over political authority ultimately would settle the issue. Meanwhile, Washington County planters salvaged what labor they could from a species of property that slipped further from their grasp. Jackson, Prince, Jim, Stephen, Mary Jane, Dick Lake, Jenny, Jack, Venus, Edith, Glasgow, Amy, Clarky, Charlotte, and the others teetered on the edge of freedom, dealing cautiously, even gingerly, with the vestiges of their masters' power in a revolutionary situation.

Finally, there is the strange case of Peter. Peter was owned by Charles Pettigrew, who had lent the slave to his brother, General James Johnston Pettigrew. In early June 1862, General Pettigrew was shot during a battle in Virginia, captured by McClellan's army, and taken to a hospital in Maryland. Northern newspapers mistakenly reported Pettigrew dead. Meanwhile, in the course of the fighting, Peter became separated from his master.

After a few days, the slave made his way back to Richmond where he stayed most of June, evidently inquiring from time to time about efforts to recover the general's body. One day while Peter made such an inquiry of a certain officer, Jefferson Davis happened to pass by on his horse and to stop. The officer remarked to the president that this slave had been General Pettigrew's personal servant. Davis "then expressed his sympathy for Peter & assured him that everything that was in his power should be done to preserve his master's remains from the enemy." Thereupon, the president "turned away his face and shed tears." Then, "touching his hat to Peter," Davis rode away. Two days later, William Pettigrew arrived in Richmond, hoping to recover his brother's body. The planter soon found Peter, who related the story of Davis's concern for what the president considered a grieving slave. Pettigrew viewed the episode as "touching" and an "indication of the goodness of the President's heart." Moreover, Pettigrew considered the actions of the president and the slave "complimentary to all parties" concerned. For a single moment, the contradictions of paternalism lay bare.

Peter ostensibly played the part of the faithful servant. He followed his master into battle, waited for him in Richmond, and inquired about his remains, presumably so he could take the general's body home to Washington County. Yet, for all his service, there is no evidence to suggest that Peter grieved over the loss of his master. The story, after all, contained no report of Peter himself having shed tears. Paternalism had failed to create a sense of obligation, any dependence apart from an immediate need for food and protection. A planter's power over his human property, in fact, had never been as extensive as the Pettigrews and other Washington County slaveholders had supposed.

In his effort to console Peter, the Confederate president revealed his own ignorance of the actual relation between master and slave. Davis, in fact, possessed no evidence of any sense of loss on Peter's part. He could not. He had no knowledge of Peter's past relationship with James Johnston Pettigrew. And in riding onto the scene, Davis had no opportunity to observe any manifestation of grief. The Confederate president simply projected his own beliefs into the situation. He assigned to Peter the emotions that a slave ought to feel in such a situation. Then blithely ignoring the facts before him, Davis went on to attempt a renewal of the bond between master and slave. He uncovered his head in a show of respect for the grieving slave. He touched the slave so as to establish a personal, physical relation. Here, the president simply acted out a version of the means by which planters traditionally had produced their power over their slaves. In all this, Davis failed to see a disjunction between the reality of slavery and the ideology that legitimated the practice.

William Pettigrew argued that Jefferson Davis's actions showed a "goodness of heart." This was an extraordinary thing for the planter to say. Common wisdom portrayed the Confederate president as politically incompetent. Whigs, Pettigrew among them, had vilified Davis as an aspiring monarch or dictator. What could have changed Pettigrew's opinion? The key to this reversal lay in the president's reaffirmation of paternalism, the principle for which William Pettigrew's brother supposedly had died. Davis demonstrated with a few words and a sweep of the hand the central activity of a master—the care of dependents. At the same time, Peter's apparent acceptance of that gesture reaffirmed his subordinate position. He acknowledged his supposed grief and, thus, the correctness of his service to James Johnston Pettigrew. From the planters' viewpoint, William Pettigrew had much reason to consider the episode "complimentary to all parties."

In the end, these few moments encapsulated the basic ironies and contradictions of paternalism itself. Peter in being perceived as grieving completed the realization of James Johnston Pettigrew as a master. This occurred at the same time the general, even in his death, prevented Peter from becoming a person in his own right. Yet, by removing his hat and touching the slave, Davis acknowledged Peter's essential humanity. The president admitted Peter's capacity to think and feel, to be a person. All the while, Davis led a war to perpetuate a government that denied any such aspirations among slaves.

How could a slave be both property and person? Did not the one status negate the other? Washington County slaves thought they did. So, too, did some unionist farmers. In mid-1862, only local planters and the federal government remained unconvinced.

4

A Question of Sovereignty

· I ·

By late February 1862, Charles Pettigrew stalked about his plantation "fully armed." "The low whites are not to be trusted at all," he believed. "They would betray or murder any gentleman." The planter probably exaggerated only slightly. Many poor persons from Washington County had fled to Roanoke Island, seeking protection after the battle at Hatteras. In February, they returned to their homes feeling confident that Union troops would intervene if planters did unionists any harm. After all, federal gunboats controlled the entire Sound, and the federal commander for the Albemarle region had resolved "to arm these people and organize them as North Carolina's reserve."[1]

Having returned home, Washington County unionists began to exploit the connection they had forged with federal troops. In early March, local unionists contested for control of the militia again; in Cool Spring, they refused entirely to muster under planter leadership. Therefore, George Collins, only recently elected captain, disbanded the neighborhood company. "There is more to apprehend from the agrarianism so rampant in that section," wrote one planter, than from any possible slave uprising. Some planters excused the unionists' actions, arguing that while the militia harbored some anti-secessionists, most were Southern men. These secessionists now feared to leave their families unprotected from federal incursions.[2]

Events just across the county line, however, suggested otherwise. Farmers in adjacent Tyrrell County held a unionist meeting
in which they declared themselves "subjugated" by the federal
government. In addition, they resolved that no one should leave
the county, that is, be allowed to desert to the Confederacy. In
response, planters around Columbia arranged for the local colonel,
a man named Davenport, to call a general muster of the Tyrrell
County militia for the first week in March. The muster, planters
expected, would be a public test of every man's loyalty to the
South.[3]

Residents of East Lake, the neighborhood in Tyrrell County
near the Washington County border, however, complained to the
U.S. commanders at Roanoke Island, who subsequently traveled
to Columbia. The officers told Davenport that since "many did not
wish to go," it was the federal government's "business to protect
them." To this, the colonel replied that he already had countermanded the order for a general muster. Moreover, his men would
"pursue their peaceful occupations, should they not be molested
by the Enimy." Davenport's words seemed to settle the matter.
The federal soldiers returned to Roanoke. But Colonel Davenport
had lied. A few days later, unionists near Lake Phelps traveled
once again to Roanoke Island, saying that "the Malitia" "certenly"
would be "called on Saturday." Worse, they reported that one
thousand Confederate cavalrymen would descend on the assembled unionists and march them westward into Confederate territory.[4]

The federal commander at Roanoke became enraged when he
learned of Davenport's duplicity. In retaliation, two thousand
Union troops raided the town of Columbia. While there, the soldiers looted the homes of several secessionists who had fled the
county earlier. At one man's dwelling, the troops "destroyed his
furniture [and] carpets [which they then] tore & dragged about the
streets." They also "took his Bacon." Afterwards, S. S. Simmons,
representing the town's planters, went to the federal flagship and
requested an interview with the commander. Simmons was told
that Union troops would leave Tyrrell County in peace, provided
local leaders never mustered the militia again. But the federal
commander warned that if planters persisted in these efforts he
would "with fire & sword devastate the county."[5]

Planters in Washington County followed these events very closely. D. G. Cowand, by then in Confederate service, advocated fighting a local guerrilla war in retaliation. He sought permission from the North Carolina governor to organize a cavalry company recruited from among his friends and neighbors. They would be based just west of Plymouth alongside the Roanoke River in Confederate-held Bertie County. But other Washington County secessionists politely opposed Coward's idea. They knew that a guerrilla war would destroy the last social ties by which they now barely controlled the county. Besides, the very men Cowand proposed to recruit had been alienated from planters by recent events. One writer explained that these men blamed the "leading secessionists of the county," who had fled earlier, for exposing them to the ravages of federal troops. "Some of the people," the man reported, "think those who have left did wrong in so doing."[6]

Washington County's unionists also scrutinized federal actions in Tyrrell County. Therefore, when in April 1862 Colonel Davenport called out the Washington County militia, local unionists immediately appealed to the U.S. commander at Roanoke. How Davenport, the militia colonel for Tyrrell County, presumed to have authority over Washington County troops remains a mystery. There is no evidence to say that he acted on special orders from Governor Henry Clark or the Confederate army. Whatever the exact arrangements, Davenport ordered the men assembled for an enrolling procedure "as the present law requires," but "some men took fright." Many simply disappeared into the swamps. Four, however, made their way to Roanoke, seeking protection as the unionists from Tyrrell County had done earlier.[7]

These four men told the same story as the Tyrrell County unionists; they claimed that "the Cavelry" were after them "with a large force." In response, the commander dispatched a gunboat to Columbia to seek another interview with Colonel Davenport. This time, however, the federal troops came away unconvinced. They saw no evidence of Confederate cavalry. Davenport again denied that he had mobilized the local militia. Therefore, the federal officers censured the Washington County unionists for spreading false stories. But just in case Davenport had lied as before, the federal commander threatened "to place an army in Plymouth to keep the Militia of Tyrrell & Washington from leaving."[8]

By late April 1862, Washington County unionists had observed that federal forces would intervene on their behalf. They had only to take the oath and claim that they had received some abuse at the hands of secessionists. That accomplished, yeoman farmers might rule the county with impunity, if the federal government chose to make its presence permanent.

· **II** ·

On Thursday, May 15, 1862, a small federal fleet anchored in the Roanoke River at Plymouth. Commanded by S. C. Rowan, the flotilla consisted of three gunboats and four transports carrying several dozen U.S. Marines. After a short while, a launch commanded by a young lieutenant named Chaplin approached the shore. When the boat docked, H. G. Spruill, the militia general and mayor of Plymouth, presented himself and Major Henry Gilliam. Gilliam had commanded Washington County's volunteers in the battle for Fort Hatteras in August 1861 and had been captured with his troops, imprisoned at New York harbor, and paroled in April 1862. Spruill also introduced the town's commissioners, John Latham, Sr., Alexander Woodhouse, R. H. Bennett, and E. W. Jones. All were invited on board the federal flagship to meet Commander Rowan.[9]

Rowan took the opportunity to describe his policy toward Washington County. He told the officials that he did not intend to "interfere with the people or to trouble private property." Instead, he hoped that Washington County residents would "pursue their business and remain quiet." If they did so, they would "not be disturbed." His only purpose was to "maintain the authority of the government." Rowan also explained his policy toward slaves: He considered them "just as Artillery horses because they aided the enemy." If local residents made slaves into implements of war, then the blacks could be seized as contraband. But should local planters choose to employ their slaves in peaceful pursuits, such as growing crops, the commander would have have no need to interfere. This policy meant that planters could reclaim their slaves who ran away, by force if necessary, as long as they remained peaceable. The federal government, however, would not expend its time and effort in compelling slaves to labor for their masters.

In fact, Rowan's sailors already had enforced his policy toward slaves. The day before, two federal gunboats had stopped at a plantation landing on the Roanoke, just upriver from Plymouth. There, the crew confiscated rod iron from the plantation's master. But the Union sailors refused to allow any slaves to return with them to Plymouth on the boat. The crew declared, wrote one planter, that "they were not after negroes & would not have them."[10] This point was of special concern to Washington County planters because less than a week earlier Major General David Hunter had declared slavery incompatible with the martial law then in force along the coasts of Georgia, Florida, and South Carolina. Should Rowan's presence be interpreted as an application of military rule to the county, slavery might be endangered. But Rowan's words soothed Spruill and his friends; local power and property appeared safe.[11]

Yet in all this, there lay several unanswered questions. Was the local government empowered by the Confederate state of North Carolina or by the federal government, or did town and county authority derive from local votes only, from the people of Washington County? At the core of these concerns lay the issue of sovereignty. How could political power be created? By whom? And by what means? The struggle for answers would begin on Saturday, May 17, with the arrests of two local secessionists. But one thing had already become clear. The fight over local sovereignty would not turn on discussions of abstract principles. It would focus chiefly on the power to defend claims in property—both land and slaves.

After Plymouth's officials left Rowan's gunboat, the commander continued to receive visitors through the evening and into the next morning. In that time, local unionists bent the naval officer's ear with tales of abuse at the hands of secessionists. They particularly focused their attention on Henry Gilliam, arguing that the major had violated his parole "by assisting to raise a company of [Confederate] volunteers" and by "persecuting the Union men" in the county. The next day, Rowan ordered Lieutenant Chaplin ashore to arrest the major.[12] Then Lieutenant C. W. Flusser, who would command at Plymouth after Rowan's departure, arrested a second secessionist, Jesse G. Griffen, owner of a fishery on the Roanoke River. Some unionists had "represented" Griffen to the lieutenant "as a violent secessionist and a persecutor of Union men." They specifically accused Griffen of "selling fish to the rebel army," a practice which violated a U.S. Navy proclamation against taking fish in the Sound, except to catch a few for one's own use. In fact, Flusser did not feel the evidence against Griffen sufficient to prosecute him. But imprisoning a hot secessionist, he thought, would "exert a good influence on others."[13]

The two arrests raised a fundamental political question: Who ruled Plymouth? Commander Rowan had agreed to allow local officials, a North Carolina government in the secessionist view, to function normally. Hence, the arrests of Gilliam and Griffen cannot have been legal; the two had broken no state law or municipal ordinance.

Immediately upon hearing the news of Gilliam's arrest, H. G. Spruill made his way to the wharf, boarded the federal flagship, and held a short conversation with Commander Rowan. In the discussion, Rowan explained that he had been confronted with "unmistakeable evidence that the Major had violated his parole." Spruill did not attempt to dispute this. Instead, the mayor pointed out that to secessionists, Gilliam's arrest "implied a breach of honor"; Rowan's subordinates had violated the agreement between himself and Confederate authorities. Worse, the arrest was made with only the slightest evidence and at the behest of local unionists. According to Spruill, unionists had shifted the balance of power toward themselves by military force. If by this means they dominated the community, how could the local government continue to exercise any authority?[14]

H. G. Spruill moved immediately to reassert the power of the planter government. On the very day of the arrests, May 17, the mayor told Lieutenant Chaplin that in two days the county court, an administrative body, was scheduled to meet as usual. Spruill further informed Chaplin that the county needed to levy a tax to pay for "our county and town charges and expenses." These included both alms for the poor and "support of the wives and children of [the Confederate] Volunteers." Spruill reminded the lieutenant that the court was bound by North Carolina law to levy a state tax. By these initiatives, Spruill sought first to retain his secessionist constituency by caring for the dependents of committed Southern partisans. Then he hoped to implicate the federal government in establishing a principle of home rule for Washington County. Finally, by collecting a state tax, the mayor attempted to force U.S. officials to acknowledge North Carolina's sovereignty over the local government. The mayor concluded: "It is very important that the Court be held."[15]

Lieutenant Chaplin, however, expressed several reservations about this plan. He told the mayor that he had "no objection to collecting a tax to support the poor; and [to] ordinary county and town taxes." But Chaplin argued that "many persons in the country," meaning unionists, "were opposed to the war and in favor of the U.S. Government." Therefore, he did not think it "fair to compel them to pay a tax to support the families of soldiers who were fighting against their own side." The lieutenant then announced some limitations to the agreement Rowan had made with the county's officials. Some local unionists, he told Spruill, "had claimed his protection and were in favor of his government." Therefore, "if any one of these men be arrested by your authority," Chaplin said, "I will arrest two secessionists for every one of them."

On the next day, Sunday, May 18, the lieutenant requested that the county court be suspended for a time. Spruill, fearing that an open confrontation would destroy his authority, agreed.[16]

Having failed to gain the local autonomy he sought, Spruill anticipated a reaction by the Confederate army. His fears were confirmed that evening. Local secessionists told Spruill that "a [Confederate] cavalry dash would be made to arrest the county's leading unionists." Therefore, the secessionists suggested that Spruill and John Latham, acting as town commissioners, go to Williamston, twenty miles west of Plymouth, to "represent the matter to the [Confederate] authorities."

The two men went on Monday and "asked their cooperation," Spruill reported, "in preventing any arrests." Specifically, Spruill and Latham reported that secessionists in Plymouth thought the Confederate cavalry would attempt to "arrest some of the citizens" in the town "called 'union men.'" In that case, the Washington County representatives pointed out: "The Yankees would arrest two 'secessionists' for one union man," just as Lieutenant

Chaplin had announced. Therefore, the commissioners "wished the authorities in Williamston to use their influence to prevent any such arrests of union men at Plymouth." In the end, the Confederates decided not to interfere. Spruill communicated all this to Lieutenant Chaplin, and the question of local political authority seemed settled. Washington County's unionists, however, had other ideas.[17]

· **III** ·

Early on, Washington County unionists sought a federal presence in the area. When U.S. gunboats first arrived on May 15, "the Union inhabitants of Plymouth" made an "earnest entreaty" to Commander Rowan requesting him to keep at least one gunboat stationed at the town wharf. Rowan agreed to do this. Then within a week, unionists from throughout the county appealed for more help. On May 19, fifteen men from the Cool Spring militia district, twenty-five or thirty from Scuppernong, about fifty from Germanton, plus large numbers from Lees Mill and the three Plymouth districts assembled in the county seat. The unionists presented a petition to Lieutenant Chaplin, "asking the Old United States for protection." They "begged" Chaplin to station his men ashore, to form local unionists into companies under his command, and to request that General Burnside send more troops to the town. Finally, the men demanded that a federal recruiting officer be detailed to Plymouth. Some claimed that the Union army could recruit as many as sixty men in one precinct. Those men would bring their own horses, if needed. Others "offered to volunteer" on the spot. Washington County unionists "only wish[ed] a leader in order to take arms in their own defense."[18]

At about the same time, some Washington County unionists organized themselves for local military duty without waiting for federal help. On May 23, fifty-three farmers in the Scuppernong neighborhood met at Joseph Basnight's home to form themselves into a "company known as the home guards." The farmers elected John Davenport captain, Warner Smith first lieutenant, Jesse Furlow second lieutenant, and John Patrick orderly sergeant. All of these men cultivated corn and herded hogs on a very small scale. Evidently, farmers with interests more like landless men had replaced substantial yeomen in local unionist councils. Whatever the case, Scuppernong's unionists acted in the knowledge that Lieutenant Chaplin already had promised to supply them with "powder, ball & muskets." They also received permission from Chaplin to "get provisions where ever they can get it," in a word, to seize supplies from the county's plantations. The unionists agreed among themselves to "drill one day in the week."[19]

By all this activity, Washington County's unionist farmers hoped to "keep everything right." To Chaplin, the phrase mainly meant preventing people and provisions "from going out of the county." Washington County's unionists, however, implied much more when they vowed to "keep everything right." Some continued to insist on the arrest of active secessionists, including several more Plymouth residents, for what one secessionist planter called their "virtuous conduct." Among those arrested was a physician who had threatened rather loudly to cut Lieutenant Chaplin's throat. The unionists also provoked a federal expedition to Mackey's Ferry, on the Sound five miles east of Plymouth. Unionists there pointed Union troops toward a certain suspicious trader who had come from federally held Morehead City to the south and who carried a U.S. permit but "had violated the stipulations" it contained.

"There are so many mean tories about," it appeared to one secessionist, that "they may be informed of almost anything they wish to know." And worse, local unionists had made it their business to "report every man that has done any thing for the South."[20]

Washington County unionists also attempted to force secessionists to take an oath to defend the Constitution of the United States. Some of these secessionists so confronted refused, packed their personal belongings, and set out on the road to Williamston. They reported themselves "fearful of violence" to their persons if they remained in Plymouth. Others stayed at home but reported that local unionists had handed them a "paper" in an "abrupt manner" and told them that they "must sign it." If they refused, the unionists threatened to place their names "on the black list." Secessionists objected saying that "it would be improper for them to sign the paper" and that "such signatures might involve them in difficulties hereafter," presumably with the Confederate army. Washington

County secessionists did not fear the federal troops as much as "violence from our own citizens."[21]

Some local unionists sought to provoke quarrels with leading secessionists. On May 23, for example, John Phelps, Jr., accosted Jesse G. Griffen, the fishery owner and secessionist arrested a few days earlier. As the two stood in the town's main street, Phelps asked Griffen "how he liked that Flag on the Customs House." The day before, unionists had raised the Stars and Stripes with great ceremony over the building. "I had nothing to do with it," Griffen replied, "and wish to say nothing about it." But Phelps could not be satisfied. "In angry manner," he declared that the secessionist must comment. "Well," said Griffen, "if I must speak of it, I don't like it." Thereupon, Phelps struck Griffen, or at least made the attempt. Griffen ran around a corner with the unionist, hurling bricks, close behind. Finally, Phelps cornered Griffen in a lot behind a store and "renewed the attack." By now the dispute had attracted several men who followed the two. Charles Latham, a leading local unionist, at last intervened to stop the fight.[22]

These acts, taken together, produced a second crisis in local authority. H. G. Spruill explained the facts in the cases involving Griffen and Phelps to Captain Flusser (then in command of the gunboats off Plymouth) and advised the federal officer to take no action himself. But the mayor did seek a statement from Flusser exhorting local authorities to enforce existing local "regulations." This message could be used to threaten unionists with arrest for disturbing the peace. Later, Spruill intervened personally to smooth over matters in the Phelps case. The mayor explained to young Phelps's father the political danger his son had created for both secessionists and unionists. The mayor also threatened to arrest the boy. At this, the elder Phelps "seemed excited and begged that no such steps be taken, that it would only provoke evil, and he deeply regretted" the incident. Phelps blamed his son's "ungovernable" drinking for the provocation. "Nothing of the kind should again occur," John Phelps, Sr., told Spruill.[23]

In all this, Spruill had acted cautiously and had done so with good reason. Washington County's political controversies came under the close scrutiny of Confederate authorities in eastern North Carolina. On May 24, Plymouth residents observed a large number of "strange men," supposedly Confederate soldiers, "lurking bout the edge of town," presumably "acting as spies." The Confederates evidently had come to gather information about the treatment of secessionists in the county. In addition, some local secessionists had begun to perceive the town government as no longer loyal to the Confederacy. Spruill learned by a rumor that he had been "severely criticized" by his friends for his course in recent events. The mayor and his local government now walked a tightrope between two sovereign authorities, both of which claimed jurisdiction over Washington County. Finally, federal officers began to talk about leaving Plymouth. This prospect alarmed Spruill greatly. He begged them to remain, saying that their "presence might be useful to us," presumably in controlling landless unionists.[24]

In the last week of May, Henry Gilliam, recently released by federal officials at New Bern, at last came to the local government's rescue. He went to Williamston where he represented the planters' delicate position to the Confederate commanders there. Hoping to achieve local political stability, Gilliam urged the officers to restate their position in a letter. This was the bargain: If the federals allowed town and county authorities to make all arrests in accordance with local law and if they continued to respect all existing rights in property as they already had done, then "no matter what they hear, no Confederate Cavalry will visit Plymouth." The letter went on to emphasize that the difficulty lay in arrests made earlier, in the question of whose law should prevail in Washington County. With regard to the enforcement of property rights, the Southern officers had no quarrel with federal actions. In fact, they expressed themselves quite "pleased with Captain Flusser's treatment to the negroes." Gilliam himself carried the letter to Lieutenant Flusser at Plymouth.[25]

Flusser made no objection to the Confederate proposal. It seemed to confirm his existing policies. He evidently had no intention of making further arrests. All seemed promising in this truce. But neither Confederate nor federal officials reckoned with the impact troops stationed in Plymouth might have. Washington County's unionists had requested a U.S. garrison in late May. The following month, General Burnside granted the unionists' wish.

· IV ·

As early as June 8, 1862, rumors began to circulate in Plymouth about federal troops possibly being stationed in town soon. The rumors began with a visit by Colonel Rush C. Hawkins to Plymouth on June 7, and they had some basis in fact.[26] Hawkins had found that among "the non-slaveholding population" around the Albemarle Sound many "professed sentiments of loyalty to the Union," and others had "expressed a determination never to serve in the ranks of the rebel army." In this opinion, Hawkin was confirmed by Lieutenant Flusser's account of unionists at Plymouth. Flusser had become "deeply impressed" with their "truthfulness and sincerity." In conversation, he told Hawkins that "many of them had successfully resisted rebel conscription, and had never given their allegiance to the rebel cause." The gunboat commander had found that Washington County unionists "worked in their fields in parties, with arms near at hand, during the day, and at night resorted to the swamps for shelter against conscripting parties of rebel soldiers." By this method, Flusser explained, the unionists constantly remained "on the alert."[27]

Acting on his observations, Flusser wrote to Colonel Hawkins urging him to occupy the town. The naval commander also advocated an effort to "organize the Union men of that vicinity into regiment of soldiers." "We will miss the golden opportunity," Flusser wrote, "if we do not promptly send small detachments of men to the towns on the Sound and arm the loyal people." "They are eager to be enlisted." "If I had 350 or 400 muskets, with ammunition," Flusser concluded, "I could soon find Union-loving men to take them and use them well in our cause." Hawkins, for his part, wrote to General Burnside recommending Flusser's plan. Finally, Burnside approved an effort to organize and arm unionists at Plymouth.

On June 12, S. C. Rowan, commander of naval forces in the Sound, and Colonel Hawkins met with local unionists in order to "ascertain the extent of existing Union sentiment" and "see to what use, if any this sentiment might be put for the public service." While Hawkins's soldiers loitered about town, several unionists boarded the federal flagship to see Commander Rowan and Colonel Hawkins. The men sought aid and told the officers that many others in town wished to speak with them. Therefore, the group adjourned to Plymouth's customs house where about 250 local unionists had gathered. After some "patriotic speeches" by Rowan and Hawkins, a "free interchange of views" took place "in relation to the affairs of the country." "The anxiety of these loyal North Carolinians seemed to hinge upon one point," as Hawkins put it later: "What will become of us in case we are captured by the rebels?"[28]

Rowan and Hawkins assured Washington County's unionists that the U.S. government would "protect them and their families to the last extreme; and that the Southern men who placed themselves under the protection of the flag would, by fighting in the ranks of our army and upholding the authority of the country, be looked upon as special wards of the Government; and that any outrage perpetrated upon them, or upon their families would be severely punished." The federal officers also revealed that the army intended to aid local unionists "in throwing off the tyranny that now oppressed them" in other ways. It planned to "put arms in their hands to defend and assert their rights, if they would organize into companies and come under military discipline."[29]

That was exactly what the unionists had come to hear. Roughly one hundred Washington County residents "signed their names," volunteering for federal service. They became the core of a company in the 1st North Carolina Union Volunteers to be stationed permanently at Plymouth. The remaining unionists present adjourned their meeting until June 16, vowing to return with "many more[,] enough, perhaps, to form [another] company." To encourage such action, Rowan authorized Hawkins to move some of his troops from Roanoke Island to Plymouth "as a nucleus around which the Union men can rally under the protection of the gunboats."

H. G. Spruill, of course, protested. Local unionists, he argued, "were emboldened by the presence of the Federal forces;" and that made it difficult for town officials "to enforce our municipal regulations for the good order of the town." Exactly.[30]

As if to confirm Spruill's fears, unionists persuaded U.S. authorities to begin arresting local planters again. After the customshouse meeting, a delegation from Scuppernong in southeast Washington County complained bitterly to Rowan about Henderson B.

Phelps, J. J. Lindsey, and Jordan Spruill, large planters from that neighborhood who had "threaten[ed] vengeance if Union men should take up arms." The three had acted as violent partisans in the secession crisis in the spring of 1861. Phelps, in fact, had commanded the old neighborhood militia company and still held a commission (illegally issued) from the North Carolina governor. Therefore, on the night of June 12, Lieutenant Flusser, acting on orders from Rowan, arrested the three planters and sent them to New Bern to face General Burnside.[31]

Two days later, the first occupying garrison landed at Plymouth's wharf. The force consisted of Company F, 9th New York Volunteers, perhaps fifty men in all who came from around Albany and styled themselves Zouaves after the famous French fighters of that name. They were commanded by Captain William W. Hammill, who also took command of the 1st North Carolina Union Volunteers at Plymouth.

Immediately, H. G. Spruill sought out the company's officers in order to reaffirm Rowan's policies. He did so by presenting Captain Hammill with a problem. Spruill told the officer that a few "runaway negroes about town" had committed "some depredations." The mayor hoped to arrest them but sought the captain's permission to do so. In response, Hammill announced that he "had nothing to do with it" and "wished [the local] people to do as they liked." Thus satisfied, Spruill went home.[32]

In his satisfaction, however, Spurill did not imagine what other consequences a local garrison might have upon Plymouth. In placing the town within federal lines, Hammill emboldened unionists to harass planters and slaves to leave their owners. On Sunday, June 15, Colonel Hawkins stationed pickets at the edge of town to watch for Confederate cavalrymen and spies and to prevent any person from passing who had not taken the "oath of alligiance." By requiring the oath, Hawkins carried out a general order in force throughout the eastern theater of the war. But local unionists who often stood picket duty used their position for a different purpose. H. G. Spruill's daughter, for example, "was stopped on the road at the point of a bayonet and her pass demanded." At the same time, the occupation encouraged slaves to make their escape to Plymouth. By June 25, several Washington County runaways had persuaded the New York Zouaves to shelter them on board federal gunboats. Then, the protected slaves began "coming on shore" and "talking to the [planters'] negroes." Also, slaves from as far away as Halifax County, sixty miles up the Roanoke River, began to trickle into the federal post. Finally, the proximity of Union troops persuaded unionists that they might succeed in confiscating absent planters' crops. In the Scuppernong neighborhood, some men showed a "disposition to appropriate" William Pettigrew's corn, as the planter phrased it, "without making such remuneration as common honesty demands."[33]

By late June 1862, the U.S. government's presence at Plymouth had profoundly altered the terms of truce between local federal and Confederate forces. It encouraged unionists to organize and arm themselves, subjected secessionists to further arrests and intimidation, and persuaded some slaves in Plymouth that the time had come to flee to Northern troops. All this undermined the authority of local officials, but it did not create an alternative means of governing the county. Federal troops had produced confusion and something approaching political anarchy.

· **V** ·

On the evening of Sunday, June 29, Edward Stanly, the military governor of North Carolina appointed by President Lincoln, arrived in Plymouth. He was well known and respected among exactly those Constitutional Unionist planters who, before the confrontation at Fort Sumter, had opposed all efforts to promote disunion. Before the war, Stanly had been elected a Whig congressman from eastern North Carolina. In 1858, he had moved to California and, thereby, avoided making enemies in North Carolina during the secession crisis. Hence, Lincoln considered Stanly the only man capable of returning the state's planters to the federal fold. As a first step toward that goal, the governor determined to produce organized government once again throughout the Albemarle region. In Washington County, he hoped to do so by securing a mandate from the local elite. Stanly sought a government of unionist planters.[34]

On Wednesday, Governor Stanly gave a public speech in Plymouth "to a large number of people." In it, he denounced secession, condemned North Carolina secessionists for their part in leaving the Union, lauded the federal states, and described the dire consequences for North Carolinians of their own rash actions. Finally, the governor urged North Carolina to repeal its secession ordinance and to rejoin the Union. In all this, Stanly hoped simply to restore all forms of prewar dominance. He expected planters to rule, property claims to be enforced, and slaves to submit. The governor, however, also made some suggestions bearing on local affairs. He urged in his speech that "Union men ought to organize themselves into a company of 1 or 200 as a home guard for the protection of themselves and their property." "If they would do so," Stanly promised "to arm them." Should they still need protection, he promised to deploy Union troops on their behalf. Finally, the governor announced that a public meeting to organize local unionists would be held on July 12 in Plymouth.[35]

Governor Stanly failed to understand the implications of his own suggestions. He evidently intended to address himself strictly to planters. Should they rally under the U.S. flag, local slaveholders could run the county as they wished. The governor even suggested that planters use the home guard to retrieve their runaway slaves now living on Roanoke Island. In saying this, however, Stanly revealed his ignorance of the state's new political realities. Washington County residents counted alligators and black flies that could kill a horse among the area's fauna, but nothing so exotic as a unionist planter. The governor, evidently, did not know that the unionists to whom he spoke at Plymouth already had vowed publicly to drive Washington County planters off their lands. Stanly had made no allowance in his thinking for the political consequences of secession, war, and federal occupation. He could not see that his plan would result in complete destruction of the very political economy he hoped to restore.

H. G. Spruill was extremely upset. In a private conversation later, the mayor told Stanly that, if the governor armed local men and withdrew U.S. troops, "those of us who were known to be strong Southern men [would] be compelled to flee for safety." "If these men [armed unionists] were turned loose on us," the mayor claimed, "we should be ravaged." Moreover, local unionists would free the slaves, the mayor thought, and therefore, Spruill begged that federal troops remain at Plymouth. He argued that many of "the recruits" now in the local home guard were "lawless violent men." "We fear them," he told the governor, "and we ask that they be controlled by officers of discretion." To Spruill, all this seemed a "strange anomoly" indeed. Planters in Washington County appealed to men they considered enemies in order to protect their lives and property from the "violence of our own people."[36]

Stanly replied to this outburst with reassuring words. He told Spruill that the Union troops at Plymouth would remain. United States forces, Stanly contended, never "abandon[ed] any post [of] which they took possession." Moreover, the Union government had no intention of interfering with the administration of local government. As a show of good faith, Stanly urged the mayor to undertake the relief and feeding of the wives and children of Confederate volunteers now out of the county. Such relief had been specifically prohibited earlier. At the same time, however, Stanly warned that a failure to cooperate with the U.S. government would result in political chaos. "Every effort would be made to down the Rebellion," the governor told Spruill, "and if they went on until all were exaspurated, that the end would be to incite the negroes [to rebellion]." "This," he argued, "cannot be avoided by an advancing army." Stanly's words gained considerable resonance over the next few weeks.[37]

During the month of July 1862, U.S. Navy gunboats made four expeditions into North Carolina's coastal plain. On one of those expeditions, Lieutenant Flusser, commanding two gunboats loaded with about one hundred soldiers from Plymouth, sailed up the Roanoke River. The party intended to burn the town of Hamilton, which had harbored a Confederate cavalry company. As it happened, Flusser's men found the town deserted and decided not to destroy it. But while they surveyed the situation, blacks from miles around converged on the place, seeking federal protection. Flusser told them to go home, but many stayed the night and followed the U.S. boats back to Plymouth.[38] On July 17, H. G. Spruill complained that Plymouth was filling rapidly with runaway slaves from the upcountry. In ten days, the mayor claimed, "there would be 500 in town," if the captain permitted them to enter federal lines. The U.S. government must "make large provisions" the mayor told Hammill, "for feeding negroes."[39]

Captain Hammill, however, preferred to avoid the question of emancipation, if at all possible. He allowed none of his troops to harbor runaways, and he vowed not to give the refugees from up-river "one iota" of food. In addition, the captain ordered his pickets "not to permit a negro to come in the lines without a pass." By July 17, he had "driven off over a dozen" and promised to continue to "search the town and drive off every vagrant negro." Hammill's officers were in agreement with this policy. One man, a certain Captain Graves, boasted that he would give the runaways some "Gov[ernment] protection." When asked to explain his remark, the captain said that he had a rope "which he called 'protection,'" and when slaves came to his boat seeking asylum, the captain gave them "a dozen stripes." That, Graves revealed, "stopped the request for 'protection.'" By July 20, however, runaway slaves in Plymouth had become numerous enough to make Hammill "embarrassed." He vowed to "get clear of them" and by nightfall he had driven all the blacks out of town.[40]

Stanly had failed in his effort to revitalize local planter rule. Instead, he inadvertently encouraged an alliance between U.S. officers and unionists, and unionists used that relationship to arm themselves, to form a home guard, and to harass the very planters Stanly had hoped to aid. In addition, federal expeditions encouraged slaves from the Roanoke Valley to seek refuge in Plymouth, even if turned away by Union troops. This development, of course, produced no friends for Stanly among planters west of the town. Moreover, it burdened planters who remained in Washington County with what they thought was their responsibility for controlling a mass of runaway slaves. In the end, Stanly would succeed in fostering an organized government but not the one he had envisioned.

· **VI** ·

On June 12, 1862, a convention of unionists met at Plymouth and determined to place the county under martial law. In making this decision, Washington County unionists did not act alone. During the summer, Tyrrell, Martin, Bertie, Hertford, Gates, Chowan, Perquimans, Pasquotank, and Camden counties all formed organizations "not only for self-protection against rebel guerillas," according to a unionist newspaper printed in New Bern, "but for the purpose of expatriating all the rebel families from their limits." In addition, the unionists in each county had started petitions, "extensively signed," which they directed to President Lincoln, requesting "authority to carry out these purposes." "To enforce these objects," they promised the president "a loyal regiment from each county, which are to be maintained as a standing army." Finally, unionists around the Albemarle Sound proposed to "appropriate all the property, of every kind, belonging to rebels within these counties, to the support of this armed force."[41]

The convention at Plymouth elected John Phelps provost marshal for the county. Phelps, thus, replaced the county court and its magistrates as the chief administrator for Washington County. As marshal, Phelps also took on military powers as the head of the local militia—the home guard. In addition, the unionists formed a cavalry under the direction of John Giles. The new government came into being with a vote by unionists present at the convention on a set of written resolutions. Shortly afterwards, the resolutions circulated through town to the alarm of planters and to the annoyance of federal officers.

The unionists' resolutions began with a vote of "full confidence in the virtue and integrity of the Government of the United States, under whose laws all good citizens have been protected at home and abroad." "We are still willing to abide by and defend the same," vowed Washington County's unionists. They then castigated secessionists for "trying to break up the Government of the United States" and for "the dreadful consequences" which that effort "brought upon the whole country." By contrast, local unionists expressed "confidence" in the federal officers at Plymouth, saying that they merited "respect" from "all good citizens." Finally, the convention recommended that "the people of the State" call upon their representatives to the Constitutional Convention still in session at Raleigh "to vote the State back into the Union." Specifically, local unionists instructed William S. Pettigrew "to use all his influence to accomplish that end" and voted to send him a copy of the resolutions.[42]

H. G. Spruill went immediately to see Captain Hammill. He goaded the officer, saying that he "presumed" that local unionists had "superceded him." Hammill thought so too when he first read the resolutions. He vowed that "if any of them interfered" with his authority, he would "imprison him or them." But by Tuesday, the captain had calmed himself. John Phelps told Hammill that he "did not intend to come in conflict" with federal authority. Phelps planned to station soldiers only "outside of [Hammill's] pickett." By this means, Washington County unionists hoped simply "to prevent any who had not taken the oath of allegiance from leaving the county." In other words, Phelps proposed to extend Hammill's policy in Plymouth to cover all of Washington County. Finally, Phelps assured the captain that local martial law "should not affect anybody here" in Plymouth. Phelps promised to "control and regulate" his men.[43]

On July 18, 1862, however, John Phelps posted notices throughout the county which required all persons to take an oath of allegiance to the United States. This represented a distinct change in local policy toward secessionists. Hammill had been content to respect rebel sentiments as long as such men neither left the county nor aided the enemy. Now local unionists demanded that all men submit to the U.S. government. Spruill naturally protested to Captain Hammill and then to Lieutenant Flusser. The mayor urged the officers "to stop it." Otherwise, Phelps's efforts "would result in a guerilla war in the county." But the officers saw things differently. They argued that the local unionist government constituted "an organization with the people" over which the U.S. government had no control. Besides, the federals had no quarrel with unionist aims. Therefore, they would neither interfere with nor encourage Phelps. But they did insist that the marshal be allowed to post his notices in the town.[44]

With that vote of neutrality in mind, Phelps targeted men who had claimed unionist sympathies but had not joined their organization. He did so not expecting to convert many furtive secessionists but in order to drive a further wedge between U.S. officers and local Confederates—which could be used for a larger purpose. Unionists, for example, confronted Wilson Ambrose, one of the men who had helped Hammill round up runaway slaves earlier that week. But he refused to take the oath. That turned the federals against men like Ambrose who claimed to be both unionists and slaveholders. Hammill declared that "he had no use for such Union men." He warned that Union troops would "afford him no protection or privilege." The captain told Ambrose to his face that he "did not want him to come to town any more." The reaction pleased Phelps, who sought to exploit Hammill's anger. Specifically, Phelps hoped to create a constituency within the county for martial law by feeding poor people without levying a local tax. To do so, the county marshal planned to seize grain from plantations belonging to secessionists absent from the county, grain which he would distribute to landless unionists.[45]

· VII ·

At ten p.m., July 21, 1862, U.S.N. Captain Thomas Woodward, twelve marines, and John Giles, the newly appointed captain of the local unionist cavalry, reached Josiah Collins's Somerset Place. Collins had long since fled to Hillsboro, Orange County, in the North Carolina piedmont, leaving behind about two hundred slaves, an overseer, and George Patterson, a local Episcopal priest and friend of the family, to care for the plantation. Just east of Somerset Place lay Bonarva, Charles L. Pettigrew's smaller plantation, where the planter remained to manage about eighty of his slaves. Woodward acted on Captain Hammill's orders when he steered his gunboat, the *Shawsheen,* up the Scuppernong River.[46]

When the troops arrived, Captain Woodward introduced himself to George Patterson and assured the minister that he "should not be annoyed in any way." He promised that "none of the servants or the property on the plantation should be troubled." Woodward then said he wished "to examine the house" to see if there were "any arms, or ammunition." Patterson obliged. Afterwards, the two agreed upon sleeping arrangements for themselves and the troops. But before Patterson and Woodward retired for the night, they had a long conversation. The captain explained the purpose of his visit. On "orders from his government," Woodward said, he must "take away a lot of corn and wheat." The grain was to be transported "to Plymouth to be distributed among the poor." Patterson asked him whether or not the U.S. government intended to pay for the grain, and the officer said no. The minister did not object, but he should have. The seizure was, in fact, illegal. Woodward later admitted that he took the grain "before we had seen the President's proclamation concerning the confiscation act."[47]

The next morning, Woodward and his troops supervised the preparation of corn by Collins's slaves. After milling, the slaves packed the grain into barrels, rolled barrels onto flatboats, and floated boats and barrels down the plantation canal to a U.S. schooner waiting in the Scuppernong River. Patterson watched all this closely. He explained later to Josiah Collins: "Altho' Captain Woodward had assured me that the Federal Government did not wish our negroes, that they were not allowed to go within their lines, & that our servants should not be carried off in his vessel, still I thot it best . . . to go down to the Scuppernong River with the Capt, his men, and our people." The minister wanted to "see for my self that our negroes neither ran away, nor were carried away." To make sure, Patterson "remained either on board the [U.S. gunboat], or in the neighbourhood until the vessel was loaded, & all our servants were on their way back to the Lake." Altogether, the troops took 1,080 bushels of corn and 238 bushels of wheat.[48]

Unionists on the scene acted cautiously, but they did not hesitate to take advantage. John Giles *"apologized"* to George Patterson aboard the schooner "for taking away of our corn & wheat." He said, by Patterson's report, that "he did all he could to prevent it." The unionist leader also told the minister that he "regretted the war & its consequences upon [local planters] & the people of our neighbourhood." Not likely. Giles's actions before and after this conversation revealed very different opinions indeed. Here, he simply hoped by his words to grease the wheels of the new unionist government. In this aim, Giles succeeded. The unionists got their grain to Plymouth. Others took advantage as well. Durham Lassiter, a small farmer and strong unionist in the Scuppernong neighborhood, for example, sought and received permission from Captain Woodward to haul away two barrels of grain free of charge. When Patterson protested, Giles said that Lassiter "was a *poor* man & unable to work."[49]

Two weeks later, Washington County unionists used Union troops to exact a further levy on absent planters in favor of the county's new government. On Sunday morning, July 27, John Giles, Captain Woodward, and thirty soldiers from Plymouth again visited Somerset Place. When George Patterson and Charles Pettigrew found the captain, he was examining horses in the company of Giles at the plantation mill. Woodward saluted Patterson, explained the purpose of his visit, and gave the minister a copy of an order for twelve horses. Giles had convinced Captain Hammill, who was in command at Plymouth, to issue the papers to equip the county's unionist cavalry. After reading the orders, Patterson begged the captain "to leave us some horses, particularly our Carriage horses & Conrad." The horse named Conrad had "belonged to a deceased member" of the Collins family. But the captain explained that he must take whatever horses "would be of use to his Government," including Conrad. John Giles, meanwhile *"seemed* most anxious to take those that were most valued by the family."[50]

Woodward, however, found only seven horses in Collins's stable fit for military duty. Therefore, he sent Giles to Bonarva with permission to seize five of Charles Pettigrew's horses. Giles, who had evidently conflicted with Pettigrew before the war, did so with relish. He led the troops directly to Pettigrew's stable, "called for the horses by name," and told the soldiers "on which side they drew in harness & c." In the end, Giles "selected all the carriage horses, & one of the very best farm horses," including one out of which Giles claimed Pettigrew had cheated him. "That's the one [Pettigrew] fooled me out of," Giles said pointing to the horse. After dinner, Charles Pettigrew came to the Collins mansion to protest. The planter told Woodward that "no Government could prosper which took away the property of the people against all law & order."[51]

The show of federal might encouraged unionists in Scuppernong to seek to appropriate the plantations for themselves. Two men applied to U.S. authorities "for permission" to take over William Pettigrew's Belgrade plantation, but the officers refused. In one planter's words, the unionists "find great fault with the Yankees for not allowing them to sack the plantations." Moreover, "many a severe quarrell" broke out among unionists "as to the division of the lands of Mr. Collins," Charles Pettigrew, and his brother William Pettigrew. "In some instances," one planter claimed, "they have come to blows.!!"[52]

John Phelps and his military government had forced dramatic changes in the county's politics. First, Phelps's actions—especially the effort to force sessionists to swear an oath of allegiance to the

U.S. Constitution—defined sharply and publicly who might or might not be considered a unionist. That drove a wedge between U.S. officers and propertied unionists—whose civil liberties would no longer be protected as under an earlier informal truce. Second, the expedition to Somerset Place set a precedent for the confiscation of personal and real property. Those actions negated the bargain between local C.S.A. and U.S. officers not to interfere in property claims. Finally, yeoman farmers found themselves able to settle old scores, especially to retrieve that which they believed planters had taken from them unjustly. The result was bitter fighting, just as H. G. Spruill had warned.

· VIII ·

In late summer 1862, politics in Washington County became confused and violent. During the last week in July, Confederates, for example, captured two black soldiers from Plymouth who had been detailed to a road in southwestern Washington County. The blacks had been "sent out as emissaries to induce others," slaves living alongside the road, "to run away and enlist." According to the blacks' captors, the two "had U.S. money and enlistment papers with them." The prisoners were then brought before a certain Colonel Williams, who, after presumably interrogating his prisoners, had them hanged.[53]

Then on August 17, a man named Gardner, a secessionist still living in Plymouth, was arrested for threatening to kill Captain Todd, a U.S. officer stationed in town. H. G. Spruill interviewed Gardner after the arrest. Based on that information, the mayor claimed that the unionists had told "a set of lies" about Gardner. But Captain Hammill was not persuaded; the secessionist remained under guard. A day later, a rumor circulated in Plymouth that two men had been arrested for murdering Captain Flusser. In fact, the two had been imprisoned, but not for murder. They had enlisted for duty on Flusser's gunboat while it was operating near their homes on the Roanoke River in Bertie County. But when the expedition returned to Plymouth with the two on board, they deserted. For that reason, they were arrested. Flusser was away on leave at the time.[54]

Executions, murders, and rumors of assassination plots unnerved federals and unionists alike. Captain Hammill warned Spruill that if anyone not belonging to the Confederate army shot one of his men, "he would look upon it as murder, and he would hang the murderer." Hammill's troops acted even more skittishly. Some of his marines forged the captain's name to an order permitting John Phelps, the unionist marshal, to call out the U.S. cavalry (not the unionist cavalry). Phelps ordered the troops to post themselves on the county's roads and bridges, but Hammill found out and countermanded the order. He sent for Phelps and his compatriots that evening and "read them the law." The captain told Phelps that if he "gave another order," he would be "committed to jail."[55]

Meanwhile, the Confederate army in eastern North Carolina had been organizing companies for local guerrilla service. Lieutenant Colonel D. G. Cowand, then serving with Washington County's troops near Petersburg, Virginia, again proposed that the North Carolina governor allow him to form a guerrilla company of one hundred Washington County recruits, arguing that "good sharpshooters in all of our eastern counties would annoy the enemy more than a good force of any other brand of the service." His purpose was to "drive the miserable traitors from our county," especially John Giles. "Giles should be hung without any trial." Cowand did not get his wish, for the moment anyway. But the Confederate army did form several guerrilla units, one assigned to the Roanoke River region.[56]

At the same time, Confederate, federal, and unionist troops already in Washington County fought several small guerrilla battles of their own. John Giles mobilized the unionist cavalry first to burn two bridges in the northern part of the county connecting Plymouth and the area's largest plantations to the east. As one planter put it, the unionist action "cut off all retreat from below." Then the unionist cavalry began arresting prominent secessionists in that part of the county cut off from Confederate troops. One secessionist escaped by swimming across a creek where a bridge had been before Giles set fire to it. The secessionist had heard that the unionists planned to "arrest him in a day or two." At the same time, Giles and his men began seizing secessionists who carried letters to and from the upcountry. Planters responded by sending their reports by more secure means. "The only way we have to send letters," one planter revealed, "is by the 'Underground Rail Road.' "[57]

In early September 1862, Confederate and federal cavalrymen engaged in a series of more serious conflicts. The immediate cause lay in federal efforts to control the roads west of Plymouth. Sniper fire from that direction convinced the U.S. commanders that the Confederate cavalry now posed a greater threat than before. In fact, the Confederates had moved their camp from Williamston, about twenty-two miles from Plymouth, to Jamesville, only eleven miles distant. Therefore, Captain Hammill ordered regular patrols outside his usual pickets, and he increased surveillance of civilians leaving and entering the county. In response, the Confederate cavalry began to attack Union patrols at every opportunity. On August 30, roughly fifteen Confederates fought "quite a skirmish" against an equal number of federals near a plantation on the Williamston Road west of Plymouth. There were no casualties on either side, and only one Confederate trooper was captured by the federals.[58]

During the first week in September, a very large skirmish took place west of Plymouth. On the first of the month, a Confederate company of infantry and a company of cavalry marched from near Tarboro to a place on the Williamston Road three miles west of Plymouth. There they camped on the evening of September 1, apparently planning to attack on September 3. In the night, however, a unionist resident of the neighborhood, "knowing the intention of the rebels, came quickly to town and reported it to Captain W. H. Hammell." Hammill woke his troops, a company of the the New York Volunteers and a company of the locally recruited 1st North Carolina Union Volunteers. Most of the soldiers, including all the officers, were ill, evidently from malaria then prevalent in Plymouth. But all rose in the night and prepared for battle.

At dawn, the federal force marched west out of Plymouth and surprised the Confederates still "bivouacked in the woods." "A Rebel [picket] intended giving the alarm of the approach of our forces by firing his piece," wrote one of the federal soldiers, "but it missed fire." "Our boys took this as a signal of alarm, and they dashed upon them with great earnestness, fighting the whole force [of Confederates] for an hour." In the end, the federals captured the Confederate commander, a lieutenant, and forty other soldiers, "together with many of the cavalry horses." "The rebels lost thirty killed, with the ordinary proportion of wounded." Unionists from Plymouth evidently inflicted many of these casualties. "The loyal North Carolinians," according to a federal report, "were fast and fierce in the pursuit of their rebel neighbors. The chase was given up only when the enemy was completely put to flight."[59]

Afterwards, tempers in Plymouth became brittle. The Yankees and unionists in Plymouth appeared to planters "as becoming more and more audacious—disturbing the [secessionist] citizens in town and country more & more." In mid-September, H. G. Spruill was attacked. He had "started downtown on some business" when a Zouave called to him from the troops' barracks. The soldier asked whether "there was any news outside." Spruill wanted to know "if he alluded to Confederate forces or an attack on this place." The man said he meant both. The mayor answered that he had been outside the lines the day before and had found that Confederate cavalry forces had concentrated in Pitt County, some distance southwest. "From what I could learn," Spruill told the soldier, "no attack was proposed on this place." All this conversation was conducted "in a pleasant manner." Then, "in a moment" the soldier took a swing at Spruill with his fist and swore an oath. The man "seemed furious" and kept striking at the mayor's face. Spruill at last subdued his attacker with several blows from his cane.[60]

In the end, a large force of Confederates did reach Plymouth. On September 23, at about four in the afternoon, a squad of fifty cavalrymen rode toward town, but they were driven off by heavy artillery fire from federal gunboats in the Roanoke River. The Confederate raiders, therefore, confined their depredations to the town's outskirts. First, they stopped at a house occupied by a free black, two New York Volunteers, and Captain Todd. Todd had been supervising several freedmen who were cutting down trees near town, presumably so federal gunboats could get a clear shot at Confederates who might approach from that direction. Evidently, the living arrangements Todd had undertaken—blacks and whites, officers and enlisted men all together—attracted Confederate attention. Whatever the reason, the Confederate cavalrymen arrested all three whites and killed the black man. "It was a cruel affair," H. G. Spruill wrote of the murder, and likely to "result in retaliation." Then, the cavalry raced along Morattock Road south of town, where they arrested two unionists.[61] As a result of the Confederate raid, Spruill thought "there are many good men [secessionists] in town and country who may suffer innocently."[62]

· **IX** ·

Sovereignty in Washington County had finally by late September 1862 boiled down to a matter of guns and bullets. But the exercise of power had not been so simple or brutal just four months earlier. Federal occupation, unionist aspirations, and the continued operation of a local Confederate government combined to pose many complex questions relating to sovereignty. Secessionist planters, U.S. officers, and local unionsits each formulated a different and distinct version of how power might be constructed. All claimed the mantle of popular approbation. But whom those constituents might include, how a government might be structured, and what force might be used legitimately by any government remained at issue. In the end, might prevailed. All local government dissolved. Washington County residents had raised questions of sovereignty such as had not been discussed since the Revolution. Despite four months of struggle, they had arrived at no common answers. The local war would continue, and the county's unionists dedicated themselves to winning it.

On October 8, "a large and spirited meeting" took place in Plymouth, at which Samuel Newberry, "a prominent citizen of the town" and the man who in 1851 had predicted secession and a bloody war within ten years, presided. The audience included "Union citizens and soldiers," among them the "company of North Carolina Union Volunteers stationed at that point," who heard an address by Charles Foster, who was running for a North Carolina seat in the U.S. Congress. The meeting closed "with three hearty cheers for the Union, the Constitution, and the enforcement of the [federal] laws." As a result of this demonstration, wrote a federal newspaper correspondent, "authority has since been given" by Major General John G. Foster "to raise a company of cavalry, in addition to that of infantry already there; and the prospects are most encouraging that it will be completed at an early day."[63]

5

The Emancipation
Proclamation: Beginnings
of a Property War

· I ·

In mid-1862, slaves remaining in Washington County saw little chance of freeing themselves soon. True, local unionists had promised them "absolute freedom" and "equality with white men" if they joined in an effort to dislodge local planters from their land. A few white men had actively aided Washington County slaves in their efforts to escape. In early March 1862, for example, three unionists arranged for several boats to be left at the mouth of the Scuppernong River for slaves wishing to flee to Roanoke.[1] But local slaves still faced an official federal policy that defined them as property. Captain Hammill had helped planters retain their slaves, and even the abolitionist-minded New York Volunteers in Plymouth divided among themselves. On July 19, a New York soldier "cut the cords from one of the negroes" who had been taken up by secessionists in Plymouth. But within minutes, five other soldiers arrested the New Yorker and abused him for his action. "The negroes were better off here than he was at home," they told him. Besides, the soldiers did "not want the negroes North."[2]

The Collins slaves, therefore, "behaved with great propriety," according to George Patterson, when in July Captain Woodward had led his troops to Somerset Place. Similarly, when the officer inquired "very closely" of Charles Pettigrew's slave Tom at Bonarva, the slave feigned ignorance as to "whether any [Confederate] soldiers had been there" and "if any cotton was hidden." Tom also answered with an underestimation after having been asked "how many men his master had sent up the country." Finally, one of Pettigrew's slaves, Edward, went along to protect his master's interests when Woodward sent a party to the residence of Pettigrew's overseer in search of saddles. After the men had found no saddles and "began prying about for other matters," Edward told the soldiers: "If you do that I'll report you to the Capt. He said you must not trouble nothing other & there ain't no saddles here."[3]

The slaves at Somerset Place and Bonarva had good reasons to keep their own counsel. The wrong word spoken to the wrong person, secessionist or federal, might result in a whipping or worse. Not surprisingly, "so far as [Patterson] could learn," not one "was desirous to run away." Moreover, caught between two contending powers, the slaves became easy victims to unscrupulous federal soldiers. During the first visit to Somerset Place, one man "shamefully ravished" a slave woman named Lovey. He "threaten[ed] her that she should be shot, if she resisted or made any noise." Later, he drove away "by threats" some of Lovey's fellow slaves who went to her assistance. Captain Woodward promised afterwards to "severely punish" the soldier. But the damage had been done, both to Lovey personally and to the slave community's faith in federal soldiers. Hence, when Union troops returned to Somerset Place, the people there displayed a skeptical attitude. Woodward's soldiers "talked to some of the servants about freedom." The Northerners asked "if they would not like to go away with them, where they could work, & receive wages for their work." But the slaves saw little prospect of that; they gave the soldiers no encouragement.[4]

Still, a few slaves took a chance in July 1862 when federal troops visited Somerset Place. Fred Elsy, for example, left his post when George Patterson, thinking that Union soldiers would steal fruit from an orchard behind the plantation mansion, assigned the slave to guard the place. Elsy went instead to the grist mill, where Woodward and John Giles had begun selecting property for confiscation. There, the slave bridled several horses for the two. Later, Patterson "remonstrated" with Elsy about his conduct. But the slave replied with "impudent words." And, Elsy's "conduct *afterwards*" was "extremely wicked," Patterson reported.[5]

Other slaves as well might have acted boldly had they known Abraham Lincoln's plans for them. In September 1862, hints of a change in federal policy toward slaves began to appear around the Albemarle Sound. In New Bern, Governor Stanly decamped suddenly for Washington, D.C., to see President Lincoln "in order that he might know what [the federal] policy was on the slavery question." Stanly strongly supported slavery and evidently had perceived some movement in the government towards abolition. On Thursday, October 2, a small steamer pulled up to the wharf at Plymouth "bearing dispatches" to Captain Flusser. But the captain had left town a short time before; therefore, the reports remained unread and their contents unknown, pending Flusser's return.[6]

· **II** ·

On October 3, 1862, another mail boat arrived in Plymouth carrying news of President Lincoln's proposed Emancipation Proclamation. "It is entirely changing the prospect here," wrote H. G. Spruill. "Some [planters] who can are running off their negroes," evidently sending them upcountry. "The rest are wild." In a matter of hours, a number of slaves in the countryside fled their masters and headed for Plymouth. Word had spread among them that the soldiers would let slaves enter federal lines for the first time and that the U.S. government would transport the refugees to safety. "The town is filling up with them." "The white seaboard will be devastated," thought H. G. Spruill, "and the country must be abandoned."[7]

The proposed procalmation meant that the federal government no longer conceded to secessionists their absolute claims to property. The U.S. Congress had moved in that direction earlier with the passage of the Confiscation Acts in 1861 and 1862. The Emancipation Proclamation, however, specifically extended a principle of confiscation to cover slaves. "I had no fear of losing but few of my negroes until this Proclamation," H. G. Spruill admitted, but

"this settles the matter and shows us the issues of the war."
William Pettigrew agreed: "There is no mistaking the meaning.
The slaves of the loyal men [secessionists] will be taken from
them, nor do I think there is any probability that the slaves of the
disloyal men [unionists] will much longer fare otherwise." This
would be a "property war," just as Washington County's unionists
had predicted in the fall of 1861.[8]

But how might the Emancipation Proclamation be implemented
in Washington County? Hoping to find out, H. G. Spruill went
immediately to see Captain Hammill. As far as Hammill could tell,
Lincoln's proclamation did not apply to Plymouth. Since that territory remained under federal control, all laws then pertaining to
slaves had to be enforced, as in Maryland, Delaware, Kentucky,
Tennessee, and Missouri. Besides, in Hammill's mind, the proclamation implied nothing about freedom or citizenship. Therefore,
he refused to aid runaway slaves in any way. In fact, the captain
encouraged the county's planters to remove their slaves to the
upcountry while they still could. "The owners ought to get them
off," Hammill told H. G. Spruill. For the moment then, Lincoln's
announcement had little impact on local federal policy. The course
of events over the next two weeks, however, would give the Emancipation Proclamation life and effect apart from Hammill's opinions.[9]

Within days, a multitude of slaves had made their way down
the Roanoke River to Plymouth. Most of H. G. Spruill's slaves
left his plantation in Martin County for Plymouth. "Nearly all of
mine are all in town," the mayor wrote, and "keep out of my
sight."[10]

By October 7, Captain Hammill was anticipating "an attack on
this place" as a result of "the congregating of negroes." According
to reports gathered by Flusser, the Confederates had built three
gunboats and a large artillery barge covered with railroad iron at
Halifax on the upper Roanoke River. In addition, the Confederate
army had concentrated two regiments of infantry and one of
cavalry in Martin County just west of Plymouth. Flusser wrote "in
haste" to his superior: "The avowed objects of the rebels are to
burn this place, destroy the boats if possible, and sweep the lower
counties of conscripts [meaning unionists], horses, and provisions."
The Confederate threat, however, only encouraged slaves to flee

more quickly to the town in hopes of getting there before the federals left.[11]

By Friday, October 17, Plymouth had become jammed with runaways. Therefore, Captain Hammill announced publicly that all slaves in town faced two alternatives. They could depart on Saturday aboard a special boat bound for Roanoke Island. The boat had come on General Foster's orders and was supposed to carry able-bodied male slaves to New Bern where the general hoped to put them to work building fortifications. Hammill served his own purposes by allowing women, children, and the elderly to board as well. Otherwise, the fugitive slaves would be drummed out of federal lines. In the end, about five hundred blacks left the town by boat, including "nearly all the runaways" from upcountry, plus "a large portion of those whose masters lived here." H. G. Spruill lost thirteen slaves. Ten more told him they intended "going on the next boat." All the while, Washington County unionists had made every effort to convince local slaves to desert their masters. John Phelps, the unionist marshal, personally persuaded H. G. Spruill's house servants to leave the mayor's household. (To add insult to injury, Phelps hired for wages one of Spruill's slave cooks.)[12]

The Confederates, however, did not attack immediately. Meanwhile, local slaveholders saw clearly enough where this war in Washington County was headed. By October 25, Spruill could see "no discipline or control of negroes." "They work when and where they please," he lamented, and "quit their owners and go to the next house." Thereafter, local planters undertook to relocate all the slaves then remaining in Washington County to the North Carolina piedmont.[13]

By mid-November 1862, Washington County planters had salvaged their property in slaves. William Pettigrew estimated the number refugeed so far "not falling short of two thousand." But this was accomplished at a great cost to all concerned. Washington County slaves lost their customary rights in dependence. As hirelings, they would receive a minimal upkeep specified in their contract, if that. Planters gave up their mastery of slave labor. They would no longer direct slaves but simply receive rent from their property's labor. The greatest losses for Washington County planters, however, lay not in slaves but in the land and personal property they left behind. The Emancipation Proclamation had transformed the local conflict into a struggle over property of all kinds.[14]

· **III** ·

Events following news of the proposed proclamation convinced Confederate commanders in eastern North Carolina that Plymouth must be destroyed. The town had become a base for federal attacks against secessionists living deep in the interior, and it served as a safe destination for thousands of slaves who slipped away from their masters in the Roanoke and Chowan valleys. If secessionist property was to be saved, Plymouth must be attacked and the federals driven away. The Confederates began their preparations in October, two days after the proposed proclamation became known.

The federal commanders followed Confederate actions closely. On October 18, Lieutenant Flusser hired an "intelligent negro" for $100 to "visit Halifax and Hamilton" and to return "with all the information he can obtain." By such means, the captain found out about the floating artillery batteries and the iron-covered troop barge at Hamilton. He also learned that the Confederates were building elaborate fortifications at Rainbow Banks, a bluff overlooking a bend in the Roanoke River three miles east of Hamilton. In addition, the Confederate army had dispatched perhaps three thousand soldiers—two regiments of infantry and one of cavalry—to Martin County.[15]

Federal prospects looked bleak. The army had only about 150 regular soldiers, plus perhaps 100 locally recruited unionists, stationed at Plymouth. The town had no fortifications, and pickets stationed around its perimeter depended entirely on gunboats to provide artillery cover. Finally, the three gunboats stationed at Plymouth drew too much water to pursue the Confederate artillery barges upriver.[16] Therefore, Rear-Admiral S. P. Lee, commander of the North Atlantic Blockading Squadron, advocated a preemptive strike, a combined operation directed at Hamilton. The admiral suggested to S. K. Davenport, U.S. naval commander on the Sound, that he propose such an operation to General John G.

Foster, commander of Union troops for eastern North Carolina. This Davenport did. In response, Foster assured the naval commander that within three weeks he would march several thousand soldiers from New Bern to "cooperate with our gunboats in an attack upon the enemy."[17]

Confederate troops, meanwhile, raided Washington County's plantation districts. On October 29, rebel troops marched along the Washington Road south of Plymouth, arresting as they went "many persons who were supposed disloyal," meaning unionists, "traitors in arms and without arms," as one planter put it, plus "conscripts, negroes belonging to traitors, &c." Altogether, about forty unionists were seized, lodged in the county jail at Williamston, and later transported to the Confederate prison at Salisbury in the piedmont region of North Carolina.[18]

Among the conscripts taken was Thomas Hassell. He owned ninety acres of land valued at $1,000 in 1860. Like many small farmers in Washington County, Hassell had remained loyal to the United States in the secession crisis of 1861. "At the beginning of the war," he explained, "my sympathy was with the Union." Hassell also let his opinions be known in the neighborhood. James A. Wilson, who had known Thomas Hassell for several years, "saw him often during the war" and "heard him express himself" "concerning the war & its progress." Therefore, when the Confederates swept through Washington County in early November 1862, Thomas Hassell became a target. "I was arrested [and] threatened several times by the rebels on account of my union sentiments." In the end, Hassell "was conscripted" by force and removed from the county when the rebels retreated to Jamesville.[19]

When news of the Confederate raid reached Plymouth, federal commanders prepared to be attacked. At nine in the evening on Thursday, October 30, an alarm was sounded, warning local residents of imminent battle. The rebels failed to show. That night, however, a Confederate soldier deserted to Plymouth and told Captain Hammill that his fellows had camped alongside the Morattock Road three miles south of town. And he warned that they intended to attack Plymouth on Friday night. Hence, as a precaution, the next day federal gunboats fired a "heavy cannonade" over the town, about thirty shells in all, evidently hoping to persuade Confederate troops that an attack would be suicidal. The tactic succeeded. By three in the afternoon on Sunday, November 3, Charles Latham, the local unionist politician, reported that "the whole force had left." The Confederates had retreated temporarily upriver.[20]

Before word of the Confederate departure had reached federal headquarters in New Bern, however, General Foster was on the move, as he had promised earlier. On November 1, he left New Bern with roughly five thousand soldiers, passed through Washington, North Carolina, and then proceeded directly northward to Williamston on the Roanoke River in Martin County. Foster planned to cut off the two Confederate regiments which he believed had been foraging in Washington County. When Commander Davenport heard of Foster's movement, he sailed three gunboats upriver to meet the army at Williamston. But the federals found Hamilton deserted. On November 3, "hundreds of people" from Williamston had fled from the Yankees as the soldiers approached town. Confederate forces had withdrawn to Tarboro, thirty miles further inland, two days before Foster had marched from New Bern. Hence, on November 5, Foster's army set out overland in pursuit of the Confederates. But suddenly the federals beat a hasty retreat. Foster had heard reports of large reinforcements being sent from Richmond to Tarboro via the railroad. He and his troops, therefore, marched along the Roanoke River under cover of Davenport's guns back to Plymouth, where they boarded transports and returned to New Bern.[21]

In strategic terms, all this maneuvering came to nothing. Foster claimed his expedition had succeeded in saving Plymouth from "destruction and capture." But the Confederates had already done their damage and had moved on. Not only did the federals fail to defeat a Confederate army, they did not even locate one. Moreover, Foster's troops held no more territory than they had before. The Confederates did no better. They had hoped to take Plymouth, to drive away the troops and gunboats from the town, and, thereby, to "give the people of Martin, Washington, and Tyrrell Counties an opportunity to bring out their provisions, &c." In fact, Confederate actions only convinced the Union army of a need to hold the position. In late November, the federals sent more gunboats into the Roanoke River and stationed additional infantry troops at Plymouth, part of the 27th Massachusetts Volunteers. In political terms, however, the movement of Union troops and gunboats proved crucial in expanding Washington County's property war.[22]

· **IV** ·

While the federal expedition marched upcountry, rumors and reports of all kinds began to reach Plymouth. One story circulated that "Federal troops [had] sacked Williamston, busting open homes and stores and taking what they wanted." Another reported that Hamilton had been burned "because some one fired at [federal troops] from a house." Later, rumors filled in details or corrected earlier reports. At Williamston "damage was done to furniture," and only "a part of Hamilton was burned."[23]

On November 7, Foster's troops returned to Plymouth, where they confirmed all that local residents had heard. Some admitted burning Williamston and Hamilton. They reported that the army had "devastated the count[ies] through which they went, taking all the horses and killing all the stock." H. G. Spruill learned that "a part of the Army" had quartered itself at his plantation and had "destroyed fences and stock." "My mules are now being sent off," he lamented, evidently in federal schooners to New Bern with General Foster's troops. "I hear that my farm was entirely stripped of every thing that could be got hold of." "So my property is all destroyed," the mayor concluded.

Later, Confederate reports told the same story. A certain resident of Williamston returned to her home and found the town "pretty much in ruins" and her own property and house "greatly destroyed and stolen." Similarly, A. G. Jones, a rebel infantryman detailed to Hamilton the last week in November, surveyed the damage. Foster's troops "burnt eight or ten fine houses [here] in Hamilton," he wrote. In addition, they "carried off a great many horses & mules & shot all the cows, hogs & sheep they could find." "They also destroyed a great deal of corn." Most perplexing to Jones was the destruction of fences. "It is not at all strange," he observed, "to see large corn fields without a particle of fencing around them." "There's no fencing left wherever they went."

When Foster's troops returned to Plymouth, they brought with them another kind of property—slaves. On November 10, Spruill reported the streets of Plymouth "filled with troops and negroes." "The latter are over 1000," he believed, "brought down by the Boat[s] with the Army." They remained in Plymouth because federal naval officers had forced them off the transports to make way for Foster's troops who were to be taken to New Bern.[24]

"The expedition of Gen. Foster we cannot comprehend," wrote H. G. Spruill of himself and his planter friends. "He left Newbern with some 8000 infantry, 1500 cavalry, and 40 pieces of Artillery, all well provided (such are the number reported) to go to Tarboro and cut off the R[ail] R[oad] at Rocky Mount." (That was not Foster's plan.) "The corps [then] proceeded within a few miles of Tarboro and there retreated in haste to this place where transports are taking them off." "It must have been a mortifying failure in a military point of view," the planter concluded. So why all the sound and fury on the part of the federal army? Spruill thought he knew. "They have taken a large amount of what they termed contraband property. At least 700 horses and mules, worth $70,000, many buggies, wagons, and carriages worth $15,000, and all the stock on the way." And he noted: "At least 1000 negroes came with the Army or in the boats worth nearly $5,000,000." So, the planter believed, "in a money point of view, the expedition paid."[25]

Certainly, the expedition added to the Union army's provisions and stores, and it deprived the Confederate army of the same. But the implications of Foster's expedition went much deeper than Spruill indicated. It had been primarily an attack on property—the first such attack by the federal army in eastern North Carolina. Moreover, the burning and stealing had been directed mainly against planters—their town homes in Williamston and Hamilton, their livestock and fences, and their slaves. The expedition in practice, although not by design, had attacked a particular economic class, those men who lived by their investments in property. The rules of war, thereby, had been altered in Washington County and the Albemarle region.

Within days, some federal officers in Plymouth began denying to local secessionists having taken any part in the sacking of Hamilton and Williamston, portraying themselves as protectors of all property claims. They argued that secessionists in Williamston and Hamilton had torched their own houses, presumably to deny the federal government the benefit of their goods. The officers also claimed that "some persons" from Plymouth, unionists serving in the 1st North Carolina Union Volunteers, participated. But officers with the Massachusetts troops blamed Captain Hammill and his New York soldiers. The Massachusetts men claimed to have been "opposed to the pillage and plunder and insisted that it was not done by their men but by the Zouaves." General Foster, for his part, simply neglected to mention any burning or looting in his reports. In these efforts, the federal officers attempted to avoid taking responsibility for the change in policy. Their message, and Lincoln's too, had been communicated to planters, but they feared Confederate attacks on unionist property.[26]

The Confederates, however, had no intention of letting such a breach of decorum go unnoticed. In late November, C.S.A. Major General S. G. French, commander of the Department of North Carolina based at Petersburg, Virginia, made a personal inspection of Foster's line of march. He came away appalled. French wrote to Foster complaining that "many wanton acts of destruction of private property and many depredations were committed by the troops under your command." Then he gave a list of particulars: "Negroes were forcibly abducted from their owners; many isolated houses in the villages of Hamilton and Williamston were willfully burned; parlors of private residences were used for stables; family carriages were taken to your camps, abandoned, and destroyed; houses of peaceful citizens were forcibly entered, doors and windows broken and all the furniture destroyed; bedding was carried into the streets and burned; women were insulted by your soldiers and robbed of all the money and valuables on their persons, and all their clothing and that of their children, except what they had on, was cast into the fire or torn to pieces."[27]

General French wanted to know the meaning of all this destruction and inquired of Foster if "these outrages [were] committed with your knowledge and sanction." If so, had Foster altered federal policy towards property and the rules of war observed thus far between the two armies? If not, what would Foster do to rectify the situation? Would he prosecute the perpetrators in a court martial and, thereby, confirm existing property claims? French gave Foster ten days to answer. If the U.S. general failed to respond, French would assume "that you admit and hold yourself responsible for the acts charged." Should that occur, the Confederate general promised "action to be taken in the case."[28]

Foster answered quickly explaining to French that all had been done against his orders and without his knowledge. He admitted that fifteen houses had gone under the torch in Hamilton. "The fact I deplore," he claimed. He acknowledged that his troops had taken "draught animals, and in some cases carriages" plus some "beeves and pigs" and "forage." But Foster excused the destruction on the grounds that his troops had needed the livestock for food, forage for feed, and carriages for ambulances. He denied that his troops had committed any needless theft. Finally, the general sought to shift the blame onto his troops for any damage not accounted for in his letter. "The principal cause of the depredations which I know were committed was, I think, that so many houses [in which his soldiers quartered] contained apple brandy, and which escaped the eye of the provost-marshal." As for the slaves, Foster contended they had not been forcibly removed, but he did admit to having allowed them to follow his army to Plymouth.[29]

French accepted Foster's account of events and his promise to do better. But why? Foster's story was hardly credible. French had seen the damage, much of which Foster denied outright. And who could believe that Foster saw none of the fires or the livestock trailing behind his soldiers? Moreover, did not the general admit to aiding in the removal of slaves worth millions of dollars? French had his reasons. "It affords me much gratification," he wrote to Foster, "to learn that the acts of depredation referred to in my letter 'were not only not done by your orders but against them and against your strongest efforts to prevent them.' " "It is to be hoped," he went on, "no future cause for complaints will be given by your forces." French now had Foster's promise that the property war would cease. From that point forward, all conflict would be between the two armies. The Confederates would expend the bodies of poor white men, not property itself, in the defense of planters' claims to livestock, real estate, and slaves. Washington County's unionists, however, saw the matter differently.[30]

· **V** ·

In mid-October 1862, Washington County's unionists made their own attempts to confiscate local planters' property. They had appealed earlier to Governor Stanly for permission to seize planter lands and personal property under the provisions of the Confiscation Acts. Now, they sent a petition directly to President Lincoln, "urging that the rebel families [in Washington County] be expatriated & their property seized." Lincoln, evidently, did not answer. But no matter. The president already had rendered his judgment on this question. His Emancipation Proclamation invalidated planters' claims to absolute control over their possessions.[31]

Soon, Union troops and unionist soldiers in Washington County began to seize by force property of all kinds belonging to secessionists. A woman whom H. G. Spruill called "Old Mrs. Walker the mother-in-law of Dr. Bell," for example, lost all her possessions. She had gone to Halifax to stay with Bell's granddaughter and while there "had all her property of every description taken, stock, corn, fodder, provisions, carriages, and horses." "The property of all those who had left their farms were taken," Spruill claimed.[32] Similarly, unionists from Plymouth in federal service gathered horses from the Collins plantation during the last week in October, and they hauled cotton bales to Plymouth, presumably for the Treasury Department to sell under the terms of the Confiscation Acts. The unionist soldiers also attacked slaves. One Zouave committed "violence on an old negro woman," a ninety-year-old slave belonging to a local planter.[33]

Unionists focused their depredations directly on planters who had refused to take the federal loyalty oath. On November 12, some began "visiting down the county," H. G. Spruill reported, "and bringing up horses and mules." "The county is to be stripped," he feared. According to the mayor, the soldiers, "principally the Buffalo Cavalry [local unionists], are scouring the county and ransacking houses and committing violence on women and taking all the money, bed clothing, etc."

Soon, secessionist planters began to stream into Plymouth, demanding from federal officers protection from unionists. They complained that unionists had threatened to take their property if they did not submit. A certain secessionist named McKee lost all his horses and mules, even though he had maintained close relations with federal soldiers by selling them wine and brandy. These actions were not without official support. At about the same time, Governor Stanly told all the secessionists he encountered that he planned "imprisoning every man in North Carolina who refused to take the oath," as long as he had "a place in which to imprison them."[34]

By November 18, many Washington County secessionists had seen the wisdom of taking the oath. Jordan Mezell, for example, did so. He lost his horse, but at least he got a receipt in return. Most, however, did not take the oath willingly. "Many men feel compelled to take the oath," wrote H. G. Spruill, "to preserve something for their families to subsist on, whose hearts do not sympathize with it." J. C. Johnston, for one, came to Spruill "weeping and in great distress." He claimed to have been "severely treated" by local unionists who had "urg[ed] the authorities and soldiers" on him. He now believed that, if he failed to take the oath, his house would be "ransacked" and "everything he had taken." Moreover, the unionists would not allow him to leave the county. Therefore, he had appealed to the U.S. authorities. But they admitted that the U.S. forces wielded no power outside the federal pickets around Plymouth; the county lay entirely in the hands of local unionists whom the secessionists must satisfy. Johnston had no idea where to turn. He felt that "by taking the presented oath," he would be acting against his conscience. But unless he did so, his "house would be riddled." Johnston concluded that he had "no powers against the [unionist] soldiers."[35]

Washington County unionists also raided plantations in nearby Bertie and Martin counties. In mid-November, a group of slaves belonging to a planter named Mooney made their way down the Roanoke River to Plymouth. There, they cut a deal with a white man, a resident of the town, who agreed to rent to the slaves three flatboats. Twenty of the slaves would return to Mooney's plantation in the boats and strip it of all the planter's valuables. On the day agreed upon all proceeded upriver. At the plantation, the slaves "loaded up the 3 flats with cotton, wool, whiskey, and the most valuable property on the farm." They also brought out "70 or 80 negroes," presumably relatives and friends. But "while the farm was being pillaged," evidently "some of the neighbors found it out" and "collected a small force." Then, the planters "came down the River, intercepted the flats, and fired into them." Three or four of the slaves escaped to shore in a canoe, along with the white man. They appeared in Plymouth the next day "minus hat, shoes, and coats." But the other slaves and all Mooney's possessions were returned to his plantation.[36]

In December unionists raided plantations belonging to Washington County's largest planters. During the first week of that month, four privates in the 1st North Carolina Union Volunteers at Plymouth descended upon William Pettigrew's Magnolia plantation. They acted in concert with Warren Ambrose, the unionist leader, styled a "volinteer thief" by William Pettigrew's overseer, John M. Hough. When the unionists arrived at the plantation, they "called" for Pettigrew's "property" and threatened "destruction to all that belonged to [the planter.]" But Hough swore that Pettigrew had moved his property "up the country." He claimed that all the property which now remained on the plantation had passed into his possession. Pettigrew's slave driver, Henry, "seconded" these statements. In addition, the overseer showed the unionists his "protection," issued by federal officers in Plymouth.

In reality, John Hough had taken great pains to disperse and conceal William Pettigrew's personal goods. In June 1862, he reported "seeing the Proclamation of Lincan [evidently announcing the second Confiscation Act] stating that after the 4th of July all the property of citizens having left the invaded counties should be confisticated." Therefore, the overseer "thought it best," as he told Pettigrew, "to remove some of the most valuable Furniture from off your premises and out of the neighborhood where it would not be recognized as yours by visitors." Hough then borrowed a wagon, loaded Pettigrew's possessions onto it, and set out on a road alongside the Scuppernong River, looking for likely hiding places. He finally stopped at a Mr. Willis's house, where he found two of William Pettigrew's friends who seemed willing to take some of the goods. Hough "made arrangements to move the things in the night and as secretly as possible." All this was done in the knowledge that there had been "much said by the Bufiloes about hiding Property & heavy threats made against them that had it concealed for the men that had left the invaded counties." In the event, one of the two men, Mr. Cooper, "became alarmed" and implored Hough to remove Pettigrew's property. His house stood next to a thoroughfare where the unionist cavalry "road night and day." But Hough prevailed upon the faint-hearted man to keep quiet. He told Cooper to "consider it sold to him by me and leave me to *lie* myself out of trouble the best I could."

In the end, Hough's forethought and fast talking on that day in December "caused the unionists' depredations to be light" compared to "what they bid fair to be when they came." But Ambrose and his friends did break the lock on a trunk and took "a silver medle somewhat larger than a dollar." And they "killed 3 turkeis, 2 shoats that would weigh about 50 lbs per piece, besides several things belong to [Hough's] own family."[37]

· **VI** ·

The official disregard for secessionists' property claims, however, eventually lost its focus. This resulted mainly from an order issued by General Foster in November 1862 that required the confiscation of all horses in the Albemarle region for use by the federal cavalry. The order altered the class-specific nature of confiscation in Washington County by rendering all property claims indefensible by law or custom. Afterwards, property belonging to any person, including yeoman farmers, became subject to attack.

Before the Emancipation Proclamation of September 1862, unionist farmers usually received a receipt from federal forces for confiscated property. Jeremiah P. Newberry, a prosperous yeoman farmer who lived about seven miles from Plymouth, for example, had "always expressed himself very freely when it was safe for him to do so." When he did speak out, Newberry was "opposed to secession all the time & the war." He also was "in favor of the union & the restoration of peace & the union as it was before the rebellion." Hence, before the proclamation, this unionist farmer willingly allowed federal soldiers to take whatever they wished from his farm in return for written proof of the transaction. "The soldiers would go out to my house," he recalled later, "& get corn & fodder to feed their horses with & bring it to Plymouth." Altogether, Newberry supposed that the federals took about two hundred bushels of corn worth $800, five thousand pounds of fodder worth $75, and ten hogs valued at $144.[38]

After the Foster order of November 1862, however, Union troops simply seized Newberry's horse without his knowledge or permission while he was in Plymouth on business. Similarly, Isaac Harrison, a unionist farmer living about three miles from Plymouth, lost his horse, an eight year old worth about $125, in mid-November to a group of soldiers from the 1st North Carolina Union Volunteers stationed at Plymouth. Harrison protested to C. C. Brundy—one of the soldiers and also a neighbor—saying that "it was hard [of the federals] to take the last horse" he possessed. Now he "had nothing to farm with." He argued that he had always been loyal to the federal government. This Brundy admitted. "From his general reputation among his neighbors," the soldier explained later, "he was considered a union man." Therefore, Brundy advised Harrison to contact the U.S. officers at Plymouth to "see if he could not get another one that might answer his purpose." He did this, but to no effect. Harrison received neither a replacement nor a receipt. His horse went into service with the U.S. cavalry at Washington, North Carolina, and was never seen in Washington County again.[39]

Even locally prominent unionists had difficulty in protecting their property from their coveteous compatriots. Captain M. Bowan, a unionist slaveholder living in Plymouth, attempted to play both sides of the political fence in November 1862. During the summer, he had obtained permission to import salt from the North in order to sell it to those wishing to kill and dress hogs that fall. Bowan, however, dealt indiscriminately with both unionists and secessionists. That raised an outcry among local unionists, but Governor Stanly intervened on his behalf and all seemed well. Then Bowan made two serious mistakes.

First, in mid-November Bowan crossed John Phelps, Jr., a teenager and the son of Washington County's unionist marshal. The younger Phelps had been an outspoken, if not belligerent, unionist since secession; in 1862 he had hurled bricks at one secessionist in the streets of Plymouth. Now he organized a raiding party that sacked several plantations on the Chowan River north of Plymouth. At one place, Phelps seized twenty-nine bales of cotton from

the overseer of an absent secessionist. He told the overseer "that
he was acting by authority of [the] U.S." He threatened to take the
cotton by force, if that became necessary. The overseer relented.
But before Phelps could get the cotton to Plymouth, Bowan heard
about the seizure and contacted the planter who actually owned
the cotton. Bowan bought it all for thirty cents a pound. He got
an order from the federal officers at Plymouth giving him possession of the contraband when it reached town.

In late November, Bowan worked a similar scheme but on a
larger scale. H. G. Spruill had found that several of his friends,
secessionists who had fled their plantations in Martin County
across the river from Plymouth, wanted desperately to market
their recently picked cotton. Spruill, therefore, proposed to Bowan
that the planters "sell to him at 30 cents per lbs." In addition to
the cash price, the unionist would furnish each planter with four
bushels of salt which he was to give to them "unconditionally."
Bowan agreed. Sometime before November 17, the planters delivered their cotton to a landing at Welch's Creek, a small stream
that emptied into the Roanoke about a mile upriver from Plymouth, evidently hoping to keep it out of the view of local unionists.
In the meantime, however, some of the slaves who had transported the planters' cotton revealed its presence to people unknown, presumably unionists, who then informed the U.S. officers
at Plymouth. The officers, in turn, issued an order to have the
cotton seized. But Bowan found out. He then reasoned that he
could regain possession of it if he could claim that he and not
the secessionist planters owned the cotton. This Bowan did. H. G.
Spruill testified falsely to the federal officers at Plymouth that the
sale already had been completed. And they, in turn, awarded possession of the cotton to Bowan.

In making these deals, Bowan accumulated a great deal of
money and several secessionist friends. "He is a Union man and
opposed to the war on the part of the South [and] to all Secession
Movement," wrote H. G. Spruill. But he also "was trying to make
money," and "in doing so, he has had no regard to man's opinion,
and has done the southern men every favor he could." Therein lay
Bowan's difficulty. Around the first of December, unionists in
Plymouth freed all Bowan's slaves and sent them to New Bern.
The retribution fit Bowan's offense with perfect symmetry. Local

unionists deprived him of property equal to that which he had taken from them by a subterfuge.[40]

By late November 1862, all property claims had become a matter of serious contention in Washington County. The conflict began in a federal attack directed specifically at property belonging to local slaveholders. This was in keeping with the logic of the Emancipation Proclamation which legitimated the confiscation of a species of property held mainly by planters. But the attack soon wandered from that target. Federal troops began to confiscate supplies and horses from unionists. And unionists competed among themselves for the local spoils of war. Such competition became possible largely because neither the federals nor the local unionist government erected any means for establishing the legitimacy of property claims. The proclamation had invalidated planters' claims to property, but it had not created a coherent system of counter-claims. Hence, the possession of property now remained suspect and enforceable only by armed intervention. By the end of the month, the Confederate army in Martin County grasped this essential fact and, therefore, prepared to battle for planters' property.

· VII ·

At half past four in the morning, December 10, 1862, Lieutenant Colonel John C. Lamb, a native of Elizabeth City, across the Sound, led approximately three hundred rebel infantrymen and seventy cavalrymen into the heart of Plymouth. The federals were taken completely by surprise. Their pickets fell back in disarray and offered no resistance. By the time the other soldiers and Plymouth's residents awoke, the Confederates had positioned three artillery pieces on the town's wharf and had opened fire on the only gunboat then present at Plymouth. The gunboat, the *Southfield,* sustained numerous direct hits that caused it to lose power and become unnavigable. Meanwhile, the gunboat's crew weighed anchor, somehow maneuvered the boat into the middle of the river, and began to return fire—but to little effect. The gunners aimed their shots too high, overshooting the Confederate artillery. They had no choice. By this time, "the whole of Plymouth was on the banks of the river, screaming and yelling." "If I had fired promiscuously," the *Southfield*'s commander wrote later, "I should have killed more of our friends than of the enemy." After a few minutes, the gunboat began to drift out of control down the river.[41]

The Confederates then turned their attention on the town itself. They moved their cannons to within a block of the brick customs house where the town's garrison had taken refuge. But the federals raised no defense. Their captain, a man named B. Ewer, had fled to the *Southfield* and had attempted to convince its commander, Lieutenant Charles Behm, to take his men aboard. When the lieutenant said he had no room, Ewer refused to leave the boat. Later, C. W. Flusser concluded: "The fact is Ewer got frightened [and] left his men. . . ." Meanwhile, the locally recruited 1st North Carolina Union Volunteers rallied and poured a steady fire into the Confederates from the customs house.[42]

The unionists' rifle fire, however, did little to impede the Confederates, who pillaged several houses and burned the rest. Roughly two-thirds of the town went up in flames. In addition, the marauders "carried away against their consent and against the consent of their owners a large number of slaves," evidently about fifty. Most of those slaves belonged to the hapless unionist entrepreneur, Captain Bowan. Where he acquired them is uncertain, for around the first of December unionists had freed all his slaves and had sent them out of the county. Perhaps, he now dabbled in the slave trade. Some of these captured blacks, however, had simply run away from their masters upriver. After the attack, one planter's wife in Halifax County remarked: "Many negroes were killed" at Plymouth. "I hope," she continued, "their brethren will hear of it & it will be a lesson to them" about what might happen when "they leave home with their false friends."[43]

Whatever the exact details, much of the responsibility for Plymouth's destruction must rest with H. G. Spruill. When the mayor first heard pickets firing, he rode to the edge of town, found Colonel Lamb, and convinced him to rescue the few rebel families remaining, including his own wife and daughter. That accomplished, Spruill urged Lamb "not to leave till he had finished his work." The mayor complained that the Confederates "had not destroyed but half the town" and that "by pressing" Lamb "might either destroy the town or capture the enemy." The purpose in burning the town, explained one planter, was to "prevent its affording shelter to the Abolitionists & run away negroes in their train."[44]

The raid ended after an hour. At half past five in the morning, the Confederates withdrew to a place about a mile south of Plymouth, where they lingered for a day or so. By that time, the *Southfield* had returned with Flusser's *Commodore Perry*. The gunboats fired a few rounds, which convinced the Confederates to abandon their plans to capture the town. Meanwhile, Plymouth's remaining secessionists fled upcountry for the duration of the war. Unionist residents remained, however, and had plenty to say when the gunboats finally returned. One federal soldier reported "the commander of the *Southfield* has been severely censured." And they "cried and begged for the *Perry* to remain."[45]

The attack on Plymouth raised anew the specter of a property war. The U.S. military governor, Edward Stanly complained of the "barbarous and willful burning of the town of Plymouth" and seizure of slaves. And he wondered "by what rules this war is to be conducted." General J. G. Foster wrote to S. G. French, the Confederate commanding general, wanting to know first "if it was by your approval that in the recent attack on Plymouth many houses and other buildings were fired, and to that extent families ruined and rendered homeless." French denied that charge outright. "I do not think," he wrote, "the town of Plymouth was barbarously and willfully burned, but, as reported to me, a house was fired in which your troops made a stand and from which they fired on our troops." Foster then inquired about the slaves taken from their masters in Plymouth. To this charge, French admitted his troops' action, but he also justified the theft. "So many [such acts] have been committed by the forces of the United States," French wrote to Foster, "that it is now regarded as legitimate and proper, a 'fit and necessary war measure,'" to paraphrase ironically Lincoln's own words.[46]

· **VIII** ·

The Emancipation Proclamation had accomplished exactly what President Lincoln had intended. It focused the war directly on planters by attacking their personal property—houses, furniture, and slaves. But the proclamation actually freed very few slaves, in

Washington County at least. While slaves escaped by the thousands from upriver to Roanoke Island and had done so for months
without benefit of the Emancipation Proclamation, those from
Washington County found themselves transported upcountry as a
direct result of Lincoln's action. In the end, only one hundred or
so out of nearly three thousand Washington County slaves became
free people in early 1863. Those few black people resided mainly
on plantations belonging to Josiah Collins and Charles Pettigrew.

Sometime in mid-February 1863, Major Bartholomew, the new
U.S. army commander at Plymouth, rode with a small squad of
soldiers to Somerset Place, Josiah Collins's plantation in the Scuppernong neighborhood. Bartholomew gathered together Collins's
remaining slaves, sixty-six in all, and "told the negroes they were
all free." He advised them to stay where they were and try to support themselves." But he also told the newly freed people that they
"could do as they pleased" and that George Spruill, Collins's overseer, had no more authority over them. From Somerset Place,
Bartholomew made his way to Charles Pettigrew's plantation,
Bonarva, informed the slaves of their freedom, and then returned
to Plymouth.[47]

The freedmen at Somerset Place now faced a crucial decision.
Should they stay or go? Should they strike out for new places, shed
their past, and seek wage labor, or ought they take possession of
themselves and begin to labor for a subsistence? Moreover, could
they claim a customary right to the land and tools that they had
used for decades?

One young man, Jim, elected to test the waters of freedom elsewhere. He sought work in Plymouth sometime in February or early
March 1863. Meanwhile, those who remained at home "all refused
to do anything except [Spruill] should hire them." The plantation
miller, for example, declined "to attend the mill unless Spruill
should pay him seventeen dollars per month." Collins's overseer
did not pay, and "the mill was stopped in consequence." But the
Somerset Place freedpeople could afford time to dicker over terms
of employment, for Bartholomew had ordered Spruill to retain
enough corn in Collins's barns to feed the freedpeople for several
months.[48] After a few weeks, Jim returned to Somerset Place,
complaining that his Yankee employers "made him work very hard
and fed him badly." That settled the matter of leaving. Collins's

overseer, George Spruill, claimed that "the other negroes" had "all gone to work on the farm." At Charles Pettigrew's Bonarva plantation, the freedmen reached a similar decision. Bartholomew reportedly told them that "the place belonged to them." Therefore, they "determined to cultivate the place, and remain where they are."[49]

The Somerset freedpeople's decision, however, did not imply a return to the past. They asserted a right to possess not only their labor but also all things connected with the plantation—land, tools, livestock, and grain stored from the previous year's crop. They appropriated the food immediately. The Somerset freedpeople helped the federals during "three hog killing days" in early March and took a share, and the women and children continued to draw a ration of corn and other supplies. Then, the freedpeople divided the plantation lands and remaining livestock among themselves. When Bartholomew set the slaves of Somerset Place free, he had turned over to them "as much land as they wanted to tend." He also "gave them a lot [of] hogs." The freedpeople took the captain at his word. To get started, the freedmen also purchased two old plow horses from unionists who lived in the neighborhood. In May, they planted a crop, presumably of corn and vegetables.[50]

Spruill, meanwhile, labored mightily to persuade Collins's freedpeople to remain on the plantation. "I keepe talking to them," he wrote. In fact, he pretended to read "in their hearing" letters written by Josiah Collins. Spruill had received no such correspondence but attempted by this action to imply Collins's presence and his possible return to the plantation. The overseer also reported "hav[ing] given off hogs and cattle to each familey." In doing so, he committed the blacks to caring for livestock he hoped would revert to Collins's possession should the Confederates win the war. Finally, Spruill attempted to force the freedpeople to work as a gang. "I will not let the water run," he wrote to Collins. Presumably, he closed the lock where water from Lake Phelps ran into the plantation's canal system. Hence, the plots of corn planted by the residents of Somerset Place would wither unless they submitted to the overseer's discipline. In attempting to "keep them at home," the overseer hoped, "if peace should come they might be saved" for Collins.[51]

Spruill's tactics, however, did not intimidate the freedpeople of Somerset Place. In response to the overseer's letter reading, they began referring to their former master as "Old Collins" in Spruill's presence. They told the overseer to let their former master know that "if ever" he went to the plantation or sent "down there" for them they "intend to leave." "The[y] doo not cear for you at all," Spruill wrote to Collins. The freedmen responded with a threat to the overseer's control of water. "The nigroes say the[y] will go to plymouth & report all these trubales." Moreover, the freedpeople began "fearming on the[ir] own rule." Spruill "encour[aged] them to make all the corn" they possibly could, but he could exercise no control over that planting. Similarly, the blacks refused to perform any other form of uncompensated labor. Spruill, for example, had "a good stock of hogs on hand," but he could get no one to feed them. Therefore, the overseer had to turn them loose to forage in the woods. As for Collins's sheep, he could "not git them tended to [at] all."

Spruill summarized the conflict this way: "I have had to wearke evry skiam to keepe them hear on the place." But "the[y] have bin taken out of my control & I can not doo enything with them at all." And "if i doo bothear one," he complained, "I put my self in troble & likewise the fearm by report" to the unionists and federals. He concluded, "No nigro is not to bee depended on." "When the word fredom is given to them you can not doo any thing with them at all."[52]

At William Pettigrew's plantation the story was much the same. News of Major Bartholomew's visit to the Collins plantation reached the slaves at Magnolia within hours. The next morning, Henry, Pettigrew's black driver, traveled to Somerset Place in order to verify the reports for himself. There, he learned that they were free and that "all the property that their masters had left was theirs."

The former black driver returned to Magnolia a different man. "When he came back," wrote John M. Hough, Pettigrew's overseer, Henry acted "like a tyrannical king."[53] The former black driver informed Hough that he, Henry, now owned the plantation and all the property attached to it. He told Hough that if the overseer "wanted anything to use that was here" he "must buy it" from him. Henry further demanded to know what Hough had done with "his property," items that he charged Hough had "carried off." Most important, Henry sought the key to the barn for the corn and hay stored there. Before the war, Henry ordinarily had kept the key as a part of his duties. But when local unionists had raided the place in December 1862, the key to the barn had somehow passed to Hough. Hough claimed that Henry himself had offered the key to the overseer as part of an effort to deceive the unionists into thinking that the barn belonged to Hough. But the driver argued that Hough had taken the key from him by force. Finally, Henry revealed that he "would have different arrangements" on "his farm" when planting began in month or so.[54]

Henry and his wife Polly attempted to drive Hough off the plantation by intimidation. In his various conversations with the overseer, Henry spoke in "all the insulting language he could use"—in Hough's view. Moreover, Polly was "not a whit behind" her husband in the use of verbal intimidation. On one occasion, she strode back and forth on her front porch declaring that she "could not bear the sight of a poor person." Moreover, she complained that there was "a parcel of poor folks," referring to Hough and his family, "stuck up here in rich folks places," that is, on the plantation she and her husband owned. Polly went on: "Master," meaning Henry, "did not want them," poor people, on the plantation and would have run them off earlier if he had "had time." All this Polly "rail[ed] out in a loud voice," Hough reported, "so that my family could not help hearing it." In the overseer's estimation, "No doubt they thought that was the best plan they could fall uppon to get me away."[55]

Hough, of course, reacted with anger. "This was hard to bear," he reported to his employer. "I could not help myself" from becoming enraged. But there is no evidence that Henry actually attempted to become a planter. Five months later, he moved off the plantation and began subsistence farming. He never attempted to direct his fellows' labor again. Neither is there any evidence to suggest that Henry held a low opinion of any "poor folks" except the overseer and his family. Henry and his wife simply played upon the newly inverted social order to dismantle the ideas and practices of paternalism. By acting out of place, Henry and Polly lampooned the overseer's pretensions and asserted the common interests that Hough ought to have felt between himself and other poor people, black and white, slave and free. Like Henry himself, Hough was a poor man and made a living only by submitting to a rich man. Hough, however, did not see it that way. "There was but 2 ways for me" to think and act, he wrote, either "to grin and bear it" or to "kill them." Fortunately for all concerned, Hough "took the former course" and vowed to "put up with [Henry's] big ways."[56]

In short, slaves throughout Washington County understood immediately the implications of Lincoln's Emancipation Proclamation, even if it did not free all slaves at once. In late January 1863, one federal soldier then in Plymouth and a friend went "among the negroes" who had lately flocked into the town from the surrounding country." Visiting "one family in particular," the soldier wrote, "several times we engaged breakfasts of which the principal portion was *corn cake.*" "They were very intelligent," he thought, and "although they could neither read nor write, yet had their ideas upon matters pertaining to themselves." In particular, the soldier found his hosts "quite well informed upon the President's Proclamation, at least the portion relating to their own immediate change of condition, viz. freedom." "There is no use," he concluded, "in repeating that they are not capable of taking care of themselves and that they do not desire their freedom, for it is wholly false."[57]

In the end, Washington County planters failed to redeem their property in slaves left at home. George Spruill recommended to Josiah Collins that he re-enslave the freedpeople remaining at Somerset Place and remove them to the North Carolina piedmont, but that was not an option open to the planter. He possessed no plantation upcountry on which to work them. He could find hired employment for only a few of the slaves he had removed already. Therefore, some Somerset Place freedpeople remained in Washington County for the duration of the war. Similarly, slaves belonging to the Pettigrew brothers moved about in the neighborhood but never worked for their master again. These events foreshadowed the conflict over land and labor that would begin in 1865, but they remained exceptional for the time being. Most slaves from Washington County now resided in the upcountry, refugees in their own country and from their own freedom—victims, not beneficiaries, of the Emancipation Proclamation and the property war it had engendered.

Refugeeing: The Second Crisis in Paternalism

By January 1863, Josiah Collins, master of Somerset Place, had moved to the town of Hillsboro in Orange County. His slaves now resided in three separate groups. Sixty-six, mostly older men and women, remained at Somerset Place with George Spruill in charge. The Reverend George Patterson, "transporting their children and their household stuff in the farm wagons" by way of Tarboro, had led a second group to Hurry Scurry plantation in northern Orange County. And a third group went to Northwood plantation in Vance County. But these were not satisfactory arrangements from a planter's point of view. Who could control slaves scattered over half the state, out of the planter's sight, all hoping for freedom as federal armies pressed further inland? How could a slaveholder's power be produced in the upcountry?[1]

Collins's strategy, according to one of his friends, consisted of "keeping them together." The planter made every effort to do this. Of the thirty-four households recorded on a list of families made at Somerset Place in 1860, nearly all arrived intact at Hurry Scurry or Northwood. Only two children were missing. Fifteen of these families, however, were recorded without a male head of household present. But the exceptions proved the rule. These men had been hired out to the North Carolina Railroad at Company

Shops, only a few miles from their families at Hurry Scurry. Similarly, Collins sent several young single men, but no married men, to work at the Confederate hospitals in Raleigh. When forced to separate male slaves from their families, Collins often paid their railroad fares so they could visit family members from time to time. In 1864, he paid $18.75 on one occasion "for fare of Sam & Augustus to see their families," as the planter explained in his accounts.[2]

Josiah Collins also sought to motivate his slaves to work hard for their new masters. Some skilled slaves were encouraged to make a percentage profit from their work. Ishmael, for example, early on showed an entreprenurial spirit when he was sent to work as a shoemaker for the North Carolina Railroad. There he manufactured shoes on company time, which skill he then carried off on his own at the expiration of his contract in December 1863. Subsequently, Collins arranged for the slave to make shoes at a place where he would be paid directly by the piece rather than by the day, a part of the wages going to Ishmael. Similarly, Collins rewarded his slaves, as had been his custom at Somerset Place, "for good behavior while hired out during [the] current year." In December 1863, the planter paid his slaves $205.[3]

Unlike Josiah Collins, William Pettigrew did not seek profits from his refugeed slaves. "Safety is far more important than profit for ones negroes," he wrote, "as it is a description of property which will be exceedingly valuable after peace is restored." But how to employ that property remained a puzzle for the planter. When he relocated in the eastern piedmont in September 1862, Pettigrew found the area glutted with slaves. Even at low prices, he could find employers for them only with difficulty. Finally, after some months, Pettigrew determined to move most of his slaves further west. In the northwest piedmont, he reasoned, yeoman farmers would jump at the chance of hiring one or two slaves cheaply. Moreover, there would be little competition. Communities near the mountains had far fewer plantations and, hence, fewer slaves than Chatham County.[4]

On January 3, 1863, William Pettigrew and eighty of his slaves— men, women, and children—arrived in Mocksville, the seat of Davie County. To prepare the way, the planter had sent ahead a notice to be circulated among the area's farmers explaining that he brought slaves whom he wished to hire out. "The men and women," he claimed, "are unusually good hands, and those hiring them I am sure will be pleased." By the end of January, Pettigrew had succeeded in leasing all his slaves, but at bargain prices—"the men for $125 [each] & the women for from $50 to 60 [each]." The planter did not rejoice over these terms, but he did consider himself fortunate to have hired out as many as he did. "The county is over supplied" with slaves, he thought, "& it would be difficult to hire out more."[5]

Having saved his property in slaves, William Pettigrew positioned himself to watch over them. He arranged to move his household from Chatham County to the town of Winston. From that place, he could visit his slaves from time to time without great difficulty and still travel quickly to the state capital by rail to conduct political business. Winston was located in Forsyth County adjacent to Davie County where his slaves now worked. Unlike Collins, William Pettigrew hoped to continue surveillance of his slaves, even if he did not direct their labor.[6]

Charles Pettigrew was not as lucky in hiring out his slaves as his brother and Josiah Collins had been. In October 1862, he had moved his slaves remaining at Bonarva to a place near Greensboro. There, he hired them out to Mr. Wilkes, to whom he also leased his mules. Wilkes was a contractor who had been hired by the North Carolina Railroad to rebuild a heavily used section of track about eighteen miles west of Greensboro. According to the agreement made, Wilkes evidently was to feed and house only the slaves he could use. Supplies and shelter for Pettigrew's remaining slaves, mostly women and children, would be charged to the planter's account, in effect, deducting the slaves' subsistence from wages that otherwise would be paid to their master. Wilkes himself would pay a minimal fee for using the slaves. Like William, Charles was content, for the moment, simply to preserve his property.[7]

· **II** ·

In late February 1863, Washington County's refugeed slaves resumed their agricultural routine. At Northwood plantation, the portion of Collins's slaves there began their usual work in early March.

They had brought with them plows from Somerset Place, fifteen in all, which had been stored at the town of Oxford since the previous fall. After having purchased new plow points for each and after some delay caused by heavy rains, Collins's plowmen began preparing the land for corn planting. Other Northwood slaves, meanwhile, occupied themselves in hauling corn, some to plant and some to eat, that Collins evidently had purchased from other planters in the neighborhood. Some transported fodder for Collins's cattle to eat. Finally, Josiah Collins's slaves at Northwood plantation began building permanent cabins for themselves. They had raised six by the middle of March.[8]

Charles Pettigrew's slaves at Cherry Hill plantation in South Carolina followed a similar routine, acting under the direction of Charles's wife, Caroline. The slaves from Bonarva found the soil at Cherry Hill very fertile, especially in the bottomlands. But no one had worked the land for some time, and the rains had been heavy that winter. Hence, the slaves faced a soil that was thick and difficult to plow. Jackson and Whitaker had attempted to turn the soil with light plows they had brought from Bonarva, but the plows broke, and the slaves could not "keep them in order." Therefore, Caroline Pettigrew authorized the two to purchase bull-tongue plows from a local merchant and encouraged them then to start plowing in earnest. Even so, she feared that planting time would "find us behind."[9]

But like other Washington County planters in the upcountry, Caroline Pettigrew's troubles had only begun. The slaves required so many things. "They will need clothes surely before long." And she was short of money—only $70 in the house. But no matter. She evidently could not find any slave clothes for sale in the neighborhood at any price. Indeed, even the largest textile mill in South Carolina, William Gregg's factory at Graniteville, could not supply her with coarse "negro" cloth. Besides, prices for corn had risen in the neighborhood to $1.60 per bushel. When her supply ran out, as it would soon, she would have to purchase corn until the first ears began to ripen in August.[10]

Caroline Pettigrew, therefore, concentrated her efforts on vegetables, so as to have something to eat quickly and cheaply. In late March, she sent Jackson around the neighborhood to buy as many bushels of seed potatoes as he could find. After making some inquiries, Jackson found a farmer who would sell him as many as he wanted and bought ten dollars' worth—two bushels for seed and the remainder for eating. In the next few days, Jackson and four others cut up and sowed most of the potatoes on a hillside. Mrs. Pettigrew also gave half a bushel to Jackson to plant for himself. She told the slave that, when ready for harvest, her husband would either buy the potatoes from him or allow the slave to feed his family with them. In addition, Caroline Pettigrew planted a summer garden with tomatoes and califlower among the other vegetables.[11]

William Pettigrew's slaves who remained unemployed in Winston, meanwhile, shifted for themselves. The planter, as yet, had not succeeded in arranging transport for his household goods to the house and lot he had purchased in the town. Therefore, he remained at his farm in Chatham County, while his slaves occupied the residence in Winston. To provide food for his slaves, Pettigrew directed them to spade the ground around the house and to put in a spring garden, and he arranged for a friend to supply them with seed and any advice or assistance they might need. Pettigrew also arranged to buy corn for them to have ground for meal. But this was not enough in the opinion of his slaves. By late January, Pettigrew's slaves attempted to support themselves by taking on odd jobs from white people in the neighborhood. Some of the women took in washing. John, for one, worked "about in town such as chopping wood," according to one report, thus "earning a little something for himself."[12]

Washington County's planters and slaves, however, had reestablished only part of their former routine. The planter's directions, for example, often came from a distance in a letter or through the planter's wife. Hence, planters' surveillance over their slaves diminished, although it did not cease. As a result, the slaves continued to work, but with considerable independence. They plowed and planted for themselves. Some dictated reports of their activities to their masters. And John, the slave in Winston, took it upon himself to choose among possible new masters. In January 1863, three different white men had attempted to hire him, but John turned down the offers. He had set the price of his labor for one year at $40, plus a year's worth of clothing, a price his prospective employers thought "too high for him." In setting such a sum, John evidently hoped to avoid hiring himself out to riffraff. "John says," wrote a friend to Pettigrew, "he wants a good master." But all this would change in March; routine would become crisis.[13]

· **III** ·

The contractor named Wilkes proved to be a cruel master to Charles Pettigrew's slaves on the North Carolina Railroad. In early January 1863, the planter had heard rumors to that effect while in Rocky Mount, some 125 miles to the east. Therefore, he went to Company Shops to see for himself. When he arrived, the slaves seemed "very glad to see me," as Pettigrew put it. And well they should have been. They told their master that they would have "by now starved to death" had it not been for the timely intervention of Mr. West, who lived in the neighborhood. He was a "very large strong man," observed Charles Pettigrew, and made "the white men about him afraid of him." Moreover, West told the planter that he would "stand by the negroes against oppression." He had done so already. West forced Wilkes to give Pettigrew's slaves a decent ration, much against Wilkes's will. As a result, Pettigrew told his wife, "I found them tolerably well." But many of the children had contracted "something like measles."[14]

Even after Pettigrew complained, however, Wilkes did not mend his ways. In late January, the contractor worked the Bonarva slaves without restraint. "They are not allowed a moments leisure to rest," reported the planter, "neither men nor women." And at the end of the year, they had been allowed "a holliday of only Christmas day." The contractor also continued to feed them poorly. "It is after a great struggle that Mr. West can get the allowance [of pork and corn meal] for the laborers and the women & children." Moreover, Wilkes had housed Pettigrew's slaves in crude wood shacks alongside the roadbed. "They are dreadfully crowded," Pettigrew complained. And "if summer finds them in this state," he thought, "there will be great death among them."[15]

Charles Pettigrew was probably correct. Already, there had been "a great many deaths" among the slaves working for Wilkes. A certain Dr. Fishman, whom Pettigrew met, had lost four already. In addition, "many more are sick," the planter observed. To deal with the illnesses, Wilkes proposed creating a "hospital" for slaves, but Pettigrew's people became alarmed at the idea. They thought it would be a place to dump without care slaves who had fallen ill and, in the meantime, would relieve the contractor of any obligation to feed them. Therefore, the slaves appealed to West who sent an urgent message to Pettigrew, then in Greensboro, requesting that the planter come "as soon as possible" to the camp where the slaves worked. When Pettigrew arrived, West told the planter about the planned "hospital." The planter was "greatly displeased," he explained, "because it would cause me to lose many of my people."[16]

In all this, Wilkes took care to charge the greatest possible fees at every opportunity. Half of the men he had hired from Pettigrew earned no wages at all for the planter. Their pay went to feed overpriced grain and meat to Pettigrew's slave women and children. The contractor charged $3 per bushel of corn and forty-two cents per pound of bacon. Moreover, Wilkes collected from the planter a fee for "every days sickness they have." Hence, Wilkes made money whether Pettigrew's slaves worked or not. "In fine," Pettigrew concluded, "the net profit from all those people I have on the road is only 470$ for two months." This, he claimed, would "scarcely cloth" his slaves "and pay the taxes for the year" on them.[17]

Charles Pettigrew had found employment for his slaves, but the slaves' new master, Wilkes, had little incentive to treat the slaves well. He had no long-term interest in a slave's survival. A sick slave was no loss; indeed it was an occasion to charge Charles Pettigrew an additional fee. The result was brutal labor discipline, malnutrition, poor housing, illness, and sometimes death for the slaves who worked on the railroad. But Pettigrew worried about more than the slaves' physical condition. Wilkes's abuse had violated Pettigrew's obligation to "protect" his slaves, as the slaves themselves phrased it. "Not altogether liking the treatment of the negroes," he informed his wife, "I concluded to go up the country to see if I could find a place" for them, a farm where they could work under his supervision. But he did not succeed for some months.[18]

In early March 1863, Mr. West wrote a desperate letter seeking to inform Charles Pettigrew of the continuing ill-treatment of his slaves. West had every reason to be alarmed. The Pettigrew slaves then working on the North Carolina Railroad were living in a "wretched condition." "The men are laboring on dry bread," he claimed, "the section masters and overseers" having "reduced the allowance of meat." The women and children had "scarcely anything to eat." Moreover, West claimed that the contractor was "treating the people tyrannically," all the while declaring that he "will pay no attention whatever" to the agreement made with Pettigrew.

Unfortunately for the planter and his slaves, West had contracted diphtheria and had become too ill to plead the slaves' case to their employer, as he had done earlier. Finally, West warned of certain rebellion "unless Mr. Pettigrew comes directly." "All the men will run away," he believed. And he added that it would be "out of his power to prevent it."[19]

After West's letter finally caught up with Pettigrew at Cherry Hill, the planter hastened to his slaves' camp west of Greensboro. What he saw appalled him. "I found them in a most miserable condition," he wrote to his wife, "looking squalid" and "discontented." One of the slaves, Soloman, complained of a "pain in his back." Antony had "dreadful sore legs"; "two or three others with sore legs"; "two or three others with swollen limbs and rheumatism." "If the negroes all staid," Pettigrew concluded, "many deaths would occur, as has been the case with many negroes moved from the low country." A case in point was Pettigrew's friend, Henry Bryan, who had "lost from 7 to 10" on the railroad "since his removal" from Washington County.[20]

When Pettigrew went among his slaves, they all seemed "extremely delighted" to see him. They "gathered around" the planter and "begged" him to remove them from the railroad. His slaves further told him that they had been "cheated of their allowance" and that they were "never allowed to see the light of day at their quarters." Worse, Pettigrew learned from Mr. West and some "friendly neighbors" that the contractor had "threatened" the slaves. If they did not work night and day without complaint, they would be subjected to "the most tremendous whippings" or "shot." Fortunately for Pettigrew's slaves, Mr. West had again intervened. By "great swearings and imprecations," the slaves' advocate had "not allowed" them "to be improperly punished." But West's actions had proved fortunate for the planter as well. Pettigrew's slaves told him

that they all would have "run away had it not been for Mr. West."
"This is a dreadful state [of] things," Pettigrew concluded, "and
utterly ruinous to discipline."[21]

Charles Pettigrew had no choice; he had to remove as many
slaves from the railroad as possible. In a matter of days, the
planter found a small farm nearby and bought it. The farm consisted of 340 acres, about half in fields and pastures and half in
woodlands, not nearly large enough to support all his slaves then
working on the railroad. Therefore, he determined to put only "the
invalid negroes on it." Others he accompanied a few days later to
Cherry Hill plantation in South Carolina. But some had to remain
working for Wilkes. Pettigrew, therefore, renegotiated his agreement with Wilkes. "They are to work from sunrise to sunset, and
have one hour for dinner" around midday. The dinner hour, at
least, represented some improvement in their condition. "I hope
things will work better," wrote Pettigrew.[22]

Over the next few months, life for Pettigrew's slaves working for
the North Carolina Railroad did improve somewhat. When the
planter visited them in August 1863, he found his people in better
health, although still complaining about the lack of food. The
slaves asked their master once again to "take them from the road,"
as Pettigrew put it. But the planter thought them "pretty well fed,"
or at least better off than they would be if he removed them to one
of his overcrowded farms. More to the point, his slaves would
have nothing to do but idle away their time, producing nothing for
themselves; he would have to feed them out of his own pocket.
Pettigrew, therefore, renewed his contract with Wilkes, and some
of his slaves remained on the railroad.[23]

· **IV** ·

At Cherry Hill, meanwhile, Charles Pettigrew's slaves there had
settled in to stay. They built houses, tended their livestock and
chickens, and took up their old agricultural routine. Sometime in
early August 1863, however, the slaves at Cherry Hill began to
slow down their pace at work as a conflict over the routines of
work and its proceeds began to emerge. The "spinners have fallen
off disgustingly," Caroline Pettigrew reported. The women had

been paid four to five cents per day, evidently taking in work from some contractor off the plantation. As an explanation for the slow work, one slave woman told her mistress that the days had begun to get shorter since the summer solstice in June. Hence, there was less time to produce thread. Caroline Pettigrew wondered: "What will she do in winter?"

The slaves at Cherry Hill also began to tamper with Caroline Pettigrew's garden, upon which the planter's wife now depended almost entirely for her meals. In late July, okra was one of the most prolific producers among her plants. But when she examined that vegetable, she found that her cook had left numerous pods on the plants, pods which then grew large, becoming hard, stringy, and impossible to eat. "I do believe it was being done on purpose," she wrote to her husband, "for coffee." Perhaps the slaves wanted coffee for themselves. More likely, they wanted to roast the seeds and sell them to whites. Since the blockade of the Southern coast, coffee had been impossible to buy in the Carolinas, and okra had become a substitute. In August 1863, okra sold in Wilmington, North Carolina, for seventy-five cents for a dozen pods.[24]

By the second week in August, Charles Pettigrew's slaves had become "difficult." Jackson, for example, objected strongly to Caroline Pettigrew's plan to cut growing corn to feed her hogs and horses. She had consulted with a neighboring planter, Dr. Gilbert, from whom she had bought corn in the past to feed her livestock. But the man had no more corn to sell. Therefore, he advised her to cut the tops off roughly five acres of her corn each week, along with several bushels of roasting ears. Altogether, the planter thought that she would not have to cut more than five acres. Moreover, soon her mules and horses could be turned out to pasture after laying by the corn. But Jackson was "bitterly opposed" to his mistress's plan. In fact, Dr. Gilbert had given Jackson the same advice a week earlier, advice that the black driver neglected to mention to Caroline Pettigrew. Jackson "does not like the trouble, nor does he like cutting corn," Mrs. Pettigrew explained. She thought the slaves just lazy.[25]

But Jackson had more compelling reasons for his opposition. Corn was the basis of the Cherry Hill slaves' diet. Every ear fed to a hog came from Jackson's own mouth, or the mouth of a friend or relative or child, not at the moment, but next winter and spring.

The slaves' fear of a food shortage at Cherry Hill provoked a crisis in the slave community. It was one thing to produce a subsistence and something more and then to be required to turn over to their master part of that surplus. It was an entirely different matter when Pettigrew's demands began to siphon off the slave community's future subsistence. The Cherry Hill slaves would work for their master; but they refused to starve for him.[26]

Africa organized the resistance. We do not know exactly what he planned. But the records reveal at least one thing he did. Africa directed large meetings held in the woods late at night near Cherry Hill. One night in the first week of August, Caroline Pettigrew had just gone to her bedroom between ten and eleven o'clock when she heard "a great singing in the woods." She went out onto a piazza. As the wind happened to be blowing from the direction of the meeting, she could hear the proceedings "plainly." This was not the first meeting Africa had held. Caroline Pettigrew had questioned the slave about rumors of meetings held earlier, but he had denied the reports. Now she held her tongue in fear, waiting for Charles Pettigrew to return to Cherry Hill. "I haven't said a word," she wrote to her husband.[27]

Caroline Pettigrew did not know what all this meant, but she had her suspicions. "I fear it will end in his collecting negroes from the neighborhood & having great 'carryings on' in the woods." Evidently, Africa had said something to excite such suspicions. "He is unmanageable because a fanatic." Moreover, she believed that "he will pervert every negro on the place if he goes on so." And soon they will all be "ready to join the Yankees & commit every enormity." This was not an unreasonable fear. It was well known among the slaves that the Confederates recently had suffered a crushing defeat at a place called Gettysburg. As a consequence, morale had sagged in the national government, amidst the ranks of the army, and among her planter neighbors in South Carolina. This information doubtless was learned on the many errands that the Cherry Hill slaves ran to the nearby village of Badwell after laying by the corn in late July.[28]

But not all the slaves at Cherry Hill agreed with Africa, whatever their reasons. Among them was the slave leader's wife. Sometime just before the outdoor meeting, she and Africa had had a violent quarrel, during which Africa evidently had struck her, injuring her neck. Thereafter, they each refused "doing anything for one another." Africa's wife would not cook for him. She would not even pick enough peas for two, and she refused to shell the peas without a direct order from Caroline Pettigrew. Whatever Africa planned, it was of great enough consequence to cause some of the Cherry Hill slaves to reconsider and object.[29]

What exactly came of Africa's actions remains a mystery. Charles Pettigrew planned either to punish the slave or sell him, but it is not clear whether he finally did so. Charles Pettigrew feared Africa. "He is an unmitigated villain," wrote Pettigrew, "and I shall be compelled to do that which I am unwilling to do as yet." Why was he unwilling? The planter did not say. Refugeeing upcountry had brought not only hardship but also the conditions that could produce rebellion among slaves. The war had prevented planters from meeting their basic obligations to their slaves, among them a guaranteed subsistence as long as they labored steadily. This was the very crisis Charles Pettigrew had hoped to escape when he moved his slaves to the piedmont.[30]

· V ·

In the summer of 1863, a few Washington County slaves taken upcountry did indeed rebel by attempting an escape. About the first of June, two men, Alfred and Jobe, and three women, Ruthy, Louisa, and Murrier, left Northwood plantation heading for Washington County. They evidently planned to retrace the route they had taken when Josiah Collins's friend, the Reverend George Patterson, had brought them to the piedmont in the fall of 1862. From the village of Williamsboro in Vance County, they would walk to Louisburg in Franklin County, then through Nash County to Rocky Mount and Tarboro in Edgecombe County. From there, the slaves could walk easily to the Roanoke River between Hamilton and Williamston, where they might be able to hail a federal gunboat. Altogether, they planned to march about ninety miles to secure their freedom.

Unfortunately for the slaves, the overseer at Northwood, Lloyd Bateman, realized that this was the only route they knew and could follow to the coast. To confirm that the slaves were not simply lying out in the woods nearby, Bateman inquired about what they had taken with them. He found that Murrier had carried two dresses with her, but Alfred and Ruthy had taken "only the cloas they wore." As for Jobe and Louisa, the overseer could not find anyone who would admit to knowing what they took. It was slim evidence, but Murrier would have taken nothing with her if she planned to remain in the neighborhood.[31]

Why the slaves made their escape at that particular time remains obscure. "They left without eny provicasion at all," Bateman claimed. "I have not sed aword out of the way to neither of them." Perhaps that was true. The slaves at Northwood left no evidence of conflict with the overseer that summer. Nevertheless, life at Northwood was full of suffering, privation, and uncertainty that must have become increasingly unbearable with the prospect of freedom less than one hundred miles away.[32]

Many of Collins's slaves at Northwood had fallen ill. Dick was "not out [of the woods?] yet but is getting beter," wrote Bateman. Anney was "quite low." Suckey Elsy was "quite sick yet." "She is got the bowil complaint now & has bin very bad off." "Lyda is better; but had bin very bad of." Some of the others appeared "a littal sick but nothing dangeras," thought the overseer. Shortly thereafter, a woman and a boy both died of "bowel disease." Bateman did not say why the sickness occurred, but there is a clue. A drought that summer had stunted virtually all the crops at Northwood. "It is so dry that I can hardly plow," the overseer reported. The corn looked "very bad." The vegetables had done no better. "I want to plant peas," he told Collins, "but it is not worth while until it rains for they wont cum up." Doubtless, food was scare at Northwood, especially fresh vegetables. And that may have led to intestinal disorders among the slaves.[33] Whatever the exact reasons for the escape, the five who left were not unusual in their thinking among the slaves at Northwood. "There is more in the same mind," Bateman reported to Collins. And "thay was only waiting for something for excuse" to join the five who left.[34]

William Eaton, Josiah Collins's cousin who lived near Northwood, took charge of efforts to recover the five fugitive slaves. He wrote to Hugh McNair, a resident of Tarboro and a professional slave catcher then doing a land-office business in eastern North Carolina, so much, in fact, that McNair had to subcontract his work and did so in this case. Eaton requested McNair to "put up several notices" around Tarboro and "to cause a lookout for them" on the road to and from town. He also instructed the slave catcher to send Collins's runaways back to Bateman should they be caught. At the same time, Eaton wrote to the postmaster in Rocky Mount asking him to display a notice that offered a $100 reward for the capture and return of the five slaves.[35]

Collins's slaves moved slowly, taking nine days to walk just over eighty miles. Doubtless, they took back roads, avoiding towns like Louisburg and Rocky Mount and Tarboro. McNair's men did not catch up with the slaves until they had traveled eighteen miles "below" Tarboro. Depending on the exact direction, that would have placed them within a few miles of their goal—the Roanoke River. Had they taken the road out of Tarboro heading directly east, they might have been within sight of the river, less than a mile from the town of Hamilton. On June 9, McNair's slave catchers brought to him "2 girls belonging to Mr. Collins," Louisa and Murrier. The contractor lodged them in the county jail at Tarboro. Then within five days, the slave catchers apprehended the remaining three. Finally in mid-June, McNair forwarded all five to Lloyd Bateman at Northwood.[36]

This episode proved costly indeed to Josiah Collins. The planter had authorized Hugh McNair to pay up to $50 each for the capture of the slaves. But it seems that the two "picketts" with whom McNair had contracted ordinarily charged twice that amount for each slave captured. McNair argued with the men saying that they had "had no trouble at all" with the slaves. That was probably so. When McNair's brother, E. D. McNair, transported the slaves from Tarboro to Northwood, he "did not tie them." And he "let them sleep in the negro houses" without a guard posted at a plantation where they stopped along the way. At night, they went "perfectly free," although McNair told them that if they left he would "catch them with dogs." But the slave catchers thought differently and continued to insist on their usual fee.[37]

The greatest cost, however, was borne by the runaways. The day after they were returned to Northwood, Bateman, now "very angry," "struck one with two hundred" lashes. We do not know which one, but the overseer evidently intended to inflict the same punishment on each of the runaways. "My only fear (between ourselves)," wrote E. D. McNair to the slaves' master, "is that Bateman will be too severe with those negroes." This was no small point. Part of the compact between the Somerset slaves and their master had focused on protection from abuse at the hands of other white men. McNair realized that whipping would not discipline these slaves; indeed, it would provide the excuse to leave, which the remainder of the Northwood slaves earlier had been looking for as reported by Bateman himself. Neither would it provide the food required by the slaves, the probable lack of which had caused them to flee in the first place. Collins's crisis in paternalism passed, but the planter had by no means resolved the conflict between master and slaves.[38]

· **VI** ·

By contrast, William Pettigrew's slaves labored without much complaint in the spring and summer of 1863, probably because the planter kept his slaves away from the North Carolina Railroad and off of his own small farm in Chatham County. Instead, he hired them out, one or two at a time, to individuals. And he arranged with neighboring planters to look in on the hired slaves from time to time. In doing this, Pettigrew allowed his slaves to voice their complaints. When the need arose, he could remove them immediately to better circumstances. Hence, the planter ensured his slaves' subsistence and protection from abuse, a protection they actively sought in the upcountry. According to Pettigrew's agent in Winston, those hired out in that neighborhood "are always asking me when master is coming up." "The[y] appear very anxious to see you."[39]

In late February, for example, a certain E. M. Fisher wrote his first report to Pettigrew about the planter's slaves living near Winston. Fisher told Pettigrew that they all appeared well enough, but there was one case in which a change had to be made. A certain slave girl had been hired out as a nurse to a man whose two children had taken ill. As it happened, the children died. Therefore, the man sent the slave girl to Fisher because he now "had no use for her." Fisher then placed the slave girl with another family near Winston. But that family "did not treat her as the[y] ought."

The slave complained to Fisher who agreed to move her again. "I told her," he explained to Pettigrew, "that she could not stay there being that I thought you wanted your servants treated right." Similarly in April, when a slave named John clashed with his new master's son, William Pettigrew's agent did not hesitate to relocate John. The son "was always fighting of John and knocking of him." Therefore, Fisher concluded that John "could not stay at that place," at least not "on those conditions."[40]

Moving slaves about, however, was sometimes a difficult matter, as in the case of Jack and Venus, the couple so much abused in 1862. In spring 1863, Jack and "his children" (by another marriage?) had been hired out to Dr. Martin, a resident of Mocksville in Davie County. But the doctor had no use for Venus. Therefore, she and "her children" remained at another planter's home, also in Mocksville, during which time William Pettigrew paid the slaves' room and board. Coincidentally, another of Pettigrew's agents, William C. Campbell, looked for someone to hire Venus, but he failed. Venus was ill and running up doctor bills. Therefore, William Pettigrew instructed Campbell to move the slave and her children from Davie County to Pettigrew's farm at Haywood in Chatham County. The planter was not happy about the move, but he could see "no other course" to pursue.[41]

The separation of Jack and Venus caused difficulties two months later. By that time, Pettigrew had found a home for Venus somewhere in Chatham County. Whether he hired her out or simply boarded her there, the records do not say. Whatever the case, Venus's new master did not treat her well. She complained in a letter to her husband, Jack, who subsequently wrote an eloquent plea to William Pettigrew requesting his wife's removal.

Jack began his letter with a reaffirmation of their relationship as slave and master. "I feel it my duty" he began, "to serve you." Then, Jack went on to tell how he and his children and fellow slaves now served Pettigrew by working for other masters. "I am happy to state that I have a *good* home at Dr. Martin who treats me very *kindly* & I in return try to serve him faithfully." The slave, in fact, expressed himself so pleased with Martin that he hoped "for myself & family to stay with him another year (if we ar to be hired)." Jack then looked forward to reestablishing his old relationship with William Pettigrew. "I wish you both [William and his sister Annie] the utmost pleasure & happiness & pray that the time may *soon come* when we will all be joined together as a family of Master mistress & servants."[42]

The slave then came to the point. "I rec*d* a letter from my wife dated the 30 june[.]" "She spoke of living *harder*," he explained, "than she eve[r] lived before, saying her *allowance* [of food] was to scanty &c." "Now Master," he went on, "I know your *kindness* will not allow any one in your service to suffer if you know it, hence I inform you, so that you may remidy the evil." "She spoke of her children crying for *bread* which *disturbed* me very much." "Will you *please*," he implored his master, *"attend* to thir wants & *God will bless you* for it.[43]

Jack had pulled out all the stops. By his service, he had held up his end of the paternalistic bargain. Jack emphasized that his letter was not an expression of personal opinion but an invocation of the relationship between a master and slave. "I as your servant feel it my duty to write as well as serve you." Now, he demanded that Pettigrew live up to his obligations. Specifically, the planter's position required that he act to provide an adequate subsistence for his slaves, no matter what other circumstance might arise. Moreover, the slave had only to inform his master of such a situation in order to obtain relief. This was not a matter for negotiation or discussion. If Pettigrew expected to remain master, he had no choice under the rules of paternalism worked out at Magnolia and Belgrade plantations except to remove Venus from her present situation. Should Pettigrew fail in this obligation, the relationship would dissolve, and his slaves would be justified in taking drastic action.

The records do not say whether William Pettigrew moved Venus to a better situation. Perhaps he did; for he had made a habit of relocating slaves who complained about their new masters. But perhaps he did not; the planter, evidently, had not taken at least one complaint seriously in the weeks just prior to Jack's supplication. Only days before Jack wrote to William Pettigrew, the planter lost a slave named Dempsey who ran away from his Chatham County farm "without shoes or a change of clothes." Dempsey was "23 years of age, about 5 ft 6 in. in height, of ordinary size, rather stout than otherwise for his height, neither black nor light but of a bacon [?] colour, quick in his movements, and polite in his manners." Pettigrew offered a $25 reward for the slave's capture. But

Dempsey probably was lying out somewhere nearby. Without shoes or a change of clothes, and presumably without food, he could not have gone far in any case. Dempsey, evidently, reacted to something he thought sufficient to void his relationship to William Pettigrew. Whether that something involved food or clothing or protection, we do not know.[44]

· VII ·

By September 1863, conflicts between refugeed slaves and their masters declined somewhat. Most likely as corn ripened in late August, the slaves' fears of famine in the coming year eased. In December, hog-killing days confirmed the availability of food. On Christmas Day in 1863, Caroline Pettigrew gave the slaves at Cherry Hill an extra distribution of pork sausages, beef, and sweetener. "This morning," she wrote to her husband, "I gave all the grown people a quart molasses apiece & a gallon to be divided among the children, besides a good allowance of meat." "They all seemed very much pleased & smiling." However, a different crisis had to be faced. Inflation had skyrocketed in the fall of 1863, and that created a multitude of difficulties for planters and slaves alike.[45]

Charles Pettigrew first experienced the consequences of inflation late in the year. On December 23, he arrived "ready to do business" in Greensboro. There, the planter sought to hire out his slaves already on the North Carolina Railroad for another year. To his delight, he found Mr. Wilkes "very anxious to have negroes." Pettigrew, however, was dismayed to learn that the money he would receive for his slaves would buy almost nothing. "Things are immensely high," he complained. "Corn is $12 per bushel. Pork is $2 to 2.50 per pound." Should the planter fail to hire out all his slaves, he would have to pay enormous prices to support them.[46]

Charles Pettigrew was not the only planter disturbed by the effects of inflation. "There is a general feeling of depression among the people I have met on the road" to Greensboro. They have, he reported, "no confidence in Confederate money." "And the prospect of the new tax bill seems to have but little effect in making it any better." The levy approved by the Confederate Congress in February 1864 provided for new taxes on land with discounts for planters. It was hoped that the expanded revenue would reduce the government's debt and strengthen confidence in the national currency—which it did not do. As a result of inflation, Pettigrew and his planter friends sought to purchase property and rid themselves of currency. The man from whom Pettigrew purchased a farm near Greensboro the previous summer now begged for a chance to buy it back. "And he is willing to give me a very considerable advance," wrote Pettigrew.[47]

In the end, Wilkes offered Pettigrew what the planter considered "a good price," for there was now a strong demand for hired slave labor in the piedmont. As the flight from the coast ended and the war effort expanded, slaves for hire had become scarce and expensive. No one wanted to purchase slaves because of the new tax on property; employers much preferred to rent. That fall, as a result, Wilkes had been forced to feed and house Pettigrew's slaves decently in an attempt to prevent them from complaining to their master. They reported themselves "doing better" on the road and gave what the planter called "satisfactory accounts."[48]

Inflation's greatest impact, however, fell upon planters and slaves who had refugeed on farms. Ordinarily, Washington County planters issued new shoes and winter clothes just after the harvest in December. By that time, the planter had managed to sell the first of his fall crop and had money on hand to make necessary purchases. But in December 1863, planters had little money on hand, and the cash that they possessed had lost so much value to inflation that it had become impossible to buy cloth and shoes.

Josiah Collins's overseer at Hurry Scurry plantation, Lloyd Bateman, arranged in November for the slaves there to begin making cloth. He put the women to work carding but without much success. The cards Collins sent him were "no count." Shoes, evidently, were no problem for the Collins slaves. The planter owned a skilled shoemaker, Ishmael, who made all the shoes they needed. At Cherry Hill, Caroline Pettigrew followed much the same course. The slaves there wove their own cloth for winter clothes. She even sought to purchase an additional loom. But unlike Josiah Collins, Caroline Pettigrew could not provide footwear. She had no money to buy shoes as she had done previously, and she had neither leather nor a skilled shoemaker to make them at home. Therefore, the slaves at Cherry Hill had to do without, and that led to difficulties between master and slaves.[49]

Shortly after Christmas, Jackson, for example, was assigned to take a crew of three men to "clear up a place" near a creek where there had been some flooding. Presumably, they had been sent to remove brush and obstructions to allow the land to drain properly. But according to Caroline Pettigrew's account, the slaves "hadn't shoes, so did not do much more than sit round the fire & warm their feet." The planter's wife, however, did not take offense at their lack of action. She admitted that the weather had turned terrible. After a terrific storm, the temperature had dropped dramatically, while the wind "continued fiercely, blowing violent gusts." "The cold was bitter!" she wrote. Yet after the weather had warmed a day later, Jackson continued to refuse to work. One morning he announced that he was "not well" so "he did nothing," according to the planter's wife. The next day, he "looked quite well" but "sent twice for pepper to put a cake to his side." "It seems to be a stitch." Caroline Pettigrew concluded that she would get no further labor from Jackson until he got some shoes. "No more on his acct.," she wrote to her husband.[50]

Finally in March 1864, the conflict between master and slaves at Cherry Hill was resolved, at least for a time. The demand for grain on the coast at last outstripped the rate of inflation. Hence, Caroline Pettigrew began shipping corn by wagon to Augusta, Georgia, where it brought a high price, even by the Confederacy's inflated standards. With that money, Pettigrew presumably bought shoes and clothing for the slaves at Cherry Hill. At any rate, they returned to work and began spring plowing.[51]

· **VIII** ·

Unlike the first crisis in paternalism, this one did not focus on reestablishing old rules in a new context. Refugeeing in the upcountry created new difficulties between masters and slaves. Uncertain and exploitative employment, the failure of crops, a shortage of land, and inflation made it impossible for even the most conscientious planter to meet his obligations to his slaves. Yet, slaves held their masters to standards the two parties had forged in Washington County before the war. In letters and conversation, the slaves stressed their service, their adherence to the bargain between them- slves and their masters. They pointed out in detail each planters' failure to provide an adequate subsistence, warm clothing and shoes, and protection from unscrupulous whites. Finally, when complaints went unheeded, they protested loudly, slowed down their work, and, as a last resort, ran away or plotted their revenge in secret.

Also unlike the first crisis, this conflict between Washington County masters and slaves in the upcountry never fully resolved itself. In the summer of 1864, slaves in the North and South Caro- lina upcountry became aware that William T. Sherman's army had beaten a large Confederate force at Chattanooga and, thereafter, had laid seige to Atlanta. In late August, Charles Pettigrew, writ- ing from Cherry Hill, about 150 miles from Atlanta, found "the greatest indifference among the negroes." "They either expect to go home or to the Yankees, and care for nothing that is around them," especially the crops Pettigrew hoped his slaves would plant. In the end, the planter had to threaten to whip the slaves at Cherry Hill to make them work even slowly.[52]

7

Guerrilla War

Guerrilla war in Washington County began in January 1863. Responding to unionist raids on local plantations, Jasper Spruill, the son of prosperous unionist farmer Ammon Spruill, applied to North Carolina Governor Zebulon Vance for a commission to raise a company of local secessionists. The young man proposed specifically "to kill Buffaloes [unionists]." Governor Vance reportedly replied: "Go ahead and kill the king of them and then I will talk to you about it." Therefore, sometime in early January, Spruill and two other men, Warren Snell and L. Biggs, went to John Giles's home, "waylaid" the unfortunate Giles "near his own gate," and "shot him." Giles received three balls and some "other shot" in the head and died twenty-three hours later.

John Giles had been a leading unionist in Washington County and captain of the local cavalry. Charles Pettigrew, who had lost a great deal of property to Giles and his fellow unionists, wrote: "This has ended the life of one of the worst men and most heartless villains that has been raised in any country." Yet George Patterson, the Episcopal priest who ministered to planters and slaves in the Scuppernong neighborhood, conceded that the "atrocious" John Giles "met his fate with a spirit worthier of a nobler cause." All the arrangements to kill Giles had been made in secret and would remain so. As Charles Pettigrew told his wife: This was "one piece of news you will not see by the papers."[1]

How did John Giles become the target of an assassination plot suggested by the governor of North Carolina and carried out by the son of a prominent unionist? The answer lay in claims to property. During December, John Giles had led his cavalry on a series of raids that culminated on December 29, 1862, in an invasion of William Pettigrew's Magnolia plantation. Altogether, sixteen local unionists plus a Yankee corporal stationed at Plymouth carried off virtually every movable object on the place. Pettigrew's overseer, John M. Hough, protested, saying that he owned all the property on the plantation and that he had protection papers signed by federal officers in Plymouth. Pettigrew's black driver, Henry, supported the overseer's contention. But Giles and his crew paid no attention. They removed "a Bed Matrass, Bolster Pilows & Bedstead & counterpain, 6 nice stool chairs, 12 flag seat chairs, 2 office chairs, 1 large nurse chair, 2 settees, 1 looking glass, a double set of wagon harness, 2 plow harness, 2 pair cariage cusians, 2 thermomiters, 1 stove and pipe, 5 saws, 2 bridles, 1 sadle & blanket, six [bunches of?] shingles, [and] all the ropes" on the plantation.[2]

The next week, John Hough traveled to New Bern to seek an interview with Edward Stanly, "the Military Governor of NC for the Lincan government," as he explained to his employer. Hough represented himself as the owner of Magnolia plantation and hoped, thereby, to "get some redress for the property taken." Stanly, for his part, received the overseer in a "kindly" manner. And after hearing Hough's account of Giles's depredations, the governor gave the overseer an "order for the property." From New Bern, Hough made his way to Plymouth, where he presented the governor's "order" to the commander of the post, a man named Ewer. But Stanly's directions "availed nothing," as Hough put it; Ewer dismissed Hough's claim. In the overseer's view, however, "some good did result from my going to New Bern." It caused the removal of Capt. Ewer from the Post" and that "put a stop to the Bufilows robing" or so it appeared for the moment.[3]

John Hough then appealed to Major Henry Bartholomew, the new commander at Plymouth. "I made it appear satisfactory to him," wrote Hough, "that it was my property I was trying to save." Therefore, the major assured Hough that he "would not be troubled any more." Bartholomew also promised to "look further into the conduct of Capt Ewer" and to restore to Hough "the property that he could find that was taken" from William Pettigrew's house. Unfortunately for both Hough and his employer, the federal army soon reinforced Plymouth and sent higher ranking officers to command the post. Therefore, Hough's "intercourse with Major Bartholomew was ended" toward the last part of January 1863. William Pettigrew's plantation, like most planters' property in Washington County, stood in danger of attack again.[4]

It was in this climate of frustration among planters that Jasper Spruill hatched his plan to kill John Giles. But why Spruill? As the son of a leading yeoman farmer, he might have joined Giles. Again, the answer lay in property claims. Unlike Jasper's father, Giles's unionist raiders sought to protect few property claims of their own. They were men of very small means. Of the twelve who could be located in the U.S. manuscript census for 1860, most owned less than $200 worth of real estate—the average (not counting Giles) being $179. Some, like Tom Basnight, held more land, $700 worth in 1860; others, Shadrack Jackson, for example, owned $50 worth. Only Giles himself possessed real estate worth more than $200, claiming land valued at $1,000 and personal property worth $1945 in 1860. But the unionist cavalry leader made his money from federal contracts, not from farming; he was listed in the 1860 manuscript census as a mail driver for the U.S. government. Giles and his friends, therefore, had little interest in planters and their claims to property, except to object to their hoarding of local resources.[5]

Governor Vance and Jasper Spruill had hoped by killing John Giles to disrupt unionist opposition. Instead, they simply rendered local unionists leaderless. Unfortunately, at the same time local secessionist leaders also deserted the county. Josiah Collins, William Pettigrew, and Charles Pettigrew already had fled upcountry. Now they were followed by H. G. Spruill, the mayor of Plymouth and local militia general who had attempted to moderate conflict between secessionists and unionists during 1862. Spruill moved to Raleigh where he took a job in the adjutant general's office. In addition, Henderson B. Phelps, the planter and militia captain, died suddenly in January 1863 after a bout with diphtheria. Hence, local oppositions broke down completely. Secessionist and unionist organizations both devolved into numerous guerrilla bands.[6]

· II ·

By late March 1863, the murder of John Giles had created a sensation. "Times are pretty lively around here," wrote one sailor stationed at Plymouth.[7] Then, Confederate guerrillas embarked upon a broader program of political assassinations, seeking to murder federal officers engaged in organizing local blacks and whites for their own defense. Moreover, some Confederate death squads acted with the sanction of state officials. Federal forces returned the favor. During the summer of 1863, they gave no quarter to irregular soldiers, whether involved in assassination attempts or just ordinary smuggling, and certain officers undertook a series of executions designed to terrorize Confederate guerrillas. "During the war," one resident recalled in later years, "the woods and swamps were full of men in ambush." Both played the part of "bushwackers," each "watching the movements of the others, both sides doing dirty, ugly things, causing their neighbors, friends and even near relatives, who did not approve of their ugly deeds, all manner of trouble." "There was bitter hatred between the two sides." Finally, in Washington County itself all loyalties dissolved, and people of all political persuasions became victims.[8]

The case of M. Bowan, the hapless unionist entrepreneur from Plymouth, illustrates the divisive character of the local guerrilla war. Bowan had attempted to remain friendly with both sides. He avowed himself a Lincoln man and took the federal oath. He supplied salt and other goods imported from the North to the county's unionists. At the same time, however, he attempted to ingratiate himself to secessionist planters. He had acted as a factor for some, disposing of their cotton and corn in Northern markets. In the winter of 1863, he went to extraordinary lengths to guard Charles Pettigrew's property at Bonarva plantation. The unionist had obtained a "protection" from the post commander at Plymouth. Then, he sought and received the same from Governor Stanly. During the last week in February 1863, however, the 1st North Carolina Union Volunteers removed all the furniture from Bonarva to Plymouth and put it up for sale in town. Other items also may have been taken, but Bowan could not say for sure.[9]

For his trouble, Bowan lost his remaining property and endured hostility from all sides. Local unionists already had freed all his slaves once. Bowan must have bought more, for in February his best slaves finally fled the county, evidently after Major Bartholomew had made his rounds to various plantations to read Lincoln's Emancipation Proclamation. Bowan lamented: "All the valuable portion of my slaves left and went to the yankees." Shortly afterwards, Confederate soldiers based in Martin County raided his farm and "took the remainder that had proved faithful to me." In addition, the Confederates burned his "dwelling house" and all his personal property, apparently while Bowan was absent from his place. But "worse," as Bowan put it, the soldiers "turned my children out of doors." Two were now supported by friends, and a third child he had not seen in over a year. "All this," he complained, "was done by the order of those who I have often furnished bread." Finally, the Confederates imprisoned his brother-in-law at Salisbury. Bowan was a man in the middle, much like Washington County itself. "I am an outcast," he wrote, "with thousands of others [like me] on both sides."[10]

Other men in Plymouth followed a more prudent course than the profit-seeking Bowan but fared little better. Robert S. Goelet, formerly a printer by trade and a resident of Plymouth, for example, made every effort to live quietly. He fished a little and worked odd jobs from time to time for local residents and federal soldiers. In that way, he managed "to procure food for the family," as he put it. Moreover, "by keeping a civil tongue in my head and treating all politely," he wrote, "I get on as well as could be expected in these war times." Even so, the Union Volunteers confiscated much of his property. "As for my negroes," he told his mother, "I expect they are lost to me and mine forever."[11]

· **III** ·

Guerrilla war alarmed U.S. commanders around the Albemarle Sound. Initially, the federal response was minimal. In Washington County, that resulted mainly from the appointment of a new army commander at Plymouth, a certain colonel, probably Francis L. Lee, who headed the 44th Massachusetts Volunteers. C. W. Flusser, the gunboat commander at Plymouth, for example, planned a combined expedition to rescue a captured unionist named Woodworth. Woodworth was a trader whose boat, loaded with $50,000 in goods, had been waylaid in the Chowan River. But the colonel pointed to the weather—it was snowing too hard. Then, Flusser suggested an expedition up the Roanoke River to Windsor in Bertie County. There he hoped to break up a Confederate supply dump. But the colonel argued that the roads had become impassable. Besides, he pleaded inexperience in these matters.[12]

By contrast, U.S. officers on the north side of the Albemarle Sound made every effort to hunt Confederate guerrillas. Samuel D. Hines, a U.S. Navy gunner in charge of the fortifications at Elizabeth City, spent most of his time drilling local troops in gunnery techniques. But in spare moments, he revealed, "I go out scouting for guerrillas." Writing in early February 1863, Hines reported: "I succeeded in killing one to-day. None of my men were hurt, as the enemy would not stand." He had personal reasons for seeking out guerrillas. "I came near getting killed two nights ago," he wrote, "by a ball fired by one of those murderers." Similarly, on March 1, C. W. Flusser reported from Plymouth that guerrillas had murdered a union man at Edenton. "I shall go over to-morrow and look them up," he promised. And in early March, federal volunteers stationed on the Chowan River arrested eight or ten people suspected of firing on a unionist cavalry company in Chowan County. The attackers were local men acting as guerrillas, described by Edenton planters as "troublesome, bad men"—one or two of them deserters from the rebel army.[13]

South of Washington County, Union troops engaged in pitched battles with Confederate guerrillas. During the first week in March, a U.S. gunboat, the *Lockwood,* entered the Pungo River in Beaufort County fifteen miles south of Plymouth. There, the federals found not merely a smuggling route but also a new bridge "which the enemy had built to facilitate the removal of the products from that section into the interior." After destroying the bridge, the crew confiscated a small schooner abandoned there, plus food, two cases of tobacco, some small arms, and a large quantity of bacon. In the meantime, local guerrillas had been notified of the expedition's presence. Soon they attacked. In the fight that followed, four federal soldiers lost their lives, and sixteen were wounded. The guerrillas lost about thirty men and had several captured, some of whom carried not only arms but also "passes and protections signed by Governor Stanly." One man was captured wearing a woman's clothing, bearing a federal "pass protection," and carrying a commission from Jefferson Davis.[14]

Federal officers, however, blamed not only Confederate guerrillas but also unionists, both black and white, for local violence. Sometime in early March 1863, Union troops from Plymouth marched out of town toward the south. Ostensibly, they sought to locate and engage the 17th North Carolina Volunteers based at Williamston and Hamilton. In fact, the troops marched along the Long Acre and Ridge roads between Plymouth and the town of Washington, where they "arrested all the men" for a ten mile stretch, including many of those "who had taken the [federal] oath." The roads lay in a desolate stretch of swampland inhabited mainly by poor laborers and shinglers who had been among the first to organize a unionist militia company in 1861. But these same men had accounted for many recent raids upon plantations in Washington and Beaufort counties. After a day's rest, the federals marched back to Plymouth with their prisoners. Shortly afterwards, the unionists, now thoroughly intimidated, were discharged and allowed to return to their homes.[15]

These contradictory federal actions finally destroyed the unionist coalition in Washington County between yeoman farmers and laborers. In mid-March, Charles Latham, the yeoman farmer and unionist politician, reported "all is quiet" in Washington County. But that quietude represented not calm but cynicism in unionist ranks. Latham, for example, admitted that "having stolen all the property in the county," his fellow unionists now "consent[ed] to let the people alone." And M. Bowan was reported "down on the Yankee government." The unionist entrepreneur thought the conflict "now a negro war, not a war for the Union." Among his friends, Bowan found "no Union men at all, except for *Old* [C. H.] *Willis*." Moreover, some of those local men who had joined the 1st North Carolina Union Volunteers now regretted their action. "A large portion of the Buffs," wrote Latham, "want to get out of it." "Some of them have been to see me today," he claimed, "to know if I thought they would be taken in the Southern Army."[16]

Even federal troops became bitterly antagonistic. Some Northern soldiers at Plymouth heard that "the Government was going to send some negro troops from Mass" and "swore if so, they would throw down their arms." Others, three men in particular who got "a little tight," were heard "hollowing harrah for Jeff Davis & the South" in the streets of Plymouth. The soldiers "knocked over every negro they met" and went on to "damn the negro Union" and to claim they would "be in Raleigh the first chance" they got.[17]

Jasper Spruill, the man who murdered John Giles, summed up the effect of guerrilla war and federal repression in Washington County: "You have no idea, Sir," he wrote to Josiah Collins, "of the change which has been brought about in the county within the last few months." "Shortly after you left the Union men or Buffaloes . . . bid defyance to ownership of property." They "went plundering or detroying with impunity in every direction . . . during which time several persons sustained heavy losses." "But it has finely ceased and quietness pervades the whole county."

Guerrilla war had turned yeoman farmers and landless men against each other. Charles Latham and M. Bowan, longtime unionists, now poured their troubles out in letters to Washington County's leading secessionists, characterizing their former allies, landless whites and freedmen, as plunderers and thieves.[18] The local conflict also alienated federal commanders in the area, so much so that they sought to disarm black and white unionists and to prohibit any further political activity on their part. The U.S. government had no constituency at all, a fact that North Carolina secessionists hoped to exploit.

· **IV** ·

In March 1863, the Confederate army began strengthening its forces in eastern North Carolina. The movement had its origins in Robert E. Lee's desperate search for a means to supply his army with foodstuffs. North Carolina lay close at hand. Therefore, in February General Lee detached to Goldsboro, North Carolina, an entire corps of more than ten thousand soldiers from his Army of Northern Virginia. He suggested that several "demonstrations" be made against federal posts in the eastern part of the state. Lee's purpose was not to drive the Yankees and Buffaloes from the coast. He, in fact, believed that General Foster had so strongly fortified New Bern, the Union army headquarters, that no attempt should be made to overrun it. He hoped simply to confine the federals to their posts temporarily so that the previous season's crop could be removed to the interior. To carry out this plan, General Lee assigned a North Carolina native, Brigadier General D. H. Hill, to command the troops at Goldsboro.[19]

D. H. Hill, however, arrived in Goldsboro with goals more ambitious than those envisioned by General Lee. "The planters on the Neuse, Tar, and Roanoke have sent large numbers of negroes into the interior and do not propose to raise a crop for another year." This action, he argued to the secretary of war, endangered Lee's long-term prospects in Virginia. Western North Carolina's reserve of corn and livestock had been exhausted. In addition, forage for horses and mules was in short supply. Wade Hampton, the South Carolina cavalry commander, "would find more forage in Beaufort, Washington, and Hyde [counties]," argued D. H. Hill, "than in the whole of Virginia," where he now pastured his horses. Besides, eastern North Carolina was rich in another resource— young men who could be conscripted for Lee's army.

There was, however, more at stake than food and draftees. D. H. Hill proposed to reestablish planter rule throughout eastern North Carolina. "The Confederacy cannot afford to lose the planting interest, and a brigade judiciously disposed would afford such protection as is necessary to secure confidence and encourage the farmers to plant." The rebel army must "protect the planting interest in the rich counties of the east," General Hill insisted.[20]

On March 13, 1863, D. H. Hill attacked New Bern. The Confederate general hoped to surprise the federals and surround them with troops on three sides. But when the rebel soldiers arrived, they surveyed New Bern's earthworks and balked. Hill had failed to gather any intelligence about Foster's extensive fortifications or his troop dispositions. Finally, after trading artillery fire, the Confederates withdrew to Goldsboro, marching about one hundred miles at night in a driving rain. Two weeks later, Hill's corps attempted a similar attack on the federal post at Washington, North Carolina. But again, Confederate troops failed to take the fortified town. Hill's lack of success left North Carolina's coastal plain open to federal attack during planting season. And it provided an excuse for General Foster to request reinforcements—which he did.[21]

At first, Washington County's role in all this remained ambiguous. The Confederates considered Plymouth a potential staging area for a federal invasion of the Roanoke valley. Therefore, they made periodic forays into the county to gather intelligence. During Hill's attack on New Bern, troops from the 17th North Carolina Volunteers based in Martin County staged demonstrations to prevent those troops from reinforcing the beseiged Foster. But, at that time, the federals had other, lesser plans for Plymouth. They used it only as a base for small-scale combined operations. To support such operations, the Union army constructed Fort Williams, a small defensive installation located on the south side of town.[22]

Plymouth's usefulness in offensive operations, ironically, became apparent to U.S. commanders as a result of the unsuccessful Confederate attacks on New Bern and Goldsboro. The easy defense of small, isolated posts suggested that they might be used as citadels from which federal expeditions to the upcountry could sally forth and later retreat in safety. With that in mind, General Foster announced an entirely new strategy for the Union army in eastern North Carolina. He would disperse his forces among three posts, New Bern, Washington, and Plymouth. From those places, he would concentrate his troops for lightning-quick expeditions upcountry from time to time. These expeditions would not occupy eastern North Carolina; neither would they stop Confederate troops from roaming the length and breadth of the coastal plain. But occasional forays would prevent planters from returning their slaves to the region and planting a crop in the fall of 1863.[23]

To put his plan in motion, General Foster reorganized his department into three districts. The area near the Roanoke River became the District of the Albemarle, with Brigadier General Henry W. Wessells commanding from headquarters at Plymouth. By April 1863, Wessells's troops included two brigades with 192 officers and 2,604 enlisted men present, most of them at Plymouth. In addition, the U.S. Navy continued to station at least three gunboats at Plymouth under the overall command of Lieutenant C. W. Flusser. The gunboats were considered a part of the offensive force; they accompanied all expeditions upcountry, Wessells's troops taking care to march within the protective cover of the boats' guns. In response, Brigadier General J. G. Martin, commander of the 17th North Carolina Volunteers moved his headquarters from Tarboro to Williamston in order to be nearer Plymouth. There, he hoped to maintain a close surveillance of the federal troops and, thereby, forestall any surprise raids upcountry.[24]

Between May and July 1863, the federal army in eastern North Carolina launched three raids deep into the state's interior. In mid-May, Colonel J. Richter Jones led an expedition from New Bern as far as Kinston, located about twenty-four miles inland. The federal force did little damage and did not enter the town, but they did engage a Confederate brigade stationed outside Kinston and fought to a standoff. Then in July, Brigadier General Edward E. Potter, Foster's chief of staff, led a "sizable cavalry force" on a raid from New Bern through Greenville and Tarboro to the railroad at Rocky Mount. This expedition did a great deal more damage. Potter's troops carried off property from several plantations, burned a bridge over the Tar River, destroyed military stores and cotton in Tarboro, and escorted five hundred slaves to freedom in New Bern. Finally, in late July a large force under General Foster's command sailed from New Bern up the Chowan River, disembarking at Winton. From there, the force hoped to march upcountry about forty-two miles to the railroad junction and bridge over the Roanoke River at Weldon, but a determined Confederate effort just east of Weldon stopped the federal attack.[25]

The three raids had taken no strategic position; Union troops had defeated no Confederate army. In fact, little damage of any kind had been inflicted on eastern North Carolina, except to a few plantations whose owners had fled months earlier. But the security of property had been rendered problematic once again. No planter would dare return his slaves to eastern North Carolina as long as Union troops remained. This change in federal strategy had again provoked a property war that would be fought by guerrillas. And Plymouth would become the secure base for launching raids upcountry for both the Union army and landless unionists.

In May 1863, a group of secessionist "gentlemen" from Washington County recorded their impressions of Plymouth as it then appeared. Over two-thirds of the buildings had been burned, they reported, in the Confederate attack of December 1862. Since then,

Union troops had burned a few more buildings and pulled down others, including the local Masonic lodge, from which U.S. soldiers had removed jewels and regalia. The federals also had cut down all the trees and had dismantled every fence in town. This had been done to clear an area across which heavy guns could fire unimpeded upon attackers. Moreover, the soldiers had constructed a wide canal, extensive breastworks around Plymouth, and a small fort on a hill to the southwest. This was no longer a town. There were no residences, no shops, no public buildings left standing save the federal customs house. Plymouth was a military installation.[26]

Just as the town had been transformed physically, so, too, had the local population changed. The county's leading secessionists, of course, had fled in the fall of 1862, taking with them perhaps two-thirds of the local slave population. Meanwhile, some six hundred slaves from Washington County and a handful of free blacks sought freedom among the Yankees at Roanoke Island. By May 1863, planters reported that "there are but few [blacks] left in [Washington] County except those with the enemy at Plymouth." Of the white population, "few persons except the Yankees and Tories" remained in Plymouth. Some of those men, mainly landowning unionists, now departed. Captain Bowan and his family fled to the Northern states. So, too, did E. J. Johnston. Johnston, who had been a strong secessionist in 1861, had, since that time, fallen in love with the daughter of John Phelps, the county's unionist marshal. There was "no Union feeling in the County now," Charles Latham believed, "except with those who have gone into the Yankee service."[27]

· **V** ·

In June 1863, the Confederate army sought to learn more about the federal citadel at Plymouth. "The Gen.," evidently D. H. Hill, "desired two reliable men to be sent into Washington County as scouts," an order he conveyed to the commander of a company in the 17th North Carolina Volunteers then stationed on the Roanoke River thirty-four miles above Plymouth. What Hill hoped to learn, he did not reveal. Doubtless, he wanted information on the fortifications and troops at Plymouth. But Hill most likely sought to protect "the planter interest," as he called it. Presumably, he wished his spies to inquire into local political affairs, particularly the activities of landless unionists.[28]

The general's spies, however, got caught. The two men, Benjamin Ainsley and John W. Norman, both volunteers in the 17th North Carolina Volunteers and Washington County residents, had been sent to the county on "furlough." While nosing around, Ainsley and Norman aroused the suspicions of local unionists who promptly arrested the two men and transported them to Plymouth. At Plymouth, federal officers paroled John Norman. But James Phelps, doubtless one of the unionist Phelps clan, offered evidence against Ainsley, claiming that the Confederate soldier had gone "to his house & broke open his trunk and stole his money." Another Confederate soldier who happened to be present called it "aly." "Ainsley has not been to his house at all," the secessionist argued. But the federal officers saw the matter differently. They charged Benjamin Ainsley with larceny and shipped him to New Bern for trial. The federals said they intended "to hang him."[29]

Failing to gain information through spies, the Confederates began to kidnap U.S. soldiers on picket duty. In late June 1863, Confederate raiders attacked a federal picket two miles west of Plymouth, captured a lieutenant, two privates, and two horses and "brought them away safe." When the raiding party returned to their base, the prisoners were questioned and then transported to prison at Richmond. In response, federal commanders assigned black troops to picket duty around Plymouth who, evidently realizing that capture meant death, kept up "a great deal of firing on the picket line." "I do not know whether they see anything to fire at or not," wrote one white soldier: "We cannot see anything when we are on picket." But the blacks thought otherwise, and correctly so on at least one night when a squad of Confederate cavalrymen invaded their camp, leaving three wounded and one dead.[30]

But the assigning of black troops to picket duty stopped Confederate surveillance within Washington County. This was no minor achievement for the federal forces at Plymouth. During 1860–62, the commander of the 17th North Carolina Volunteers had regularly responded to attacks on property with raids into Washington County. Now he had no way of gathering knowledge of unionist activity. In consequence, the Confederate raids ceased in July 1863, and that gave landless men a free hand in Washington County. From that time, they seized without fear property of all kinds.

· VI ·

"The people generally have been robbed," wrote one Washington County planter, "of their horses, guns, provisions, &c &c." In late May 1863, local unionists made several forays into the Scuppernong neighborhood. At Somerset Place, Josiah Collins's plantation, they "tore up things generally," according to an account given by George Spruill, the planter's overseer. Collins's library, about three thousand volumes, was "taken and distributed all around the country." Property belonging to other planters fared similarly. Spruill reported that "buffaloes houses all around the country are supplied with books & furniture taken from houses of loyal citizens [secessionists] who have come away." Washington County's landless men informed Spruill that they intended to "destroy all the property and annihilate the white people of the South," themselves excepted, rather than give up the Union.[31]

In the fall, the local unionist cavalry stationed at Plymouth also began seizing property, even from avowed unionists. They confiscated a horse from a fifty-five-year-old farmer named Harmon Harrison who lived about five miles south of Plymouth. He owned $900 in real estate and $425 in personal property from which he supported a wife, four teenage children, and an older woman, perhaps a sister. When the war began, Harrison did his best to avoid politics and armies on both sides. He neither volunteered for federal service nor did he "talk about the war a great deal," testified a neighbor. This tactic enabled him to avoid the conflict until October 1, 1863. On that day, the unionist cavalry stopped at his house and took away his last horse, a dark bay-colored mare about seven or eight years old and worth around $200. He told the officer in charge that "it would brake me up" to lose the horse. He would have nothing to plow with next spring. But the officer said that he "must have her."[32]

Charles Latham also found himself confined to his house and surrounded by armed men. He was "not permitted to leave" the premises "without a guard." And he "regret[ed] exceedingly not having left" earlier. According to one planter report, local unionists and federal soldiers made a habit of visiting many propertied yeoman farmers at "all hours of the night." Thomas S. Latham, a prosperous yeoman and a unionist, complained that he had "not been permitted to sleep a single night undisturbed since last November." He further claimed that local unionist soldiers had forced him "to be present and witness his wife's clothes nearly all torn from her person by the Yankees." The recitation "caused the tears to flow freely," according to one observer. Then, Latham said he could "go no further." Finally, unionists slaughtered or removed "all the hogs, cattle, poultry, sheep & c" they came across on Latham's farm.[33]

Meanwhile, Confederate draft dodgers living in Plymouth preyed freely upon property holders, both planters and yeomen, in the neighboring counties. One planter, John Pool, described the local implications: Bertie County lay west of the "U.S. military post at Plymouth." From that post, virtually every plantation in the county could be reached by way of the Roanoke or Chowan rivers. Moreover, these rivers recently had become federal highways patrolled as they were by U.S. Navy gunboats. Therefore, "many slaves and disorderly white persons have left here & congregated at Plymouth." Some of those "disorderly" whites were local men attempting to avoid the draft. Others were deserters from the Confederate army. Worse, these persons now found it "convenient to come by water at any time" into Bertie County "& commit depredations & indeed they have done so." In one case, Pool claimed that a certain planter had died and left his property in Pool's care. But before he could "procure a reliable person to take charge," certain "pirate bands from Plymouth, in addition to running off about eighty slaves, plundered the estate of not less than fifteen thousand dollars worth of chattle property."[34]

Plymouth also offered potential temporary sanctuary to draft dodgers who chose to remain in Bertie County in order to be closer to their prey. "Several small bands of these fugitive conscripts," Pool revealed, "have taken [shelter?] in the county." "Within the last few days," he reported, they had robbed several persons traveling on local roads at night. Others had broken into a widow's house. The widow had a "white man" living on the place, presumably to protect her. But the robbers "confined" them both "in her house" while they "broke open her meathouse and supplied themselves with provisions." "No military force can reach them," Pool complained, "because as soon as they become [alarmed?] they will go over to the enemy, either by crossing the Chowan or by signalling some passing gunboat in the Roanoke." Worse, in Pool's view, "The slaves that remain on the farms & many [white men] who have gone to the enemy are now headed by men filled with the imagined wrong of being driven from their homes" by Confederate conscription officers.[35]

· **VII** ·

Washington County's landless men, having plundered the portable goods belonging to planters and yeomen, resolved in 1863 to take over the area's remaining plantations. That act brought them into conflict with freedpeople who claimed the places for themselves. Earlier, Washington County blacks had seized several plantations by default. Landless whites had confined themselves to carting off furniture and books, the symbols of a planter's wealth, not the means of producing that wealth. But guerrilla war had changed the aims of landless white men. Now, they sought to control productive resources. They carried off absent planters' oxen, plows, and wagons—all items to which Washington County freedmen had laid claim over a year earlier. And they wanted the land. Soon, these conflicting claims led to violence. The trouble took place mainly in the Scuppernong neighborhood.

At Somerset Place, the local unionist soldiers carried off Collins's two oxen which were particularly valuable for heavy plowing. Later, a man named Hamilton Davenport was reported "driving about in [Collins's] mountain wagon." Washington County's landless men also forced the overseer "to let off water to run the mill whenever they pleased." Collins owned one of the largest mills in the neighborhood, and his canal, which channeled water from Lake Phelps to the Scuppernong River, formed the only year-round source of water power available for miles around. Similarly, the unionist soldiers seized property belonging to D. G. Cowand, the merchant and a hot secessionist. They turned over Cowand's grist mill to a local unionist, who ran it "as his own." The Volunteers also used Cowand's "new house" for target practice, leaving it "pretty well riddled." Finally, the Volunteers destroyed what they could not use or carry off. At Somerset Place, they broke up *"everything"* of value, particularly carts, plows, hoes and in fact everything used in cultivating a crop."[36]

Then in late 1863, two landless men arranged through the U.S. Treasury to rent Somerset Place and Bonarva plantations. The two men, however, did not propose to operate the plantations themselves. They apparently planned to sublet the land to fellow poor whites in the neighborhood. At any rate, the new proprietors did not need laborers and, therefore, determined to run off all the freedpeople on the two places. But Pettigrew's former slaves had made their own claims to the land and buildings and tools. Therefore, the blacks at Bonarva were "extremely unwilling to leave" when the two would-be entrepreneurs ran them off, or "so they said to persons they met on the road." Two of the freedmen, Tom and York, resisted so vigorously that they were "killed at the houses where York lives near the Lakefield" by a mob of land-hungry unionists.[37]

Similarly in January 1864, Henry, the former black driver at William Pettigrew's Magnolia plantation, got into a scrape over land with some landless unionists in the neighborhood. He had taken possession of Magnolia himself in February 1863 from Pettigrew's overseer, John M. Hough. Then sometime in July, Henry moved himself and his family off the place, taking with him most of the tools he required to produce a subsistence crop—oxen, carts, livestock, and plows. He evidently had located on one of the many "islands"—raised areas of arable land surrounded by water—in Washington County's vast swamps. But late in 1863, Henry returned to Magnolia plantation and laid claim again to the land itself. That is when he came to blows with neighboring whites who sought to divide the place among themselves. The "Buffaloes" went to Magnolia and beat him "badly," so much so that Henry felt compelled to "seek safety" among the federal officers at Plymouth. Henry claimed later that he was "to have been murdered" "by the Buffaloes in the night after the morning on which he left with the Yankees for Plymouth." Another slave at Magnolia, Virgil, testified that he "was daily expecting a similar fate when he left."[38]

Evidently, the overseers at William Pettigrew's Magnolia plantation took some part in these and other sharp dealings. "It is thought," wrote Charles to brother William, "that [Malachi] White and [John M.] Hough are anything but a protection to your property." These two were among the planters' so-called "friends at the head of the [Scuppernong] River" who "so badly treated" Henry and Virgil that "they were driven away."[39]

In December 1863, the U.S. officers in Plymouth concluded that they could no longer protect black people in Washington County from either Confederate guerrillas or landless white unionists. Therefore, they sought to refugee the county's few remaining freedpeople to either Plymouth or Roanoke Island. According to Charles Pettigrew's account, an expedition from Plymouth soon "forced" the blacks "to go with them" to town. Actually, the U.S. troops simply rode from one plantation to another, explaining the dangerous situation as they went. Henry accompanied the soldiers with the object of "induc[ing] negroes to leave their owners." At a certain planter's house, he reportedly became so insistent that he "threatened to force" one of the freedmen to abandon his home. But "the Yankee officers forbid it."[40]

In the end, these freedpeople and others refugeed to Plymouth formed themselves into a coherent community allied with the federal army. Within a month, they had organized themselves and selected leaders. On New Year's Day, 1864, "the colored people held their first Anniversary of their freedom" in Plymouth's Methodist church. A sympathetic federal soldier reported that "speeches were made, songs were sung, and a happy time was realized." "It was truly a feast of the soul," he thought, "to the people whose shakles have been loosed and bid to go free." The federal army took advantage of the blacks' enthusiasm for freedom by sending a recruiter among them. Captain Leonard Marvin spent all of January "raising a company of blacks, in Plymouth, for a regiment in General Wilde's brigade." By the end of the month, he reported his company "nearly full."[41]

· VIII ·

The spring of 1864 seemed harsh indeed to Washington County's residents, balmy weather and clouds of green pine dust notwithstanding. Guerrilla war in Washington County had fractured the alliance between yeoman farmers and landless laborers. The latter had evidently concluded that the land promised them by yeomen, that is to say the county's plantations, could be acquired more easily by a direct application of force, force that at the same time conflicted with the claims of freedpeople to the same plantations. Moreover, in acting independently, landless unionists could seize productive resources from yeoman farmers as well. In the end, Washington County's war at home became a struggle for all manner of productive resources.

But the takeover of Washington County plantations signaled much more than a simple loss of property for planters. It began a short-lived program of federal reconstruction in the county, a program in which planters would take no part and which surely pointed to a radically different future. This followed from an order issued by the U.S. secretary of war on October 9, 1863. The plan stipulated that all "Houses, Tenements Lands and Plantations, except such as may be required for military purposes, which have been or may be deserted or abandoned by insurgents" could now be "placed under the supervision and control" of special agents sent to North Carolina by the Treasury Department. The order itself implied no reconstruction. But the men assigned to administer the secretary's plans in North Carolina, like others who would follow him south after the war, had other ideas.[42]

D. Heaton arrived in New Bern sometime in late December 1863. In a newspaper advertisement, Heaton proposed leasing abandoned houses and small farms throughout the coastal plain, including Washington County, "to loyal parties residing or doing business within our military lines." He sought to rent large plantations to loyal people who would "cultivate cotton and other agricultural products," manage a plantation to "produce the largest yield possible," and pay "one fourth of the productions raised" to the Treasury for rent. In addition, Heaton required of loyal planters "that proper inducements shall be held out to laborers, white and colored, who still remain on these lands, to continue at work." Finally, the Treasury agent demanded that employers make an effort "to attract laboring and needy persons from the over populated towns."[43]

Heaton did not plan simply to rent land to the highest bidder. He outlined a program that would privilege commercial commodity production for export to the North over farming for a subsistence, substitute wage labor for bound labor, and produce a massive migration of laborers into rural districts, areas that subsequently would be dominated by large-scale employers. This was not plantation agriculture as William Pettigrew knew it. Slaveholders would occupy no place in this scheme—but neither would yeoman farmers. Moreover, wage laborers would find themselves seeking work at a very great disadvantage. Their employers would act in a partnership (or perhaps collusion) with the federal government.[44]

Heaton proposed a kind of state-supported commodity production envisioned by no one in Washington County, least of all by local planters. This course of events caused William Pettigrew to lament: "There is nothing to be hoped for from the tender mercies of the Yankees but destruction. If successful in this contest, we will have liberty and as much of our property as we can save out of the hands of the invaders. If unsuccessful, whether it be the result of defeat in battle or of reconstruction, we will be slaves to negroes & yankees; we will be deprived of property of all kinds." "In short," he concluded, Washington County's planters "will be the most downtrodden and wretched people under the sun."[45]

In William Pettigrew's mind, there could be only one solution to the planters' difficulties—military action that might subdue "the negroes and yankees." But how could Washington County's planters attack the federals and their unionist allies? The Confederate army showed little interest in eastern North Carolina except as a source of bacon and corn; General Lee thought the region of no strategic significance; and in 1862, local planters had appealed for an occupying army directly to Governor Henry Clark and President Jefferson Davis without success. There seemed little impetus, military or political, for a Confederate expedition to North Carolina's coastal plain. But events had begun that would make an attack on Plymouth a political necessity for leaders in both Raleigh and Richmond.

The Battle of Plymouth

· **I** ·

In late 1863, a peace movement emerged for the first time in North Carolina. William Holden, a Raleigh newspaper editor, and his Whig friends formed the core of the organization, although the movement never assumed the formal structure and trappings of a political party. In eastern North Carolina, Whig planters who supported Holden had suffered large property losses at the hands of the Union army. Their brothers and sons had been passed over for promotion consistently in favor of secessionist Democrats, especially those from Virginia. In the piedmont, planters endured continual raids from Robert E. Lee's subsistence officers. Therefore, many of the state's elite sought some way to bring the war to an end, preferably by striking a compromise with the Union. In the fall of 1863, their leader, William Holden, ran for governor on a peace platform. Holden, however, lost by a wide margin to Zebulon Vance, a young secessionist Democrat who had made a name for himself as a colonel commanding North Carolina troops. But the peace candidate had succeeded in splitting the state's elite into prowar and antiwar factions, even if he had failed to muster a large voting constituency.[1]

In January 1864, Holden and his Whig friends, therefore, sought broader support for the peace movement from a secret organization called the Heroes of America, commonly known as the "red

186

strings" after the red ribbon they wore to identify themselves to one another. The Heroes originated in the North Carolina piedmont and recruited perhaps ten thousand poor white unionists, both yeoman farmers and landless laborers. In this effort, Holden and his allies again found the Confederate government very helpful. Rebel recruiters had just begun to descend upon North Carolina, armed with a new conscription law. With it, they seized men on the streets and in their homes for duty in the Confederate ranks. They sometimes transferred entire local militia units illegally into Confederate service. Thus pursued and embittered, poor whites flocked to Holden's banner.[2]

Soon a political firestorm engulfed the state. In a series of sharply worded letters, Governor Vance explained the situation to Jefferson Davis. Vance hoped the Confederate president would recall his recruitment officers from the state and suspend enforcement of the conscription law altogether around the Albemarle Sound.[3] Davis, however, interpreted the situation in North Carolina not as a political difficulty but as a military challenge requiring an application of force. In January 1864, he sought and received the power to suspend all writs of habeas corpus. This would enable his officers who sought conscripts and supplies to imprison indefinitely those who opposed them—which they did. In late January, at a unionist meeting held in Greensboro, people there addressed Davis and "did not enlarge on any point so much as the prison feature of your administration." At the same time, Davis hinted darkly that this new power could be used against Whig planters who headed the state's peace movement.

But Governor Vance refused to sanction the use of force against opponents of the war. Hence, Davis undertook to defeat the peacemongers, at least those in the eastern part of North Carolina, with the Confederate army.[4] In March, the Confederate high command determined a last-ditch strategy. Davis could remove three brigades temporarily from Lee's defense of Richmond, strike quickly at the federal outposts in coastal North Carolina hoping to overrun them, and then return the troops to Lee in time to meet the expected onslaught from General Grant's more than two hundred thousand soldiers massing in northern and eastern Virginia. If successful, the Confederates would eliminate the federal presence on North Carolina's coastal plain and, thereby, both conciliate the state's disaffected planters and intimidate unionists throughout eastern North Carolina. Only one question remained: Where should General Hoke attack?

By mid-spring 1864, Jefferson Davis and his War Department had heard an earful about the Albemarle Sound region. Governor Vance complained of Confederate raiding parties in Tyrrell County that robbed farmers, unionists, and secessionists alike of their horses. A certain W. N. H. Smith wrote to the secretary of war complaining that the Roanoke valley remained "exposed to hostile visits from the enemy's gunboats" stationed in the Albemarle Sound. Smith focused his comments especially on Plymouth. "The enemy holds a strong position at Plymouth," he wrote, "and recently have made destructive raids into [adjacent Bertie] county, not alone destroying much private property, but large supplies of provisions." The secretary read the letter and then submitted it "for consideration of the President." Not surprisingly, the Confederate government directed its spring offensive against Plymouth.[5]

· **II** ·

On April 12, 1864, General Braxton Bragg, Jefferson Davis's military advisor, issued marching orders from Richmond. Bragg assigned Brigadier General Robert F. Hoke, commander of a brigade stationed at Kinston, to take charge of the expedition. To assist Hoke's troops, Bragg detailed Brigadier General Matt Ransom's brigade at Weldon and brigades from Petersburg, Virginia, and Tarboro, North Carolina. Altogether, Hoke commanded about ten thousand soldiers, including his own artillery, plus a regiment of cavalry and, eventually, an additional regiment commanded by General Martin. Martin's troops had been stationed throughout much of the war in Bertie County just west of Plymouth and had only recently been shifted to Wilmington. In addition, Hoke could count on the ironclad rebel ram, *Albemarle,* to attack the U.S. gunboats stationed at Plymouth. The *Albemarle* had been two years in the building at Hamilton on the Roanoke River.[6]

General Bragg himself formulated the plan of attack. He instructed Hoke to concentrate all his troops at Tarboro, where they would find five-days' rations waiting at the railroad station. From there, Hoke should march eastward to Williamston and then to Plymouth in two days. At the same time, the *Albemarle* would sail downriver. This was to be a fast, cheap operation. Bragg stressed that Hoke's preparations and movements must be carried out in the greatest secrecy to retain the element of surprise.[7]

This was not an altogether sensible plan from a tactical point of view. First, it proposed that a force of ten thousand soldiers move from several different points in eastern North Carolina to Plymouth in complete secrecy. In view of the number of deserters and unionists scattered about the region, a surprise attack was unlikely indeed. Second, it assumed that the forts and redoubts at Plymouth could be stormed by infantry covered by heavy artillery. But similar attacks led by D. H. Hill on New Bern and the town of Washington had failed earlier to breech a single federal entrenchment. There was little to suggest that Hoke could do better at Plymouth. Finally, Bragg hoped for a cheap victory, one that would involve few casualties. In mid-April, exaggerated Confederate intelligence estimates put Grant's forces north and east of Richmond at "four or five hundred thousand men" and "the largest amount of artillery ever known." Lee needed those soldiers in Virginia—and soon. But storming the entrenchments at Plymouth inevitably would expose Hoke's troops to enfilading fire, mainly grapeshot and canister, from several large guns. The Confederates would be slaughtered.[8]

Bragg had a reputation as being a poor tactician. But his plan's inadequacies flowed not merely from his miscalculations but also from the general's political purposes. Bragg, son of a Whig planter from northeastern North Carolina, sought a military solution to a political problem. He intended to make eastern North Carolina safe for Whig planters. He hoped to intimidate yeomen and laborers who opposed the Confederacy. To do so, he would clear the region of U.S. troops who attacked planters' property and aided unionists of all kinds. Such a purpose, however, required not merely an expedition, but an occupying army, just as Washington County's planters had argued in the fall of 1862. This Bragg did not have. Even if Hoke succeeded tactically, Bragg still had no hope of attaining his strategic goal—the restoration of planter rule in eastern North Carolina.[9]

General Bragg's orders notwithstanding, the planned attack on

Plymouth was among the Confederacy's worst kept secrets. The federals had known for months that the Confederate navy was building an ironclad ram somewhere above Hamilton. They knew in December 1863 that the ram was nearing completion and would be ready for use in the spring. Therefore, troops at Plymouth went on continuous alert beginning in late February 1864, soon after the ice broke up on the Roanoke River. Moreover, on April 14, just four days before the attack, Brigadier General Henry W. Wessells, commanding at Plymouth, obtained detailed information of the proposed Confederate operation. He informed his superiors that "a large force of the enemy," estimated at ten thousand to twelve thousand soldiers, had assembled near Hamilton "designing, in conjunction with an iron-clad boat, to make an attack on Plymouth this week; a demonstration to be made toward New Berne at the same time." This information had come from reliable spies in Bertie and Martin counties. To meet the expected attack, General Wessells requested five thousand additional troops. But his superiors, ignorant of Plymouth's political importance, declined, no doubt thinking that the Confederates attached no strategic significance to the town. Major General John Peck, commander of the District of North Carolina, sent only one additional gunboat to Plymouth.[10]

Washington County's planters also knew of the planned attack, and they looked forward to its success. One planter wrote cryptically: "If we succeed in carrying out our present program, Washington [County] will again breathe free." Specifically, the planters hoped to recapture the county in time to hold elections for the state legislature. They already had nominated William Pettigrew for a senate seat. "I think our prospects are brightning," the planter wrote, "and if every man will do his duty, all will yet be well." "We will be able to run our own councils."[11]

· **III** ·

By April 15, General Hoke had assembled his forces near the town of Tarboro, forty-two miles west of Plymouth. Over the next two days, he marched ten thousand troops eastward along a road through Martin County to the Washington County border.

At four in the afternoon on Sunday, April 17, Hoke and his troops re-formed themselves south and east of Plymouth. There they faced a formidable collection of forts, redoubts, and long entrenchments, all bristling with heavy artillery and manned by roughly 2,700 U.S. troops. All this lay in the midst of a complicated terrain.[12]

Plymouth was situated on the south side of the Roanoke River, inland from the Albemarle Sound about three miles. The town itself lay on a small rise between two creeks to the east and west, the Roanoke River to the north, and a plain to the south and southwest. A half mile to the west, Welch's Creek and its adjacent swamp formed a barrier that could be passed over on the Jamesville Road. A half mile to the east lay Coneby Creek. The swamp produced by this creek was considered impassable except by the Columbia Road that ran from Plymouth eastward to Tyrrell County. To the north across the river lay an inpenetrable swamp through which no troops could pass. If an attack came from this direction, it must be by gunboat. As a result of this topography, the only easy approach to Plymouth lay to the immediate southwest of town across a broad plain on either side of the Washington Road.[13]

General Wessells had arranged his defenses to take advantage of this difficult topography. Along the river's shore, he relied on the U.S. Navy. Commanded by Captain Flusser, a flotilla of four gunboats lay at anchor next to the town's wharf. Flusser's guns could fire over the town and into attackers on the plains south and west of town, as far as the Jamesville Road. Should the Confederates overrun Plymouth, he could rake the town point-blank with canister and grapeshot. Flusser himself believed that his gunboats alone could protect the federal garrison. Certainly, he had the firepower to do so. His own ship, the *Miami,* carried six nine-inch guns, a huge Parrot rifle that used 100-pound shot, and a 24-pounder smoothbore howitzer. The other large gunboat stationed at Plymouth, the *Southfield,* carried the same gunnery, except for a slightly smaller howitzer. Two smaller gunboats carried several 20-pounder Parrott rifles and howitzers.[14]

On land, Wessells feared an attack mainly from the southwest. When Wessells first arrived in Plymouth in May 1863, the town boasted only a single earthwork, Fort Williams. This would not

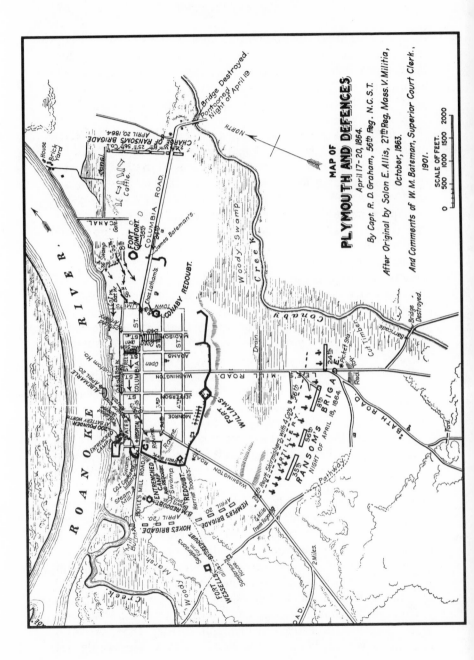

MAP OF
PLYMOUTH AND DEFENCES,
April 17- 20, 1864.

By Capt. R. D. Graham, 56th Reg. N.C.S.T.

After Original by Solon E. Allis, 27th Reg. Mass.V.Militia,
October, 1863.

And Comments of W. M. Bateman, Superior Court Clerk.

1901.

SCALE OF FEET.
0   500 1000 1500 2000

do, in the general's opinion. He, therefore, ordered construction of an elaborate system of entrenchments and redoubts designed to defend the western and southern edges of town lying alongside the open fields there. The western breastworks encompassed two small redoubts with entrenched camps capable of housing troops under heavy fire, plus a heavy artillery battery near the river called Battery Worth. Battery Worth enclosed a rifled gun capable of firing 200-pound shot. The southern breastworks included Fort Williams at the center, a large four-sided earthwork equipped with four 32-pounder rifled guns and one 6-pounder gun. The fort's guns commanded a view to the south and west with a clear shot straight down both the Lees Mill Road and the Washington Road, where the Confederate forces encamped upon arrival.[15]

Outside the entrenchments, Wessells ordered the construction of two small redoubts equipped with heavy guns and also bomb-proofs to house skirmishers. The first redoubt, Fort Wessells (also known as the 85th Redoubt after the 85th New York Volunteers who built it), was situated roughly seven hundred yards southwest of Plymouth's entrenchments. This small earthwork housed a company of skirmishers plus one rifled gun. Its purpose was twofold. First, the fort could provide an early defense of Plymouth. Its guns had a clear shot at the Jamesville Road, which was blocked from the view of gunners at Fort Williams by an intervening swamp. Second, should Confederate troops get past the fort, its guns could pour enfilading fire into the flank of Confederate troops positioned south of town or into the rear of rebels located west of Plymouth's earthworks. By contrast, Fort Grey had a singular mission indeed. Located upriver and out of sight of Plymouth, it was built specifically to pour artillery shells into the *Albemarle* when the ironclad attempted to pass down the river.[16]

The weakest point in Plymouth's defenses was on the east side of town. There, a heavily wooded swamp blocked both the eastern entrance to Plymouth and access to that side of town from the west. If the Confederates wanted to attack from that direction, they would have to pass through the swamp at least once and probably twice. Wessells, therefore, felt safe in leaving that part of town without entrenchments. He, however, did order the bridge through the swamp destroyed, and he had two small earthworks—Fort Comfort and the Coneby Redoubt—built along the Columbia

Road. These earthworks would serve as citadels to which skirmishers might retreat if attacked from the east.[17]

When Hoke's troops arrived outside Plymouth on Sunday afternoon, they drove in Wessells's pickets and halted beyond federal lines and out of artillery range. Ransom's brigade moved eastward to a plain south of town, while Hoke's brigade moved west toward Fort Wessells. Both sides threw out skirmishers, and the federals opened fire with their artillery. Kemper's brigade positioned itself upriver within sight of Fort Grey. The fighting continued sporadically until about ten in the evening. Meanwhile, commanders on both sides made their respective preparations for the next day. Hoke encamped his troops and formulated plans for attack. Wessells sent away roughly five hundred civilians aboard a transport boat destined for Roanoke Island. One man present later recalled "the hasty farewells then and there spoken (some of which were final), the pale faces of affrighted women and children, the groans of the sick and wounded, and the bustle and confusion."[18]

· IV ·

On Monday, April 18, at daybreak, Hoke's troops launched a two-pronged attack. To the west of Plymouth, Kemper's brigade, which had camped upriver the night before, opened a "terrific fire" on Fort Grey. The object was to disable the gun there so the ironclad *Albemarle* could descend the Roanoke River safely. But the Confederates had revealed their position the night before with campfires outside a house where they slept. Therefore, the gunners at Fort Grey focused their fire directly upon the Confederate attackers. The rebels were forced to abandon the house and to dig holes in the ground for protection. But the holes soon filled with seepage from a shallow water table. Therefore, they retreated beyond the range of Fort Grey's guns.

To the south of Plymouth, General Hoke positioned his own brigade along with General Ransom's troops for a direct assault on Fort Williams. But during most of the day, the two sides simply exchanged a withering artillery fire. Confederate troops prudently remained out of range of the guns firing from Fort Williams and from the U.S. gunboats. Meanwhile, most of Wessell's troops huddled underground. "Our infantry were massed in the Bomb-proofs, except those watching behind the breast works," recalled one U.S. soldier. There, the federals were "comparatively safe from danger as the Rebel Infantry kept back out of Range of muskets." Finally, both sides ordered out skirmishers from time to time in order to ascertain the enemy's dispositions. During this time, however, the Confederates made no general advance. They and the federals both waited patiently, expecting that the Confederate ironclad would arrive momentarily. "By this time," wrote one U.S. soldier, "it was generally understood that the long talked of Ram was comeing down the River, as the men in Fort Grey could see a black smoke on the river above." But the ironclad ram failed to arrive by nightfall.[19]

Ignoring his own plan, General Hoke finally determined to attack without the *Albemarle*'s help. Just after sunset, the Confederate commander massed his troops for a direct frontal assault on Fort Williams and its entrenchments. Then, Hoke moved his artillery to the fore and had them sweep the plain south of town with grapeshot and canister to force the federals' skirmishers to retreat. A company commander among the U.S. troops later recalled the action: "I deployed my reserve as skirmishers some distance to the rear of the first line." Then, he told his troops in the first line to "fall back to the reserve, firing as they did so" if the enemy advanced—which the Confederates did. From that position behind a slight rise, the federal skirmishers fired directly into the advancing line of Confederate troops. Later, Fort Williams opened fire while the skirmishers retreated to bombproof entrenchments. The result was a slaughter of advancing Confederate troops. A rebel officer was heard to exclaim: "It is of no use; we cannot endure this fire." Finally, at about eight in the evening, Hoke withdrew his troops from the field near Fort Williams, where now "the shrieks of the wounded and dying could distinctly be heard above the din of battle."[20]

General Hoke's difficulty was enfilading fire—that which his troops had endured and that which he could not bring to bear upon the federal fortifications. The solution was twofold. First, Hoke had to silence the guns at Fort Wessells, located west of town. The U.S. artillery there had fired directly into Hoke's left flank all day and had caused a tremendous number of casualties.

Second, Hoke had to destroy the 200-pounder Parrot gun at Fort Grey upriver so the *Albemarle* could pass that point safely. Once the ironclad lay opposite Plymouth, it could fire into Fort Williams from the north while Hoke's artillery shelled the town from the south.

On Monday, near sunset, Colonel Mercer, commander of the Georgia 21st Volunteers, led his troops and Kemper's brigade to a position southeast of Fort Wessells. The fortifications there consisted of a hollow square formed of high earthen embankments, surrounded by sharply spiked abatis, and included a bombproof magazine but no shelters for the troops. Inside, a company of forty-two enlisted infantrymen, twenty-three enlisted artillery gunners, two lieutenants, and a captain, N. Chapin, prepared to defend themselves. Besides their muskets, the men relied upon a small 6-pounder field piece and a light 32-pounder gun mounted on a ship carriage. The advantage in these two guns lay in the fact that they could be turned in any direction quickly.[21]

But while the garrison focused its attention on the Confederate troops advancing from the southwest, Colonel Mercer sent his field artillery to a point directly south of the redoubt. That place lay in the woods at the base of a slope that descended into a swamp behind the artillery. Not surprisingly, the troops at Fort Wessells did not become aware of the Confederate guns until they opened fire. And when they did, Mercer moved his troops forward in the confusion and surrounded the fort. Then, the Confederates made four successive charges, penetrated the abatis, but advanced no further.[22]

In response, U.S. infantrymen opened a withering musket fire and lobbed hand grenades "apparently with great effect," according to a lieutenant commanding inside the fort. That same soldier later estimated that the Confederates lost at least sixty-two killed and a "larger number of wounded" in the attack. In addition, the federals captured twenty-three prisoners who had been left behind in a hasty rebel retreat. Having failed to storm the fort, Colonel Mercer withdrew his troops and opened an artillery barrage from guns placed at right angles to the fort. The Confederate gunners fired percussion shells and concentrated on the magazine, hoping to blow up the fort and its garrison. They failed. But the percussion shells did kill three men without whom the fort's defense could not be maintained—the garrison's only trained gunners.[23]

At that point, Colonel Mercer demanded the garrison's surrender, and after a meeting of officers, the federals capitulated. As Lieutenant Butts recorded: "A large force was known to be between the redoubt and the town, cutting off communications. The cartridges were nearly expended, only half a dozen grenades were left, our gunners were disabled, the prisoners were a great embarrassment; there were no means of spiking the guns or of making signals." Besides, he saw "in the darkness no hope of efficient help from the gun-boats or from the town batteries, and the fire received from the gun-boats if repeated left no safe place in the work." Therefore, the officers surrendered at eleven on Monday evening.[24]

Later, at about three a.m., General Hoke ordered his artillery to shell Fort Grey, hoping to divert the attention of U.S. gunners from the river. The general apparently intended that the *Albemarle*'s commander, Captain James W. Cooke, would take notice of the shelling and seize the opportunity. But Hoke sent no communication to Cooke informing the captain of his intentions. And Cooke appears to have acted independently and without any knowledge of Hoke's plans or actions. At any rate, Captain Cooke weighed anchor at 2:30 a.m. and actually may have slipped past Fort Grey before the Confederate shelling began. The *Albemarle*, however, did not pass the fort unnoticed, according to Cooke's account. In fact, U.S. gunners lobbed a few shells from the 200-pounder Parrot gun at the ironclad, but to no effect whatever. Then the ironclad passed Battery Worth, a redoubt inside Plymouth's entrenchment also equipped with a 200-pounder, undetected. At about 3:15 a.m., the *Albemarle* was poised to strike the U.S. gunboats then anchored off Plymouth's shore.

The *Albemarle* was unlike any ship the U.S. naval commander, Captain C. W. Flusser, had ever faced. It had been built in a cornfield alongside the Roanoke River about fifty miles upstream from Plymouth. It had been patterned after the famous *Merrimac*. The *Albemarle* was 152 feet long, 45 feet wide, and 9 feet deep from the gundeck to the keel. It was constructed around a wooden frame, drew eight feet of water (the maximum possible on the Roanoke River, which flowed about nine feet deep in the spring), and had two propellers driven separately by two steam engines of two hundred horsepower each. The ship's armament consisted of iron plating, two guns, and a wooden ram. The iron plating, two inches thick, covered all parts of the vessel remaining above water and was thought to be impermeable to all shells then in use. The only openings in the ship's shell were six portholes, two on each side and one at each end of the ship, from which two rifled Brooke guns could be fired. Finally, the prow of the ironclad, constructed of solid oak, sloped downward into the water to form a point designed to ram other ships below their waterline. Formidable as it was, the *Albemarle* did have its weaknesses. Cooke, an experienced naval commander himself, had no trained crewmen available. Also, the engines and power train proved unreliable. And the ship's builders had failed to finish attaching all the iron plate to the wooden frame. Cooke was forced to sail down the Roanoke River with a portable forge on deck and workmen literally hammering and swearing day and night.[25]

When the *Albemarle* at last stood off Plymouth's wharf, the Confederates found the river blockaded. Captain Flusser had lashed together with chains his two largest gunboats, the *Miami,* which he commanded personally, and the *Southfield,* commanded by Lieutenant Charles A. French. He had placed the two boats broadside across the river to form a "V." To pass through this line, the *Albemarle* would be forced to ram one of the two gunboats and endure a broadside of cannon and musket fire from the other. Flusser did not expect the artillery shells to penetrate the *Albemarle*'s iron shell, but he did hope that the tremendous percussive effect would stun the rebel crew. Should that happen, Flusser's marines could board the Confederate vessel and capture it by hand-to-hand combat. Flusser had every confidence in his preparations. "I have force enough to whip the ram," he concluded just hours before the battle.[26]

Sometime after 3:15 a.m. on Tuesday, the *Albemarle* raced ahead under a full head of steam in an attempt to ram the *Miami.* But the ironclad glanced off that ship's side toward the *Southfield* and rammed the latter gunboat squarely, ripping a gash in it ten feet long below the waterline. Immediately, the federals turned their guns on the ironclad and poured a heavy fire onto its decks, but not one shell penetrated the *Albemarle*'s iron shell. Captain

Flusser, who himself manned a deckgun on the *Southfield,* was killed instantly by one of his own shells which had rebounded from the ironclad's side. Meanwhile, the crew of the *Albemarle* fired one gun and all their muskets at the U.S. ships.

Within minutes the ram had its effect. The *Southfield* began to sink, and Lieutenant French ordered his men to abandon ship. Some managed to climb onto the *Miami,* among them French himself who now took command in place of the late Captain Flusser. Others jumped into lifeboats or swam for shore. Meanwhile, as the *Southfield* sank, it dragged down the *Albemarle* with it, tipping the ironclad on its side and pushing several open portholes under water. When water began to pour into the ship, Cooke ordered his men on deck so they would not be trapped if the ship sank. Then, he ordered the vessel's engines reversed. Fortunately for the *Albemarle*'s crew, the ironclad shook loose of its sinking companion when the *Southfield* hit the river bottom.[27]

Lieutenant French, now commanding on the *Miami,* judged the situation hopeless. He saw the *Albemarle* back away from the sunken *Southfield* and move to a position from which the ironclad could take a run at the *Miami.* Therefore, the U.S. commander ordered his remaining gunboats to drop further downriver to await daylight. "The fatal effect of [the *Albemarle*'s] prow," French explained later, "had been but too fully demonstrated on the ill-fated *Southfield,* and under these circumstances I reluctantly concluded to withdraw from the river, being fully convinced that had we closed with this vessel it would have resulted in our loss." Finally, at about five a.m., Captain Cooke anchored the ironclad about a mile downriver from Plymouth, around a bend and out of sight of federal gunners. Then, he sent a volunteer by boat to seek out General Hoke and to return with battle plans for the day. The *Albemarle* now controlled the Roanoke River.[28]

By dawn Tuesday morning, the Confederates had positioned themselves for a general attack on Plymouth's main fortifications. Yet, they had paid a terrible price in killed and wounded. The failed charge against Fort Williams had produced an immense number of casualties. So, too, had the failed infantry attack on Fort Wessells. Hoke had done exactly what General Bragg feared he would do—slaughter hundreds of Confederate soldiers who might have been deployed later in a defense of Richmond. And he had done so in a situation where a simple application of artillery fire had later proved effective, that is, in the capture of Fort Williams. Why the needless slaughter? What was the point? Lacking General Hoke's correspondence and reports, it is difficult to say. The Confederate commander's actions during the next two days, however, suggest an answer.

· **V** ·

On Tuesday, April 19, General Hoke ordered another attack against the fortifications on Plymouth's southwest side. This time, however, the Confederate commander could count on favorable enfilading fire. The *Albemarle* would fire its guns from the northeast, while Hoke's artillery would pummel Plymouth from behind the walls of Fort Wessells to the town's southwest.

But the general could not be satisfied with an artillery duel. He still wanted to storm the federal entrenchments. Therefore, Hoke ordered two brigades to throw out skirmishers and drive the federals back into their entrenchments. Ironically, the rebels failed precisely because they followed their commander's orders. In forcing U.S. skirmishers back to their trenches, Hoke's infantrymen permitted them to take cover. Hence, Hoke's artillery seldom found an open target and caused few federal casualties. By contrast, Confederate soldiers now fought on an open plain exposed to artillery and sharpshooters firing from Fort Williams. According to a federal source, "Many casualties occurred on both sides, the loss of the enemy being much the heaviest."[29]

Having twice failed to breach Plymouth's defenses from the southwest, General Hoke at last conceived of a different plan of attack. On Tuesday evening, the Confederate commander ordered General Matt Ransom to move his troops through Coneby Creek swamp southeast of town to the Columbia Road. There, Ransom was to turn westward toward Plymouth and attempt a crossing of rain-swollen Coneby Creek. If successful, Ransom would find little resistance, this being the only side of Plymouth left without entrenchments. Once inside Plymouth, Ransom would be in a position to attack General Wessells's fortifications from the rear, except for Fort Williams which was fully enclosed. This was a clever plan indeed, for it alone among all of Hoke's ideas contained an element of surprise. In his report after the battle, General Wessells called Hoke's gambit "unexplained." A Pennsylvania volunteer who later summarized Wessells's report used more accurate language. "General Wessells," he recorded, "speaks of this occurrence as an unexpected disaster."[30]

Late Tuesday night, General Ransom moved his troops into position on the Columbia Road. Then, he ordered the brigade's pioneers to lay a pontoon bridge across Coneby Creek. By about nine p.m., Ransom's troops had all crossed the bridge and had re-formed themselves in a line near the Roanoke River facing Fort Comfort and Coneby Redoubt, two small federal earthworks housing perhaps a hundred soldiers on either side of the Columbia Road. Under a full moon, however, these movements could be seen clearly by artillerymen in Fort Williams, who immediately turned their guns on the Confederate attackers. "All night long," one man in Ransom's brigade recalled, the fort's shells "hurled above and around us, and sometimes exploded in our very midst." But the rebel soldiers remained motionless and silent, waiting for orders. "Then it is," wrote one rebel who endured the nightlong artillery barrage, "that thoughtful men engage in introspection and sit in judgment upon their past lives." Finally at dawn, Ransom's field commander gave the order to advance.[31]

Under a hail of fire, Ransom's troops moved across a level plain several hundred yards wide, which the federals earlier had used as a parade ground. The brigade's skirmishers fired as they went but hit no one. U.S. pickets and skirmishers had retired to the safety of the parapets at Fort Comfort. Then, artillery gunners at Forts Comfort and Williams directed an enfilading fire of canister and grapeshot at the advancing rebels. That stopped their forward movement. But after a few minutes, Ransom's main line again raised themselves from the ground and marched forward, straight into the federal guns. The soldiers moved slowly and silently without firing a shot until nearly standing in the federal entrenchments. Then, they began a long rebel yell and fired their guns as they ran to surround Fort Comfort and Coneby Redoubt. In a matter of minutes, Ransom's troops, roughly five thousand men, overran and captured the federal positions—but not before U.S. gunners "for fifteen murderous minutes" shot down rebels "like mown grass." A rebel soldier wounded in the battle estimated that five hundred of his comrades lay dead. He did not speculate on how many wounded remained on the field.[32]

While part of Ransom's troops remained to subdue the federals in Fort Comfort and Coneby Redoubt, another group marched along the river through town to Battery Worth. In a matter of minutes, the rebels overran the entrenchments there. Battery Worth had been built on the assumption that Flusser's gunboats would protect the fortification's rear. Hence, the earthworks did not extend to the east side of the battery, the direction from which Ransom's attack came. The fall of Battery Worth placed in Confederate hands the 200-pounder Parrot gun which the *Albemarle* had dropped downriver to avoid. The rebels soon turned the gun on Fort Williams, while the *Albemarle* made its way upriver in safety and began to shell the town at close range. Finally, Ransom re-formed his troops along the Roanoke River so as to march toward Fort Williams and the federal entrenchments.[33]

At this point, General Wessells sent his troops out of their entrenchments and into the streets of Plymouth. They fought in squads and companies, taking cover wherever they could find a ditch or a stone wall. But the Confederates had hidden themselves behind the various buildings in town. "We saw but little of them," recalled one U.S. soldier, "though the whizzing balls and the white smoke from their weapons told us of their presence." Finally, the federal troops saw that their fire had little effect on Ransom's troops. They became demoralized and returned to their entrenchments, while Ransom's soldiers moved forward, drawing near to Fort Williams.[34]

Early on Wednesday morning, General Hoke ordered his troops to cease fire. Then, he sent an emissary to General Wessells at Fort Williams requesting a personal interview. Shortly afterwards, the two commanders met. In a "courteous and soldierlike" manner, Hoke told Wessells that the federal defense of Plymouth had been "highly honorable to all concerned." But now he had placed the federals in an "untenable position" with no possibility of relief. Therefore, the Confederate commander demanded an immediate and unconditional surrender. In response, General Wessells requested that he be allowed to "march out with his colors, the officers retaining their side arms." But Hoke restated his demand for an unconditional surrender.[35]

The Confederate commander then threatened that there would be an "indiscriminate slaughter" of federals, according to General Wessells's account. Specifically, Hoke argued that "any further show of resistance would only result in an unnecessary sacrifice of life." Moreover, should Wessells persist "in holding the works," the Confederates would be "obliged to carry them by assault." In such a case, Hoke declared, he "would not be responsible for what followed." Wessells construed that statement "as a threat of a repetition of the Fort Pillow massacre." In March 1864, Confederate troops who overran federal entrenchments at Fort Pillow, Tennessee, had immediately afterwards executed three hundred black soldiers who had defended the place. He, therefore, replied: "You may go back and open fire." Then the U.S. commander "turned on his heel and returned to the fort."[36]

During the next four hours, a house-to-house battle raged in Plymouth. Most of Wessells's troops lay in entrenchments hastily dug around the north side of Fort Williams. From there, they fired down the town's streets as Ransom's brigade inched closer to the federal fortifications. At the same time, U.S. artillerymen in Fort Williams turned their guns on the town. According to one U.S. officer, the canister and grapeshot "did murderous execution" on the rebels for "three or four hours." The hail of federal fire notwithstanding, Ransom's brigade finally succeeded in overrunning several U.S. entrenchments on the northeast side of Fort Williams. One U.S. soldier captured there saw "dead bodies of men and animals" strewn "in every direction." And he heard the "piteous cries for help of the suffering, the groans of the wounded that had not yet been removed (the ambulance corps not having yet been able to reach them)."[37]

Finally, General Hoke arranged his artillery and sharpshooters in a semicircle around the fort so it could be bombarded from every direction. "This terrible fire had to be endured without reply," wrote General Wessells, "as no man could live at the guns." The fort was "struck by solid shot on every side [and] fragments of shells sought almost every interior angle of the work," although most of Wessells's soldiers crouched safely in bombproof bunkers.

Yet, the federals could offer no resistance. Finally at ten on Wednesday morning, April 20, Wessells agreed to surrender. An enlisted man inside Fort Williams "mounted the parapet and waved as a flag of truce a white woolen shirt fastened to a musket." Then he hauled down the garrison flag, and the battle of Plymouth ended.[38]

· **VI** ·

The surrender began in a gentlemanly fashion. General Hoke rode on his horse into Fort Williams, where General Wessells waited. Upon alighting, the Confederate commander clasped Wessells's hand, expressed his respect and sympathy, and told the U.S. general that he could "bear the fortune of war without self-reproach" after "such a gallant defense." Wessells offered his sword, but Hoke graciously refused it. The U.S. commander then requested that his men not be "robbed," specifically, that they be allowed to keep their clothing, overcoats, and blankets. Hoke agreed to this. Wessells was later taken prisoner, separated from his troops, and on Saturday transported with his officers to Libby Prison in Richmond, Virginia.[39]

The rebels then sacked Plymouth. Shortly after the surrender ceremony, troops outside the town's fortifications gave "one of those indescribable Confederate yells," stacked their arms, and then heard a few words from General Hoke. Among other remarks, the Confederate commander informed his troops that they could "help themselves to whatever might please their fancy except the horses and wagons." Thereupon, the Confederates "rushed into town" to begin pillaging. About ten minutes later, they were joined by a mass of rebel camp followers who had been waiting a mile or so from the battle, hoping to share the spoils of victory when it came. The man detailed to control the mob reported to his superiors that he was "unable with my few men to hold my position." He was ordered to withdraw "permitting the crowds that had gathered to rush into the town."[40]

Confederate looters, according to a rebel officer present, entered the few houses that remained standing and "cut open the bedding, broke the costly mirrors to get a piece of looking glass, ripped the strings out of the pianos to hang their tin cups on, [and] loaded themselves with female wearing apparel." Other rebels raided U.S. supply dumps, which had been well stocked indeed. The soldiers found twenty thousand new Colt muskets, which they distributed among themselves, as well as "a large amount of rations, such as flour and bacon." Some simply robbed their prisoners of the belongings they carried. A U.S. sergeant witnessed such an incident by "an officer, evidently in a state of intoxication." "Riding up to one of our boys," the captured soldier later recalled, the officer "drew his sword and demanded his watch, using threatening and insulting language." The Confederate soldier promised to "split open [the prisoner's] head if he refused."

Rebel scavengers also picked among the personal effects that the federal garrison had left behind. When one U.S. officer returned to his quarters on a pretext of "getting some linen bandages," he found "half a dozen Jonnies," as he called the rebels, "in there hauling over my wardrobe" and "appropriating" whatever they fancied. The U.S. officer rescued his "blanket, a cavalry jacket, a pair of new shoes and a satchel" containing his personal papers. He attempted to retrieve a dressing gown from a rebel who was trying it on at the time, but the man "could not be persuaded to give it up," having become well pleased with its "bright colors and fit of the garment." In the looting, the Confederate soldiers from cavalry and artillery units fared best. According to a Confederate report, they "loaded their horses, wagons and caisons with all kinds of plunder."[41]

After an hour or so of pillaging, Confederate officers began to reassert control over their troops. Hoke ordered most of his soldiers to march out of town a mile or so down the Washington Road. There, they camped in pastures and slept beneath pine trees. Other rebels guarded the U.S. soldiers captured that day, a number which by a Confederate count reached 2,197. The prisoners were marched out of town along the Lees Mill Road to farms the rebels assumed to be occupied by loyal Confederates. But there was much confusion among the Confederates at the same time. As a result, the rebels could not account for many U.S. soldiers who should have been prisoners by now. When the battle began, General Wessells recorded 127 officers and 2,707 enlisted men available for duty—a total of 2,834. What happened to the 637 others who fought at Plymouth?[42]

Some U.S. soldiers began to slip away as early as Tuesday evening, April 19. By that time, General Wessells had concluded that he could not hold off the Confederates for much longer. He, therefore, told locally recruited troops that "they must take care of themselves as best they could." "There was a general skedadling among the citizens for their homes," wrote a unionist later. They acted on the assumption they would be "killed by the Rebs for taking up arms."[43]

Others with good reasons to leave, however, remained, fighting to the end, and then attempted an escape. One who did, a former druggist from New Orleans named Appleton, had seen Confederate service before deserting to the Union army, in which he became a medic. After the battle, Appleton attempted to kill himself. "Surrender meant death to him," recalled one of his friends, "and when our flag went down, he, in his desperation, swallowed a dose of morphine to end his life." But a surgeon and some other soldiers "prevented him from sleeping until the drug's power had passed away." Thereafter, the soldier resumed his duties as a medic but lived in "continual dread of being recognized and shot as a deserter." Finally, as the federal captives prepared to board a train for prison, a Confederate officer with a squad of infantrymen approached and asked for Appleton. The Confederate deserter shaded his face with a slouch hat, but one of the rebels recognized him. Appleton was arrested and his comrades never heard from him again.[44]

Some unionists also scattered among regiments other than their own, "assuming names of men absent, sick or on detached service." A black sergeant from the 2nd U.S. Colored Cavalry, Samuel Johnson, in town to take charge of some new recruits for his unit, quickly created a new identity for himself. According to Johnson: "When I found that the city was being surrendered I pulled off my uniform and found a suit of citizen's clothes, which I put on." After being captured, Johnson pretended to be a local slave and was employed for two weeks in attempting to raise the U.S. gunboat from the bottom of the Roanoke River. Then, Johnson was sent to Raleigh, where his captors assigned him to be the personal servant of a Confederate officer from North Carolina fighting near Richmond. Five days later in Virginia, Johnson escaped, passed through federal lines, made his way to Washington, D.C., and then to his old regiment stationed in eastern Virginia.

Finally, some unionist soldiers simply took to the woods. Within a week, a newspaper in New Bern reported that four members of Company E, 2nd North Carolina Union Volunteers, had reached the U.S. headquarters safely after escaping "from the enemy at the surrender of Plymouth." In addition, "some twenty colored soldiers" reached New Bern on Sunday after a five-day trek.[45]

These reports, however, do not account for all of the roughly six hundred U.S. soldiers, most of them black, whom the Confederates failed to take prisoner. For their story, we must turn to a Washington County resident, a certain Mr. Darden. What he saw all took place at about three on Wednesday afternoon, April 20. By that time, Hoke's troops had finished their looting and had begun to loiter about the streets of Plymouth. They had disarmed themselves and their prisoners and, hence, were "not suspecting any further trouble." But nearby, several hundred black troops remained quartered in houses. Suddenly the blacks began to fire into the Confederate troops. Where they obtained guns no one knew. Neither was it known "what caused them to start firing after the surrender." Darden speculated later: "It might have been caused by fright or nervousness, certainly it could not have been orders from the officers of the regiment."[46]

No doubt, the reason was fright. According to Samuel Johnson, the black sergeant who pretended to be a slave: "Upon the capture of Plymouth by the rebel forces, all the negroes found in blue uniform, or with any outward marks of a Union soldier upon him, was killed." Johnson personally saw "some taken into the woods and hung." "Others I saw stripped of all their clothing and then stood upon the bank of the river with their faces riverward, and there they were shot." "Still others," Johnson recalled, "were killed by having their brains beaten out by the butt-end of the muskets in the hands of the rebels." A different U.S. soldier witnessed executions near Fort Williams. Alonzo Cooper, a lieutenant in the 12th New York Volunteers, reported that "the negro soldiers who had surrendered, were drawn up in line at the breastwork, and shot down as they stood." "When the company of rebs fired, every negro dropped at once as one man." "This I plainly saw from where we were held under guard," he later recalled, "not over five hundred yards distance." The blacks who fired on their captors had plenty to fear.[47]

In response to the black soldiers' attack, the Confederates "charged them with every conceivable weapon in their possession," according to Darden's account, "whereupon the negroes ran, taking refuge in Coneby Creek swamp and the flats beyond, scarcely a mile away." The rebels, now "infuriated," followed close behind, overtook the blacks, and "slaughtered" them "like rats." "They must have slain at least 500 of the negro troops," recalled Darden in later years. Alonzo Cooper, who had been taken from town to the Johnston farm where the Confederates held him prisoner, heard "the crack, crack of muskets down in the swamp where the negroes had fled to escape capture." When some of the Confederates later passed by the Johnston farm, they "laughingly" told Cooper that they had been "out gunning for niggers." The blacks were "hunted like squirrels or rabbits," wrote Cooper, "I can think of no better comparison."

The rebel soldiers did not even bother to bury the bodies of their victims. B. D. Latham, a twelve-year-old boy living in Washington County, later recalled that he and some "other boys of the community" went to Coneby Creek swamp the following Sunday morning. There they saw "hundreds of slain negro troops," their bodies having been left to decay for four days.[48]

· **VII** ·

In the battle of Plymouth, the Confederate government achieved virtually all it sought. At the national level, the victory lifted the spirits of secessionists everywhere. The *Richmond Examiner,* for one, argued: "Repeat Plymouth a few times and we shall bring the Yankees to their senses." But it was not at the national level that the battle's consequences exerted the greatest influence. As one planter's wife put it: "How thankful we should be to God for this signal triumph! Plymouth has been a thorn in our side & the garrison there a perpetual uneasiness to us." In the Albemarle

Sound region, the battle of Plymouth checked unionist opposition to the war.[49]

The Confederate victory intimidated both yeoman farmers and white laborers. Some simply fled to federal territory. Speaking of Plymouth refugees recently arrived in New Bern, a local newspaper noted: "They seem to have a deep seated dred of the horrors attending rebel rule." Others chose to remain in Washington County but altered their opinions, at least in public. One planter found a "material change" in local political opinions "since the fall of Plymouth." Elsewhere in the region, locally recruited U.S. soldiers lost their nerve. A U.S. colonel commanding the 2nd North Carolina Union Volunteers at Morehead City reported: "Since the arrival of the news from Plymouth," his troops had become "most excited." "I cannot place the least dependence on them," he contended, "for the defense of Beaufort or any other place." "They are utterly demoralized and will not fight." "Indeed," he claimed, "they are already looking to the swamps for the protection they have so far failed of getting from our Government."[50]

Similarly, the battle terrorized blacks throughout the region. Those serving in the Union army fled whenever the opportunity arose, some immediately after the battle, as in the case of those who made it to New Bern. Others had left earlier. Henry, the black man who had acted as William Pettigrew's driver at Magnolia plantation, "shouldered a musket" for the federals in Plymouth on Sunday and Monday. But by Monday night he could see the inevitability of a Confederate victory. Therefore, before dawn on Tuesday morning, he slipped away in a boat to the far side of the Roanoke River, where he remained in a swamp for sixteen days, living on frogs and a few crackers that he had carried with him. Eventually, the prospect of a slow death from starvation became more terrible than his fear of execution at the hands of Confederate soldiers. "Nearly exhausted from famine & exposure," Henry crossed the river to Plymouth. But by this time, only a small garrison remained, and they paid the ex-slave no attention. After a while, Charles Pettigrew's overseer, Jacob Spiers, heard of Henry's condition, took charge of him, and transported the former driver to his old home at Magnolia plantation.[51]

The battle of Plymouth created a constituency in North Carolina for continuing the war. On May 23, 1864, the North Carolina House of Commons voted its thanks and congratulations to Generals Hoke and Ransom. At last, a North Carolina officer (Hoke) had won a victory on North Carolina soil, planned by a North Carolinian (Braxton Bragg), directed by North Carolinians (Hoke and Ransom), and fought mostly by North Carolinians (Hoke's, Ransom's, and Kemper's brigades). That victory created a symbol—the immense number of Confederate dead—around which North Carolina secessionists could rally the fainthearted and draw them away from the peace movement. As William Pettigrew put it in a speech after the battle: "The gallant soldier who, wrapped in his blanket, rests in the bed of glory beneath the turf of the battlefield seems to whisper my work is done, but yours is not."[52]

Epilogue: The End of a Plantation Community

After the Confederate victory at Plymouth, Washington County planters supposed that they might return home to rule as before, and for a time they made the attempt. But in reality, there was little left of the Washington County they had known in 1860. Plymouth was destroyed. It would never again be the port it had been before the war. Yeoman farmers, who had supported planters in the Whig party during the slaveholders' regime, had found a hero in William Holden and had joined the peace movement. Laborers who had cut timber on contract to planters now farmed for a subsistence, often squatting on the county's large plantations. The planters' slaves had been scattered—some were still in their owners' possession, some had escaped to or had refugeed at Roanoke Island, some were in the Union army, some were dead, others had simply disappeared forever. Besides, planters' fields grew weeds, fences lay broken, mansions were emptied, livestock had gone wild in the swamps. In April, it was too late to put in a crop for 1864. Laborers could never be assembled, tools found, plow points ordered, wagons repaired, seed purchased, and weeds cut in time.

When William Pettigrew went home for a few days in May, he became profoundly discouraged by what he saw. His plantations,

Belgrade and Magnolia, "appeared very differently from what they did when I first left them." He found them both "overrun with weeds and bushes." At Belgrade, "the fences were in such condition as to admit the cattle to feed where ever they might choose." At Magnolia, the fences had fared better, having been made of a more durable wood, juniper. But there he had lost some furniture and much livestock. Yet, Pettigrew considered himself fortunate compared to his neighbors.[1]

After examining his own property, William Pettigrew walked to Josiah Collins's plantation, Somerset Place. Here the county's unionists had done their worst. "There was not a piece of furniture remaining" in the mansion, Pettigrew observed, "the shutters and doors were much injured; the papering had been peeled off in many places, and in some places, the plastering was broken." Even the front steps to the planter's house had been removed. Henry, Pettigrew's former driver at Magnolia, told the planter that he had heard the Yankees say they had taken $18,000 worth of goods from Collins's home, including a library of three thousand books and a trunk containing the family's personal correspondence. Other ex-slaves told Pettigrew that the Collins mansion had housed up to one hundred unionists at a time when they came to Scuppernong on pillaging expeditions.[2]

Not surprisingly, some Washington County planters despaired of ever restoring their power. Several continued to live as refugees with their families in Martin County after the fall of Plymouth, among them John B. Chesson, one of the county's largest slaveholders. But others hoped to reestablish planter rule. Local slaveholders had begun plotting their political resurgence long before the battle of Plymouth. Washington County's planters had known of General Hoke's plans and had hoped he might succeed. When he did, they expected to "run their own counsels" at home. To do so, they had selected candidates to campaign for seats in the North Carolina legislature before the battle.[3]

For the senate seat that encompassed Washington and Martin counties, planters in Martin County approached William Pettigrew. They told him that they had floated his name among their friends and that "every prominent man without hesitation declared for you." The Martin County planters further assured Pettigrew that others elsewhere, "the army vote" in particular, would support him. There was little doubt in the support of the army. Pettigrew's friend, D. G. Cowand, wrote from Virginia to tell him that he would "get all the vote" from the troops in the 17th North Carolina Volunteers, most of whom resided in Washington County. Pettigrew would run as a Conservative, favoring continuation of the war and in opposition to a peace candidate.[4]

Despite the encouraging words, William Pettigrew's candidacy carried with it certain liabilities from the start. There was the ambiguity of his political opinions and party affiliations. Pettigrew had begun his political career in 1860 by opposing the war as a conditional unionist within the Whig party. Then in the secession crisis he became a hot proponent of the war and sought voters among Democrats. Lately, he had become a strong supporter of Governor Zebulon Vance, an advocate of the war. But the planter's past opinions and associations left him open to unfounded rumors of sympathizing with the peace movement. This would undercut his support among ex-Democrats who formed the bulk of the Conservative party. Worse for Pettigrew's chances, his sponsors had thought it unnecessary to inquire closely among the area's yeoman farmers for their preference in candidates. Many supported a peace candidate named Carraway; others preferred a certain Dr. Pugh. Hence, Pettigrew's supporters thought the yeoman vote divided; therefore, the planter would have little trouble once nominated by the Conservative party.

The nomination, however, was not assured. Charles Latham, the chief organizer of Washington County's yeoman farmers before the war, had returned recently from a self-imposed exile in New York. Colonel E. W. Jones, the unionist leader and former militia commander, had also made his way back to Plymouth. Now the two unionists began to agitate against Pettigrew's candidacy from within the Conservative party itself. Latham and Jones spread a rumor in Williamston "to the effect," in Pettigrew's words, "that I am not even the choice of my own county." But the planter had no way of knowing all this when he accepted the Martin County committee's invitation to run for the state senate. In the meantime, he prepared a campaign speech to be delivered at Williamston on July 12, 1864, during court week there.[5]

William Pettigrew's speech was remarkable for the clarity of its position, not for its novelty. In it, he outlined the world as seen from a planter's piazza. The view thus surveyed was composed of masters and slaves, nothing more. "All history teaches," Pettigrew informed his listeners in Williamston, "that mankind runs from the extreme of liberty to the extreme of slaves." Hence, a war designed to free slaves must of necessity enslave those who were now masters. But the Yankees "have no right to enslave us," Pettigrew went on. We must certainly decline "being placed under our negroes—of being made the slaves of slaves." "No man," he concluded, "is so lost to self-respect as to consent to that." For Pettigrew, there was no middle ground, no alternative to a society of planters over slaves, except slaves over planters.[6]

Such a view, however, persuaded few farmers who held no slaves and, hence, could be neither master nor slave. Pettigrew, therefore, appealed to yeomen's interest in property holding. The planter asked: "What have you at stake in this contest?" "If we are subjugated, what will be the consequence?" "I will tell you," he replied to his own question: "The confiscation of the property of every man in the country, sooner or later—slaveholder or non-slaveholder." Pettigrew went on to explain that Lincoln's course, including the Emancipation Proclamation, had little to do with blacks, but everything to do with attacking property in both slaves and land belonging to secessionists—planters and small farmers alike. "Think not my friends [that] you are secure because of your owning no negroes." The Yankees "wish your money, your lands, your [live]stock as much as your negroes." And "if they subjugate us," Pettigrew told local yeoman farmers, "they intend to have every thing in the land."[7]

To prevent a total loss of property, Pettigrew told his audience that there could be only one solution. Southerners must be "independent of these people." The "machinery to accomplish your independence is in the hands of the Government at Richmond." Hence, Washington County voters ought to support that government and its war if they wished to retain their property. By support, Pettigrew had in mind more than simple encouragement. He meant approval of recently enacted currency laws, a bill allowing the purchase of substitutes by wealthy draftees, and the suspension of the writ of habeas corpus. All these measures had sowed the seeds of disaffection among small farmers throughout the South. Now, Pettigrew defended each as a necessary war measure, painful suspensions of civil rights in the defense of interests in property.[8]

William Pettigrew had learned nothing from four years of political wrangling in the midst of guerrilla war. He still could conceive of no government except one run by planters. His world was one of extremes, as he put it, masters and slaves, one in which a few dominated and many submitted. A cooperative republic imagined earlier by the county's yeoman farmers, landless laborers, and slaves was simply inconceivable to Pettigrew. He could acknowledge no such possibility when he attempted to persuade small farmers to support the war. He could stress only the necessity of protecting property claims, a need that yeoman farmers had explained in the secession crisis could be fulfilled perfectly well by the Republican party. Not surprisingly, Pettigrew's speech persuaded no one but the few planters whose interests he so narrowly defended.

Pettigrew first heard of the opposition to his nomination when he arrived in Williamston. Yeomen from Washington County had set themselves against Pettigrew and would not be moved from that position. The planter concluded that the campaign "would be an unpleasant one" and "would array parties against each other in the Counties which would be highly injurious to the welfare of the people," not to mention the Conservative party and himself. He, therefore, withdrew his name when he stood to address the convention of Conservatives. Pettigrew claimed that General Stubbs, the other Conservative candidate, had told him he intended to run, whether Pettigrew chose to do so or not. But Stubbs later denied it. Whatever the case, the general had the support of area yeoman farmers. He, therefore, would have little trouble in beating either the peace candidate or Pettigrew.[9]

In the end, General Stubbs and the yeoman Conservatives prevailed. But that had to do mainly with the presence of the Confederate garrison at Plymouth, which did not take kindly to voters who preferred peace candidates. The civilian vote at Plymouth in August 1864 was 338 for the Conservative ticket to zero for Holden and the peace candidates. Despite the apparent unanimity, Washington County remained as divided as it had been from the beginning of the war. As long as planters hoped to rebuild their old regime, there existed no possibility of forging a new political alliance among the county's various constituencies.[10]

· **II** ·

In the summer of 1864, Washington County planters had no better luck in restoring the local economy they once had dominated. But their failure was not for lack of trying. After the battle of Plymouth, the first order of business was to sort out conflicting property claims. "For a long time after we came in possession" of the county, recalled a rebel soldier stationed at Plymouth, "we were almost contin[u]ously engaged every day in restoring such property [as secessionists claimed] to their rightful owner." This was so, he explained, because in 1863 and early 1864 the U.S. officers commanding at Plymouth seemed to have followed an "established precedent" designed "to transfer the property of loyal citizens [secessionists] to the 'buffaloes.' " Moreover, the county had been "under the dominion of the arbitrary will of some tyrannical Provost Marshall," referring to John T. Phelps, Sr., "who decided capital cases and the titles to real estate."[11]

To revive his claims to land, Charles Pettigrew, for one, hastened from the upcountry to his plantation, Bonarva, just days after the Confederate victory at Plymouth. When he arrived, Pettigrew found his house occupied by Tully Davenport and John A. Norman, local unionists who had leased the plantation from the U.S. government. The two, however, now claimed to be ardent secessionists and appeared "anxious at seeing me," Pettigrew reported to his wife. They supposed the planter "would be extremely displeased" that they had "come into the house." "It was evident," Pettigrew observed, "they thought that I had come down armed with the whole power of the Confederacy."[12]

Before breakfast on the morning of April 24, Charles Pettigrew surveyed his property from the nursery window of his house. "What struck me most was the wild appearance of everything." "The trees are much larger and the garden entirely destroyed by weeds." Otherwise, he found the place "looking very naturally." "No building was missing," he reported, "and every tree in its place." His house seemed in good order. But only a few sticks of furniture remained, and some of those pieces had been damaged. Most of Pettigrew's household goods had been taken to Plymouth by local unionists in order to furnish their quarters. After the battle, all that "was carried from Plymouth by the southern troops as pillage."[13]

After breakfast, Charles Pettigrew sought out the blacks who remained at Bonarva, forty-seven in all. He reported them all "extremely glad to see me." "I was almost destroyed by the violence of their demonstrations of affection." "They said," Pettigrew wrote, "they had gone through dreadful times and they now wished me to come [to] them again." Indeed, they had suffered; several had died. Many had been treated harshly by unionists and federals alike. And some had been forced off the plantation by Davenport and Norman. The two would-be planters had no use for these blacks who evidently refused to plant a cash crop. But the slaves (as they became under Confederate rule) at Bonarva did manage to secret small patches of corn around the plantation which had done very well that spring. Pettigrew reported "every negro is at work for himself so that they are quite industrious."[14]

The blacks at Bonarva, however, worried about their safety now that the county had returned to Confederate rule. As they had done in the secession crisis, the blacks sought a master to protect them. "They all say," wrote Pettigrew, "that they are anxious to turn over all the corn to me when I return." But after considering the offer, the planter declined. "If I could be assured that Plymouth would not be recaptured," he wrote, "the place is ready for me to move to immediately." But, he continued, "I am afraid to do anything until there is victory on our side." In a word, the battle of Plymouth had returned Bonarva to Pettigrew's possession, but it did not render his claims to land and slaves secure and defensible.[15]

By contrast, Charles's brother William never considered the possibility of resuming commercial production at Magnolia or Belgrade plantations. Instead, he simply attempted to salvage what he could from his property remaining in Washington County. William Pettigrew did so by employing overseers on each plantation through a barter arrangement. Each man, John M. Hough and Malachi White, lived in one of Pettigrew's houses and used the planter's land in exchange for attending to Pettigrew's business interests.

In the summer of 1864, for example, John M. Hough farmed

for a subsistence and small surplus with his family at Magnolia plantation. "I try to raise each year a little more than my Family needs to consume," he explained to Pettigrew. And because "I raise it on your land and through your means," he continued, "you ought to enjoy some benefit from the surpluses." But how? He could not sell his extra grain for cash to send to Pettigrew—as Hough noted, "Money is of no use to us here." He could get no one to take the grain in exchange for "a days work or a yard [of thread] spun." The county now operated on a barter economy. Therefore, Hough arranged to shear Pettigrew's few remaining sheep and have the wool converted into cloth, which he could send to the planter upcountry. "As to the spinning and weaving," Hough revealed, "I pay for in the products of the Farm such as Pork, corn, Potatoes & flax."[16]

Hough also looked after Pettigrew's other property, especially his cattle and corn. In 1863, the former overseer had driven most of Pettigrew's cattle into the swamps to keep them out of the hands of unionists and the Union army. Though the cattle were out of sight, however, they were never out of mind. When two died in the winter, he skinned them and "taned them myself to save all I could." He also watched over Pettigrew's two remaining oxen. In all this, Hough kept up a running dispute with Henry, Pettigrew's former black driver. Henry had occupied part of the plantation in 1863. When he removed to Plymouth in late 1863, the former black driver took a large portion of the wool Hough had sheared that winter in addition to one of Pettigrew's oxen, all of which Hough was determined to recover.[17]

In late summer 1864, William Pettigrew began to liquidate his movable property. He responded to a gloomy assessment of the political fallout from the elections in July. According to one of his supporters, the success of Washington County's yeoman farmers in electing General Stubbs had diminished planter influence there. "Again," wrote Joshua Swift, "there is I fear a growing agrarian feeling in our [Albemarle] country." "I almost shudder sometimes at the future," the planter concluded. So, too, did William Pettigrew. In late July, he instructed a friend of his to take control of his sheep, those still on the plantations and others "that may have wandered in the country." He also requested that another friend sell the cattle remaining at Belgrade to the Confederate government. Rebel supply officers recently had toured the Scuppernong neighborhood and had informed everyone that they wished to purchase cattle. Cattle which the supply agents could not purchase they would "press."[18]

Washington County planters at last gave up. They had surveyed the political and economic damage at home, and had determined that, short of federal capitulation, there remained no circumstance under which planters could restore the society they had known in 1860. The routines of power, so laboriously constructed after the Revolution, now lay in ruins. Moreover, their claims to property in land and slaves could not be defended, even in the wake of a Confederate victory at Plymouth. Although Washington County's planters could walk their land in safety and although their former slaves now sought their protection, poor whites, both yeomen and laborers, remained defiant. Without an alliance among property holders, planters could never produce the votes that would enable them to dominate the county. Without political power, plantations could not exist. In October 1864, all Washington County planters could do was to wonder what new disaster might befall them next. They did not have long to wait.

In the last week of October 1864, a small federal flotilla attacked the C.S.S. *Albemarle* at her moorings in the Roanoke River at Plymouth and sank the ship. Shortly thereafter, the U.S. Navy invaded the town itself, then garrisoned by only 350 Confederate soldiers. In the end, the town fell and thirty-seven rebels were captured, along with twenty-two cannon, two hundred stand of arms, and a "large quantity" of ordnance stores. The captured soldiers had been conscripted only recently from the surrounding countryside and "gave themselves up in the hope of being released," wrote a Confederate planter's wife who sifted reports after the battle. "The Yankees handcuffed every man of them," she continued: "Perhaps, however, that was for effect."[19]

· **III** ·

The fall of Plymouth to federal forces plunged Washington County's planters into a final despair. "The capture of Plymouth hangs like a pall on our spirits," wrote one planter's wife. "It has shrouded 'In sack cloth and ashes' the good and loyal people of Washington and contiguous counties," thought a Confederate soldier who escaped to Williamston after the federal attack. Moreover, he wrote, "The gloom which it has cast is heightened by the remembrance of former injuries." Planters recalled bitterly the time during which "the Yankees previously held Plymouth." "The poor defenseless widow, with many little helpless children," they claimed, had been "turned out of her house without a morsel of bread—without any other place to seek refuge, because she had sons in the Southern Army." And "all loyal citizens [secessionists] were forewarned that if they afforded her protection, they themselves should be similarly dealt with." In truth, the federal commander at Plymouth had forbidden the local government to aid families whose sons and fathers fought for the Confederacy in 1862. But planters, of course, suffered little from such federal directives.[20]

In fact, the planters' anxiety focused mainly on their loss of property. As one observer put it: "They expect their perishable property to be devastated—their houses to be burned to the ground, and their families to be reduced to want." Moreover, he warned that "an expectation of such destruction will frighten many into taking the oath of allegiance to the federal cause." Actually, few planters remained in the county to be coerced. Most voiced their dismay from a distance. Writing from South Carolina, Charles Pettigrew pronounced himself "quite shocked" at reading in the papers of the fall of Plymouth to the U.S. Navy. He supposed that "there will now be an effort of the enemy at Plymouth to destroy the crops on the Roanoke." And "the scamps who ran away to avoid our conscription," he thought, "will now return to the country and have all things their own way." Pettigrew concluded: "We are to have another four years of war; indeed war will become a normal condition with us and suffering [?] continue to increase until civilization will scarcely exist."[21]

The war did not officially last another four years, but it did become a normal condition again. The Union army garrisoned Fort Williams, but with only about three hundred troops this time. As it turned out, that was sufficient to restore the county to its previous condition. Small farmers and ex-slaves continued to farm for a subsistence, a surplus being of little use in a barter economy lacking access to outside markets. A handful of unionists resumed their attempts to operate the plantations they had leased in the Scuppernong neighborhood. Confederate smugglers reopened their clandestine trade, and the U.S. Navy responded with periodic raids on their camps and landing places along the area's many rivers and creeks. Washington County planters viewed the spectacle from a safe distance and were unable to exert any influence over the county's affairs or even to visit the property they claimed.

In November 1864, Washington County's planters faced the awful truth—their regime had ended. The world they had learned to command as young men had passed into history. To some, the thought proved too much; they gave up the ghost by slipping into illnesses against which they found little will to fight. Josiah Collins died in exile at Hillsboro. James C. Johnston, William Pettigrew's confidant and political advisor, expired at his home in Chowan County across the Sound. Other planters responded in very practical ways. Charles Pettigrew gave up his temporary residence in Greensboro, from where he had looked after his slaves hired out to the North Carolina Railroad. In joining his wife at the family's plantation in South Carolina, he assumed a permanent home upcountry. Finally, some planters sought ways to change themselves, not just their surroundings. For William Pettigrew, the end of his world posed deep questions of personal identity. If not a planter, a master of slaves, a patriarch, what could he be? Who could he be?

William Pettigrew's personal crisis began with the marriage and then the death of his sister, Annie, in the fall of 1863. Annie became betrothed on May 14, 1863, to an Episcopal minister named Mr. McKay. Annie and the minister had met during the fall of 1862 after William Pettigrew had fled upcountry. Pettigrew and his sister, both devout Episcopalians, had settled in Harnett County, as it happened, in McKay's parish and had met him through the church. William approved of the marriage and thought highly of McKay.

The loss of Annie, first by marriage and then in death several months later, worked a great hardship on William Pettigrew. The planter had been a guardian and protector to his sister for nearly thirty years. Moreover, the relationship was crucial to him because it substituted for a marriage that never came to be. When William

Pettigrew was a young man, he had courted a young woman named Caroline, and she had agreed to marry him. Near the wedding date, William had had to leave Washington County for some weeks on business. When he had returned, Caroline had fallen in love with another man and had promised to marry him. The suitor was William's brother, Charles, whom Caroline married and lived with happily until her death. William and Caroline got on well all those years, but perhaps only because his role as a head of family could be enacted in the relationship between himself and Annie. Not surprisingly then, Pettigrew struggled to deal with the death of his sister. He grieved in letters to friends. He memorialized his sister in poetry. He struggled to make sense of it all and began to have dreams.

His first recorded dream, dated February 2, 1864, dealt straightforwardly with the fact that Annie had passed on to another world. Pettigrew saw himself at his boyhood home, Bonarva plantation, walking in his mother's garden. He understood the garden as the place where he ordinarily slept. There, Annie returned to visit him for several hours. Mostly, they walked and talked until she became fatigued. As she tired, Annie began to stumble and totter. William supported her. Finally, Annie left and returned to heaven. William Pettigrew laid down in his mother's garden to sleep, wishing all the while that he could go with Annie. In a second dream two weeks later, Pettigrew was forced to confront his sister's relationship to her husband. In this dream, Pettigrew saw Annie alive and her husband dead. As a result, the question of where Annie would reside arose. Annie wanted to remain in her deceased husband's home and out from under her brother's authority. William Pettigrew objected. But Annie's in-laws intervened on her behalf, and she disappeared. "I saw my dearest no more," Pettigrew wrote when he woke up.[22]

William Pettigrew had begun to reinterpret his position as a paternal figure. Even in her death, Annie at first had remained both dependent on the planter and a source of comfort to him. Moreover, this relationship continued, as it had in life, within a context of his mother's love and succor to both of them. Annie then had simply passed from one form to another without altering her essence or her relationship to William Pettigrew. The planter remained a paternal figure to his sister. Yet, there remained the conflict over who should claim authority to speak for Annie in death, whether brother or husband should administer her memory. In the end, Pettigrew could not resolve this conflict to his satisfaction.

All these private musings might have amounted to nothing more than the self-healing of one man. But the questions about authority over a man's dependents raised in Annie's death coincided with a loss of mastery over the means to support his other relatives, his slaves, and his poor white clients in Washington County. When confronting the larger loss, Pettigrew drew upon his dreams about Annie for a language and logic to ponder his difficulties. In doing so, Pettigrew searched for the causes of his troubles and found the source, not in the Yankees or unionists, but within himself and his conduct during the conflict.

On April 1, 1864, William Pettigrew first connected his difficulties with the war itself. In a dream, Pettigrew and his sister checked into a hotel much like those at the Virginia mountain springs they had frequented before the war. There, William Pettigrew caught up on his correspondence. His sister proofread the letters and commented on their contents, as she ordinarily did for her brother. After awhile, William and Annie went outdoors to attend a public meeting "the object of which was to promote the vigorous prosecution of the war." It was a convention of "gentlemen" who spoke in an "animated" fashion. Annie viewed the spectacle from the hotel piazza, while William plunged into the meeting, losing sight of Annie altogether while he spoke. When William returned to the hotel, Annie had left her seat and had gone into the hotel parlor. Those who remained on the piazza criticized Pettigrew for abandoning his sister "in such a crowd." They told him that such "was no place for her."[23]

In that dream, Pettigrew finally confronted his own role as a secessionist in Washington County. In life, he had taken an active part in many such secessionist meetings, including the Constitutional Convention that removed North Carolina from the Union. And in doing so, he had abandoned his plantation and all his dependents for months at a time, just as he had left Annie alone on the piazza. Now, Pettigrew began to see the paradox of his life and of the war itself. To preserve the paternalist's power as a whole, to preserve a society of masters over slaves, he had abandoned his dependents and thus had doomed his efforts from the start. Indeed, his dependents had sickened and died before his very eyes. In the spring of 1865, Pettigrew dreamed that his sister was unwell, sick in bed, and drawing near death. On August 16, she died in one of his dreams.

In a sense, all of Pettigrew's dependents had died. The relationship that he had forged with his slaves before the war could be enforced only by capturing them at gunpoint, jailing those who became insolent, and isolating each one from all unionists and Yankees. The same can be said of the planter's conduct toward poor white men, Pettigrew's shingle-making clients, in Washington County. In the end, the planter's war to preserve his world had destroyed it and himself.[24]

· **IV** ·

The world of Washington County's poor people had come to an end as well, if only because there remained no employers and masters. What kind of social relations might arise instead? In the aftermath of the battle of Plymouth no one could imagine. Just as the county's planters could envision no world except the one they had learned to command as children, men and women of small means could not at that moment formulate a plan for a new society. During the war, the best poor people could do was to draw on past experience for models with which to meet particular crises. When the need for government arose, they created a military regime in the image of the Union army of occupation at Plymouth. And when land became available after local planters fled the county, poor men simply squatted as they had before 1860 or attempted to become planters themselves. The poor people's alliance suggested by yeoman farmers in 1861 had been nothing more than a political bargain (which failed in the crucible of war), not a comprehensive vision of a just society.

Yet, there were hints of what might be, of how life and labor in Washington County might be restructured to afford every person a decent and honorable existence. The situation of Benjamin E. Bailey, a white tenant farmer, illustrated the possibilities.

When the Civil War began, Bailey was a twenty-six-year-old farmer residing in the Lees Mill neighborhood of Washington County, where he remained until sometime in 1861. He was a unionist and voted against William Pettigrew in the election for a seat in the Constitutional Convention. But he preferred to avoid conflict, if possible. "I was unwilling to aid either side," he testified some years later. This was so because he was a tenant farmer who depended upon a planter to lease him land each January.

Bailey found himself drawn into the war nonetheless. He was drafted into the Confederate state militia shortly after Hatteras was captured, and he served as a picket several times. But when the opportunity arose, he avowed himself a loyal citizen of the United States. After federal troops first occupied Plymouth, he went to Major Bartholomew seeking official protection, which he received after taking "the oath of allegiance to the U.S." He did so again in late 1864 at Plymouth, shortly after the town was recaptured by federal troops. In all this, Bailey showed neither by word nor action that he sought to overturn Washington County's social order, as some unionists did. But circumstances would lead him to defy that order, whether he realized the consequences of his actions or not.

In late 1861, Bailey sought a new lease but did not find one in his immediate neighborhood. Perhaps the man from whom he ordinarily rented land had fled the county, or perhaps Bailey's landlord took exception to his tenant's unionist sympathies. Whatever the case, Bailey soon found land elsewhere, just east of the Washington County border with Tyrrell County.

His new landlord, however, was a yeoman and a strong unionist. Relations between landlord and tenant soon differed immensely from the typical arrangements made between planters and their poor whites. Bailey had been "induced" by a certain Richard Iredell Hassell to "take charge of his farm, by offering me better wages," that is, a bigger share of the crop, "than I was getting" from his previous landlord. Hassell owned about 350 acres—most of it under cultivation and located near the town of Columbia—out of which he assigned about seventy acres to Bailey. We do not know what the tenant's exact share was to be, but we do know about two aspects of the sharecropping arrangement that set it apart from typical leases signed between planters and their tenants before secession.

First, about half the land leased to Bailey was wooded. This is important because woodlands could be a source of subsistence apart from crops that had to be shared with the landlord and that could be confiscated by him in case of a dispute. On woodlands, Bailey could hunt, harvest nuts and fruit, let his hogs and cattle roam and feed freely, and cut timber and shingles for his own use and for sale. This part of the agreement assumed that Bailey ought to have some livelihood apart from the cash crop produced for his landlord.

Second, Bailey took up residence in Hassell's home. In so doing, the tenant and landlord demonstrated an equality of social relations that had become possible between yeoman property holders and landless laborers as a result of the war. William Pettigrew, Josiah Collins, and Henderson Phelps would never have allowed such living arrangements on their places, and for good reason—their power depended upon dominating other men, even if planters did tip their hats to small farmers and laborers at neighborhood election grounds.

Such small differences portended a radically different society in Washington County after the war, one in which men (although not men and women) associated on a basis of equality with all others, even if one possessed more or less wealth than the other. Implicit in such a society was the notion that every household head deserved the means to produce a subsistence for himself and his family, even if employed for wages or shares, because in an independent subsistence lay the seeds of an individual's social and political power. Such power would prove antithetical to a concentration of land and labor power in the hands of a small elite. Planters would fail, and a multitude of poor men would rule the county.

Bailey, however, had drawn no blueprint for a new society—that would come later in Washington County. But he had repudiated the rules by which local society had been organized before the war. In doing so, he and other local farmers and laborers began to restructure power in the county so as to leave no place for planters at war's end.[25]

· **V** ·

In the summer of 1865, Washington County's residents, black and white, rich and poor, returned to their old homeplaces. Freedpeople formerly belonging to Josiah Collins climbed aboard wagons provided by the planter at Northwood plantation and made their way slowly to Somerset Place. Yeoman farmers who had refugeed in New Bern and on Roanoke Island caught federal schooners and mail boats to Plymouth. White laborers began to emerge slowly and cautiously from the swamps. When they returned, some located houses and outbuildings and personal possessions they had owned before the war. Others did not. But no one returned home. There was no home to be found in the summer of 1865. The community had destroyed itself, body and soul. Physically, there was little left. Socially, practically nothing survived. The ties that bound Washington County together in 1859, however affectionate and intimate, however inequitable and resented, had been destroyed in four years of bloody, murderous, terrifying war.

Whatever the confusion, the war at home had settled at least one matter—slavery—and that was no small question to resolve. Washington County's planters would never hold black people in bondage again. Although blacks would have to wait for the states to ratify that fact in the Thirteenth Amendment, the deed had been done in practice, and for that much, local freedpeople rejoiced. So, too, did many whites. They could see in black people political allies. Blacks were, after all, poor people, like most white unionists, and they could be turned against planters when the county's civil government resumed.

Washington County's war at home, however, raised many more questions than it answered. With slavery dead, how might labor be managed and by whom? Would planters attempt to substitute another form of bondage—debt peonage, for example? Certainly, there was precedent. Before the war, many poor white tenants had purchased their goods at plantation stores under compulsion of debt; they owed men like Josiah Collins and Charles Pettigrew for land rent, supplies, seed, and many more items. Or would yeoman farmers move to fill the gap left by failing planters in local commodities production? Then what? Would yeoman farmers simply mobilize the labor of their relatives, or would they employ for wages neighbors and friends? Would free labor come to dominate the county, and would the federal government aid this effort? Or would poor whites and blacks insist on managing their own labor? Would they attempt to move off the plantations and into the swamps, to hunt and fish and farm for a subsistence only, spurning commodities and labor markets entirely and turning their faces against capitalism altogether?

And what of all the property that had been so hotly contested in Washington County's war at home? The war for property had destroyed the planters' claims to much of the wealth they had accumulated as a result of slavery. But could those claims—at least in land—be revived? Or would farmers and laborers continue their campaign to dispossess planters of their lands? Would blacks begin to claim land for themselves as they had at Somerset Place and Magnolia in 1863?

It was to such questions that Samuel Newberry addressed himself in late July 1865 when he spoke before a crowd assembled in Plymouth. He recalled his prediction made in 1851 of a bloody civil war to come and of the desire of local planters to rule through what he called a "land and negro oligarchy." He went on to point toward a new day when planters would only be a bitter memory and when ordinary people would rule and live in harmony and prosperity.[26] But such words were only a hope in the summer of 1865. The reality of the Great Rebellion was destruction, and its legacy would be further conflict. Washington County's war at home had destroyed plantation society, but it did not establish the basis for a new community. Questions about the social meanings of freedom would continue both to perplex and inspire local residents throughout Reconstruction and beyond. A struggle, borne in the crucible of war, for a just society had only commenced.

Statistical Appendix

Who supported the Confederacy and who supported the Union during the Civil War are questions that continue to plague those who ponder the conflict, even after more than one hundred years. This is not surprising, however. People on both sides had reasons to change their minds during the course of the war and afterwards, to hide their true opinions or to shape them for the exigencies of the moment. Loyalties are slippery sentiments indeed.

In this study, I have allowed the course of events and the participants' own words to suggest who supported each side and why. To recapitulate briefly: Large planters and their various dependents—their sons, the merchants with whom they dealt, the lawyers and clergymen they patronized, and the poor white men who worked as day laborers and who contracted to cut shingles on swampland owned by planters—tended to be Confederates. Secessionists were an alliance of the very rich and the very poor. Unionists in Washington County tended to be men of middling means—yeoman farmers and their sons, many of whom owned land, most of whom owned a substantial amount of personal property, but seldom any slaves. Moreover, both sides divided by age into small, older cores of leaders and much larger and younger constituencies.

Both Confederate and Union supporters had many reasons for advocating their respective causes—among them, long-standing loyalties to family, friends, and political parties. Many changed their reasons and sometimes their allegiance during the course of the war. But as I argue throughout this book, a struggle over land and labor lay at the heart of the local conflict in Washington County. Hence, it should not be surprising that divisions among Confederates and unionists had something to do with economic status and prospects.

The conflict in Washington County, however, did not become a war between rich and poor, for, indeed, many poor men (mainly day laborers who worked for planters) fought for the Confederacy, and a few rich men (mainly merchants who traded with yeoman farmers) supported the Union. Instead, the local conflict was waged between two discrete social formations—one dominated by planters, and one dominated by yeoman farmers. But because each of these two local groups included men with diverse interests, there arose internal tensions on both sides and a certain fluidity of membership. That tension and fluidity eventually destroyed the alliance between unionist yeoman farmers and white wage laborers. And it caused many rebels to desert the army that they had joined with enthusiasm early in the war.

Although economic status did not determine every Washington County resident's political opinions, it was a major factor in shaping the course of men's actions, as Washington County's planters and yeoman farmers themselves admitted. The influence of economic status upon political action may be demonstrated by examining the 1860 federal manuscript population census for Washington County. The tables that follow describe the economic resources, first, of the men who led each side and, second, of the men who fought in the two armies. I have not attempted to draw statistically significant samples from a total population. Such a project is possible but not feasible here; it would require checking several thousand names in the county population census against the service records for Civil War soldiers in the National Archives. For my purposes, representative samples of two matched groups will suffice—for both leaders and their constituents.

It should be noted that a few of the leaders and many of their constituents were very young men, often only fifteen or sixteen years old. They, of course, are recorded in the population census as having owned no personal or real property. While this is technically true, it is not a good indicator of their economic status or prospects. Indeed when such men joined the Union or Confederate armies, they represented not so much their own interests as the economic status and prospects of their families. Hence, in such cases I have recorded the property holdings of the head of the household in which a young man lived. To make sure that this did not skew the overall findings, I have listed such cases separately in my tabulations, but the data have been added into all final totals.

The list of Washington County leaders was drawn from my research in the Pettigrew Papers and the printed *Official Records* of the armies and navies. If a man had either acted or publicly expressed an opinion in favor of one side, that man qualified as either a Confederate or unionist leader. By this means, I identified thirty-two Union leaders and thirty-three Confederate leaders. Of this list, twenty-eight and twenty-four respectively were in the 1860 manuscript federal population census for Washington County.

The occupations of Washington County's unionist and Confederate leaders are shown in Table 1. Most unionist leaders (57.1 percent) were farmers, while a substantial number labored as

Table 1 Occupations of Leaders

	*UHH*a	*UNH*	*CHH*	*CNH*
Farmer	16 (57.1%)	1 (3.8%)	10 (41.6%)	1 (4.2%)
Laborer	2 (7.4)	0 (0.0)	1 (4.2)	0 (0.0)
Blacksmith	1 (3.8)	0 (0.0)	1 (0.0)	0 (0.0)
Maildriver	1 (3.8)	0 (0.0)	0 (0.0)	0 (0.0)
Millhand	1 (3.8)	0 (0.0)	0 (0.0)	0 (0.0)
Merchant	2 (7.4)	0 (0.0)	5 (20.8)	0 (0.0)
Surveyor	0 (0.0)	1 (3.8)	0 (0.0)	0 (0.0)
Fisherman	1 (3.8)	0 (0.0)	0 (0.0)	0 (0.0)
Constable	1 (3.8)	0 (0.0)	0 (0.0)	0 (0.0)
Carpenter	1 (3.8)	0 (0.0)	1 (4.2)	0 (0.0)
Lawyer	0 (0.0)	0 (0.0)	3 (12.5)	0 (0.0)
County-court clerk	0 (0.0)	0 (0.0)	1 (4.2)	0 (0.0)
Student	0 (0.0)	0 (0.0)	0 (0.0)	1 (4.2)
Clergyman	0 (0.0)	0 (0.0)	0 (0.0)	1 (4.2)

Note: Unionist, $N = 28$; Confederate, $N = 24$.

a UHH = Unionist head of household
  UNH = Unionist not head of household
  CHH = Confederate head of household
  CNH = Confederate not head of household

artisans or low-level salaried employees of the local government. There were no professionals or students among the unionist leaders. Farmers (41.6 percent) also were predominant among the Confederate leadership, but did not constitute a majority. It should be noted that I have included with the Confederate "farmers" four men called "planters," a term which suggests that these men operated on a larger scale. Most striking is the participation of merchants (20.8 percent) and lawyers (12.5 percent) in the Confederate leadership. These figures suggest that small farmers were predominant unionist leaders while planters, merchants, and lawyers led the county's Confederates.

The disparity between unionist and Confederate leaders becomes more obvious in Table 2, a tabulation of the value of real estate owned by the county's leadership. Unionist leaders were largely men who operated large farms, but not extensive plantations. More than 40 percent owned buildings and land valued at between $100 and $499; another third operated farms that ranged in value from

Table 2   Value of Leaders' Real Estate Holdings

$ amount	UHHa	UNH	CHH	CNH
1–99	3 (10.7%)	0 (0.0%)	0 (0.0%)	0 (0.0%)
100–499	13 (46.4)	0 (0.0)	2 (8.3)	0 (0.0)
500–999	2 (7.2)	0 (0.0)	1 (4.2)	1 (4.2)
1,000–4,999	5 (17.9)	2 (10.7)	6 (25.0)	0 (0.0)
5,000–9,999	1 (3.6)	0 (0.0)	2 (8.3)	0 (0.0)
10,000+	1 (3.6)	0 (0.0)	5 (20.8)	3 (12.5)
No report/ none reported	1 (3.6)	0 (0.0)	4 (16.7)	0 (0.0)

	Unionist	Confederate
Total value real estate	$36,792	$335,265
Average value real estate per leader	$1,314	$22,302

Note: Unionist, $N = 28$; Confederate, $N = 24$.

a UHH = Unionist head of household
  UNH = Unionist not head of household
  CHH = Confederate head of household
  CNH = Confederate not head of household

$1,000 to $4,999. Only a handful held real estate worth less than $100 or more than $5,000. By contrast, more than half of the county's Confederate leaders owned real property valued at more than $1,000, while another third owned more than $10,000 each in land. Unionist leaders held real estate worth a total of $36,792 compared to $335,265 for Confederate leaders (although the latter figure drops to $135,265 if Josiah Collins and his son are excluded from the calculations). Unionist leaders held on average real estate valued at $1,314, while Confederate leaders owned on average real estate worth $22,302 ($6,148 if the Collins family is excluded).

Similar differences in wealth may be observed in Table 3, a tabulation of the value of personal property (including any slaves) owned by Washington County leaders. Almost half of the unionist leaders owned personal property valued between $100 and $499. About one sixth owned property valued at less than $100, and slightly less than one sixth held property worth between $1,000

Table 3   Value of Leaders' Personal Property Holdings

$ amount	UHHa	UNH	CHH	CNH
1–99	5 (17.8%)	0 (0.0%)	0 (0.0%)	0 (0.0%)
100–499	13 (46.4)	0 (0.0)	1 (4.2)	0 (0.0)
500–999	2 (7.1)	0 (0.0)	3 (12.5)	0 (0.0)
1,000–2,499	2 (7.1)	0 (0.0)	2 (8.3)	0 (0.0)
2,500–4,999	1 (3.6)	0 (0.0)	3 (12.5)	0 (0.0)
5,000–9,999	1 (3.6)	1 (3.6)	3 (12.5)	0 (0.0)
10,000+	2 (7.1)	0 (0.0)	10 (41.7)	1 (4.2)
No report/ none reported	1 (3.6)	0 (0.0)	1 (4.2)	0 (0.0)

	Unionist	Confederate
Total value personal property	$61,617	$316,096
Average value personal property per leader	$2,200	$13,170

Note: Unionist, $N = 28$; Confederate, $N = 24$.

a UHH = Unionist head of household
  UNH = Unionist not head of household
  CHH = Confederate head of household
  CNH = Confederate not head of household

and $9,999. Only two unionists held more than $10,000 worth of personal property. By contrast, nearly half the Confederate leaders reported possessing personal property worth more than $10,000. Unionist leaders held personal property valued at $61,617, an average of $2,200 per man; while Confederate leaders held personal property worth $316,096, an average of $13,170 per man. (The figures for Confederate leaders if the Collins family is excluded are $266,096 and $12,095 respectively.)

Finally, more than 85 percent of Washington County's unionist leaders owned no slaves, while 70 percent of the Confederate leaders possessed one or more blacks (see Table 4). Unionist leaders owned a total of 45 slaves, an average of 1.6 per man. Confederate leaders held 624 slaves (318 if not counting the Collins family),

Table 4   Slaves Held by Leaders

No. of slaves	UHH[a]	UNH	CHH	CNH
1–4	1 (3.6%)	0 (0.0%)	2 (8.3%)	0 (0.0%)
5–9	1 (3.6)	0 (0.0)	3 (12.3)	0 (0.0)
10–14	0 (0.0)	0 (0.0)	1 (4.2)	0 (0.0)
15–19	2 (7.1)	0 (0.0)	3 (12.5)	0 (0.0)
20–24	0 (0.0)	0 (0.0)	1 (4.2)	0 (0.0)
25–29	0 (0.0)	0 (0.0)	0 (0.0)	0 (0.0)
30–34	0 (0.0)	0 (0.0)	0 (0.0)	1 (4.2)
35–39	0 (0.0)	0 (0.0)	0 (0.0)	0 (0.0)
40–44	0 (0.0)	0 (0.0)	1 (4.2)	0 (0.0)
45–49	0 (0.0)	0 (0.0)	1 (4.2)	0 (0.0)
50+	0 (0.0)	0 (0.0)	2 (8.3)	2 (8.3)
No report/ none reported	22 (78.6)	2 (7.1)	6 (25.0)	1 (4.2)

	Unionist	Confederate
Total no.	45	624
Average no. per leader	1.6	26

Note: Unionist, $N = 28$; Confederate, $N = 24$.

[a] UHH = Unionist head of household
 UNH = Unionist not head of household
 CHH = Confederate head of household
 CNH = Confederate not head of household

an average of 26 for each secessionist leader (14.5 without the Collins's slaves).

In sum, two dramatically different sets of leaders emerged in Washington County during the Great Rebellion. Unionists were led mainly by yeoman farmers and artisans, most of whom owned land and personal property, each valued at a few hundred dollars, but they seldom held slaves. If they did, they owned only one or two. Confederates, by contrast, were led by wealthy men, mostly planters, but also by a substantial number of merchants and lawyers. They owned land and personal property reckoned in the thousands and tens of thousands of dollars, and held tens or, a few cases, hundreds of slaves.

The men who followed Washington County's unionist and Confederate leaders, however, were mostly younger men who represented poorer households. This should not be surprising. The county was populated in 1860 chiefly with men who earned their living by laboring for wages. It was among these men that Washington County's leaders, both Confederate and unionist, sought constituencies for or against the war.

In order to produce representative matched samples of those men in Washington County who participated in the conflict at home but who did not lead it, I compiled a list of 140 local residents who served in the Confederate army, and 107 who volunteered for the Union army. The Confederate names were taken from the volume compiled by Weymouth T. Jordan, Jr., *North Carolina Troops, 1861–1865, A Roster,* vol. 6 (Raleigh, N.C.: Division of Archives and History, 1977). Some of the men served in Company G, North Carolina State Troops, known as the "Washington Volunteers"; the company was organized in Plymouth on June 24, 1861. Other Confederates on my list served in Company G, North Carolina State Troops (2nd organization), which was organized at Plymouth on March 21, 1862. Names for Washington County unionist soldiers were taken from muster rolls of the 1st North Carolina (Union) Volunteers (Record Group 94, National Archives), organized at Plymouth on June 12, 1862. Of the 107 Union soldiers, 63 were identified in the 1860 federal manuscript population census for Washington County; of the 140 Confederate soldiers, 76 were located.

At first glance, Confederate and unionist soldiers did not appear

Table 5a Occupations of Soldiers

	UHH[a]	UNH	CHH	CNH
	Independent Proprietors			
Farmer w/land	13	0	9	1
Shingle maker	1	1	2	1
	Laborers			
Day laborer	2	7	13	2
Laborer	0	3	0	2
Year laborer	0	2	1	3
Farmer w/o land	1	6	0	9
Farm laborer	0	4	0	7
Spinner	0	0	0	1
	Artisans			
Blacksmith	1	0	0	0
Carpenter	1	1	2	1
Wheelwright	0	1	0	0
Apprentice	0	1	0	0
Cooper	0	1	0	0
Waterman	0	1	2	2
Shoemaker	0	0	1	0
Brickmason	0	0	0	1
	Other			
County surveyor	0	0	1	0
Overseer	0	0	1	1
Student	0	0	0	4
No report/ none reported	3	13	1	8

Note: Unionist, $N = 63$; Confederate, $N = 76$.

[a] UHH = Unionist head of household
 UNH = Unionist not head of household
 CHH = Confederate head of household
 CNH = Confederate not head of household

to differ much in occupational status, unlike their leaders (see Tables 5a and 5b). About a quarter of the county's Union volunteers and a fifth of the Confederates were independent proprietors, mostly farmers, but also a few shingle makers; two fifths of the Union soldiers and one half of the Confederates were laborers; comparable numbers, probably teenagers, reported no occupation. Yet differences among the various kinds of laborers are revealing.

Table 5b Occupations of Soldiers

	Unionist	Confederate
Independent proprietors	15 (24%)	13 (17%)
Laborers	25 (40)	38 (50)
Artisans	7 (11)	9 (12)
Other	0 (0)	7 (9)
No report/ none reported	16 (25)	9 (12)

Note: Unionist, *N* = 63; Confederate, *N* = 76.

Among Union soldiers, only three out of twenty-five laborers headed households of their own, while fourteen out of thirty-eight Confederate laborers headed households. Moreover, thirteen of those Confederate laborers who headed a household were "day laborers," men who depended on planters for casual employment. In sum, small farmers, shingle makers, artisans, and farm laborers working on a yearly contract fought on both sides, but day laborers, mostly older men who headed households and depended upon planters for daily employment, tended to volunteer for Confederate service.

If not occupation, what accounts for the political choices made by most Washington County soldiers (excepting day laborers)? The tabulations in Table 6 suggest an answer. Union soldiers who headed households in 1860 tended to be men of middling means; only one reported no real estate, and none owned more than $1,000 worth. By contrast, nineteen out of thirty-three Confederate household heads owned no property at all. Among the families of younger men who did not head households, the disparity in wealth proved to be even greater. Nearly all the families of Union soldiers owned some land, but the land was valued at less than $1,000 in all but three cases. At the same time, twenty-three out of forty-three Confederate families held real estate worth more than $1,000. Along the same lines, Union soldiers from Washington County owned real estate valued at a total of $19,243 (an average of $305 per man), while Confederate soldiers held real estate worth $99,916 (an average of $1,315 per soldier). These total figures, however, obscure a significant difference between Confederate heads of households and young rebels still living at home;

Table 6 Value of Real Estate Held by Soldiers

$ amount	UHH[a]	UNH	CHH	CNH
1–49	0 (0.0%)	3 (4.8%)	0 (0.0%)	2 (2.6%)
50–99	3 (4.8)	2 (3.2)	0 (0.0)	1 (1.3)
100–199	6 (9.5)	10 (15.9)	3 (3.9)	1 (1.3)
200–299	3 (4.8)	2 (3.2)	1 (1.3)	1 (1.3)
300–399	6 (9.5)	3 (4.8)	0 (0.0)	5 (6.6)
400–499	1 (1.6)	4 (6.3)	2 (2.6)	2 (2.6)
500–999	2 (3.2)	10 (15.9)	2 (2.6)	7 (9.2)
1,000–1,999	0 (0.0)	2 (3.2)	4 (4.8)	5 (6.6)
2,000+	0 (0.0)	1 (1.6)	2 (2.6)	12 (15.8)
No report/ none reported	1 (1.6)	4 (6.3)	19 (25.0)	7 (9.2)

	UHH	UNH	CHH	CNH
Total value real estate	$5,332	$13,911	$10,657	$89,259
Average value real estate per soldier	$242	$339	$323	$2,076

	Unionist	Confederate
Total value real estate	$19,243	$99,916
Average value real estate per soldier	$305	1,315

Note: Unionist, $N = 63$; Confederate, $N = 76$.

a UHH = Unionist head of household
UNH = Unionist not head of household
CHH = Confederate head of household
CNH = Confederate not head of household

heads of households, mostly day laborers, owned real estate valued at $10,657 (an average of $323 per man), while soldiers who had no household of their own, mostly the sons of small planters, lived in households that altogether owned real estate worth $89,259 (an average of $2,076 per soldier). In sum, farmers, shingle makers, artisans, and farm laborers of middling means tended to join the Union army themselves, and they sent their sons to fight as well. The poorest laboring men, meanwhile, tended to join the Confederates, along with the sons of the wealthy, although planters themselves stayed at home.

A similar distribution of wealth may be observed in Table 7, a tabulation of the value of personal property owned by Washington County's soldiers. About two thirds of the county's Union soldiers and their families owned personal property valued at less than $350, while the Confederate household figures remained divided

Table 7   Value of Personal Property Held by Soldiers

$ amount	UHHª	UNH	CHH	CNH
1–49	3 (4.8%)	2 (3.2%)	5 (6.6%)	5 (6.6%)
50–99	6 (9.5)	5 (7.9)	10 (13.2)	5 (6.6)
100–149	1 (1.6)	3 (4.8)	3 (3.9)	0 (0.0)
150–199	3 (4.8)	8 (12.3)	3 (3.9)	4 (5.1)
200–249	1 (1.6)	1 (1.6)	3 (3.9)	2 (2.6)
250–299	4 (6.3)	1 (1.6)	0 (0.0)	1 (1.3)
300–349	1 (1.6)	7 (11.1)	2 (2.6)	3 (3.9)
350–399	0 (0.0)	1 (1.6)	0 (0.0)	0 (0.0)
400–449	0 (0.0)	5 (7.9)	1 (1.3)	3 (3.9)
450–499	0 (0.0)	0 (0.0)	0 (0.0)	0 (0.0)
500+	0 (0.0)	6 (9.5)	5 (6.6)	20 (26.3)
No report/ none reported	3 (4.8)	2 (3.2)	1 (1.3)	0 (0.0)

	UHH	UNH	CHH	CNH
Total value personal property	$2,720	$14,241	$14,157	$271,506
Average value personal property per soldier	$124	$347	$429	$6,314

	Unionist	Confederate
Total value personal property	$16,961	$285,663
Average value personal property	$269	$3,759

Note: Unionist, $N = 63$; Confederate, $N = 76$.

ª UHH = Unionist head of household
 UNH = Unionist not head of household
 CHH = Confederate head of household
 CNH = Confederate not head of household

between rich and poor; one third of the rebels owned personal property valued at less than $100, while more than one quarter owned personal property worth more than $500—in some cases much more. The total amount of personal property owned by Union soldiers was $16,961 (an average of $269 per soldier), while Confederates owned personal property valued at $285,663 (an average of $3,759 per soldier). As with the real-estate figures, total amounts and averages on the Confederate side conceal a great disparity in wealth between planters and day laborers. Confederate

Table 8   Slaves Held by Soldiers

No. of slaves	UHH[a]	UNH	CHH	CNH
1–4	1 (1.6%)	5 (7.9%)	3 (3.9%)	7 (9.2%)
5–9	0 (0.0)	0 (0.0)	0 (0.0)	4 (5.3)
10–14	0 (0.0)	0 (0.0)	1 (1.3)	0 (0.0)
15–19	0 (0.0)	1 (1.6)	0 (0.0)	5 (6.6)
20–24	0 (0.0)	0 (0.0)	0 (0.0)	0 (0.0)
25–29	0 (0.0)	0 (0.0)	0 (0.0)	1 (1.3)
30–34	0 (0.0)	0 (0.0)	0 (0.0)	1 (1.3)
35–39	0 (0.0)	0 (0.0)	0 (0.0)	0 (0.0)
40–44	0 (0.0)	0 (0.0)	0 (0.0)	0 (0.0)
45–49	0 (0.0)	0 (0.0)	0 (0.0)	0 (0.0)
50+	0 (0.0)	0 (0.0)	0 (0.0)	2 (2.6)
No report/ none reported	21 (33.3)	35 (55.6)	29 (38.2)	25 (32.9)

	UHH	UNH	CHH	CNH
Total no.	1	31	18	228
Average no. per soldier	0.05	0.8	0.5	5.3

		Unionist	Confederate
	Total no.	32	246
	Average no. per soldier	0.5	3.2

Note: Unionist, $N = 63$; Confederate, $N = 76$.

a UHH = Unionist head of household
 UNH = Unionist not head of household
 CHH = Confederate head of household
 CNH = Confederate not head of household

household heads, many of them day laborers, owned personal property valued at $14,157 (an average of $429 per soldier), while the sons of planters living at home in 1860 resided in households with personal property holdings amounting to $271,506 (an average of $6,314).

A less dramatic difference between Confederate and Union soldiers may be seen in Table 8, a tabulation of the number of slaves held by households. Very few ordinary soldiers on either side held slaves, but Confederate soldiers held more slaves than Union soldiers. The sons of the largest planters either did not serve or, as in the case of George Collins whose father owned over 350 slaves, served as officers.

Washington County's leaders and that part of their constituencies who volunteered to fight in the larger war did not divide strictly between rich and poor. But each man evidently did calculate how his economic interests might best be served. Middling farmers and artisans saw a chance to break out of their earlier alliance with planters within the Whig party and to rule the county as unionists in the interests of small proprietors. At the same time, planters, both large and small, and their sons naturally cast their lot with the Confederacy, the only government they felt would act to secure their interests in slaves. The county's poorest men volunteered to serve their employers with an eye towards securing future wage labor. The Great Rebellion in Washington County was indeed a poor man's fight, but it was not necessarily a rich man's war, for every man who fought, whether at home or at the front in Virginia, had something to gain, providing the fortunes of war smiled upon him.

Notes

Prologue

1. New Bern *North Carolina Daily Times,* July 28, 1865. New-berry's speech was reprinted when he ran for a seat for the U.S. Congress from the Albermarle Sound region.

2. Emory M. Thomas, *The Confederate Nation* (New York: Harper and Row, 1979), 234; J. G. Randall and David Donald, *The Civil War and Reconstruction,* second edition (Lexington, Mass.: D. C. Heath, 1969).

On North Carolina during the war see John Barrett, *The Civil War in North Carolina* (Chapel Hill: The Univ. of North Carolina Press, 1963); Richard Bardolph, "Inconstant Rebels: Desertion of North Carolina Troops in the Civil War," *North Carolina Historical Review* 12 (April 1964): 163–89; Marc W. Krummen, "Dissent in the Confederacy: The North Carolina Experience," *Civil War History* 28 (Dec. 1981): 293–313; Richard Yates, *The Confederacy and Zeb Vance* (Tuscaloosa, Ala.: Confederate Publishing Co., 1958); and William T. Auman, "The Heroes of America in Civil War North Carolina," *North Carolina Historical Review* 58 (Oct. 1981): 327–63.

For accounts of the war that deal with social conflict see William L. Barney, *Flawed Victory: A New Perspective on the Civil War* (New York: Praeger, 1980); Ira Berlin, Barbara J. Fields, Thavolia Glymph, Joseph P. Reidy, and Leslie S. Rowland (eds.), *Freedom: A Documentary History of Emancipation, 1861–1867,* ser. I, *The Destruction of Slavery* (New York: Cambridge Univ. Press, 1985); Paul Escott, *Many Excellent People: Power and Privilege in North Carolina, 1850–*

1900 (Chapel Hill: Univ. of North Carolina Press, 1984); Barbara J. Fields, *Slavery and Freedom on the Middle Ground: Maryland during the Nineteenth Century* (New Haven: Yale Univ. Press, 1985); Michael J. Johnson, *Toward a Patriarchal Republic* (Baton Rouge: Louisiana State Univ. Press, 1977); Clarence L. Mohr, *On the Threshold of Freedom: Masters and Slaves in Civil War Georgia* (Athens: Univ. of Georgia Press, 1986); Phillip S. Paludan, *Victims: A True Story of the Civil War* (Knoxville: Univ. of Tennessee Press, 1981); James L. Roark, *Masters Without Slaves: Southern Planters in the Civil War and Reconstruction* (New York: Norton, 1977); and Drew Gilpin Faust, *James Henry Hammond and the Old South: A Design for Mastery* (Baton Rouge: Louisiana State Univ. Press, 1982).

3. W. A. Davis, *Soil Survey of Washington County, North Carolina* (Washington, D.C.: Government Printing Office, 1912), 15; Edmund Ruffin, *Sketches of Lower North Carolina* (Raleigh, N.C.: Institution for the Deaf & Dumb & Blind, 1861), 232–44; Edmund Ruffin, "A Journey Over the Farm Land of Washington County," *The Farmers' Register,* vol. 8, no. 3 (1839).

4. William S. Powell (ed.), *Dictionary of North Carolina Biography,* vol. 1 (Chapel Hill: Univ. of North Carolina Press, 1983): 404–6; Bennett H. Wall, "The Founding of the Pettigrew Plantations," *North Carolina Historical Review,* vol. 35 (July 1956): 281–309.

5. William S. Tarlton, *Somerset Place and Its Restoration* (Raleigh: North Carolina Division of Archives and History, 1954).

6. U.S. Manuscript Census, Population Schedule, 1860, Washington County, North Carolina.

7. June 10, 1786, Account of Importations 4 July 1785 to 4 July 1786, Port Roanoke, Ports, Treasurer's and Comptroller's Papers, Archives, North Carolina Division of Archives and History, Raleigh (hereafter NCA); Louis B. Wright and Marion Tingling (eds.), *Quebec to Carolina in 1785–1786, Being the Travel Diary and Observations of Robert Hunter, Jr., a Young Merchant of London* (San Marino, Calif.: Huntington Library, 1943), 265–67, 276; Tarlton, *Somerset Place,* p. 120; John Spencer Bassett, *Slavery in the State of North Carolina* (Baltimore: Johns Hopkins Univ. Press, 1899), 93.

8. Jeffrey J. Crow, "Slave Rebelliousness and Social Conflict in North Carolina, 1775 to 1802," *William and Mary Quarterly,* 3d ser., 37 (Jan. 1980): 79–102.

9. Ibid.

10. Bennett H. Wall, "Ebenezer Pettigrew: An Economic Study of an Ante-Bellum Planter" (Ph.D. diss., Univ. of North Carolina, 1946), 9, 31, 43, 46.

11. Uriah Bennett interview, *Scuppernong Farms Project* (Washington, D.C.: United States Department of Agriculture, 1936–1937), 8–9, in the Farm Security Administration Papers, NCA (hereafter cited as Bennett interview, F.S.A. Papers, NCA). The interview transcript was made in May 1937 and originally handwritten into the parish register of St. David's Episcopal Church, located near Somerset Place plantation. Bennett was born at Somerset Place about 1845 and lived there with his parents both of whom were field hands before the Civil War.

12. Frederick Fitzgerald to Samuel Farmer Jarvis, Jan 3, 1844, Miscellaneous Papers, Southern Historical Collection, Univ. of North Carolina Library, Chapel Hill (hereafter SHC).

13. Wall, "Pettigrew," p. 84, 89, 151, 158, 162, 167, 171–74, 177, 251.

14. Josiah Collins to Richard H. Riddick, Jr., March 10, 1860, Collins Letterbook, pp. 338–39, Josiah Collins Papers, NCA.

15. Bennett interview, F.S.A. Papers, NCA.

16. Wall, "Pettigrew," pp. 111–16, 208–9.

17. William S. Pettigrew to Caroline Pettigrew, May 21, 1860, Pettigrew Papers, SHC.

18. Mary Pettigrew to Charles L. Pettigrew, June 19, 1860; E. H. Willis to William S. Pettigrew, May 14, 1860; William S. Pettigrew to Annie Pettigrew, June 25, 1860, Pettigrew Papers. SHC.

19. William S. Pettigrew to James L. Petigru, May 1860, Pettigrew Papers, SHC.

1. Secession

1. William S. Pettigrew to James C. Johnston, Oct. 25, 1860, Pettigrew Family Papers, SHC.

2. Ibid.

3. Charles L. Pettigrew to Caroline Pettigrew, Nov. 14, 1860, Pettigrew Papers. SHC.

4. Ibid., Nov. 8, 1860.

5. Charles L. Pettigrew to James C. Johnston, Oct. 20, 1860, Pettigrew Papers, SHC.

6. Charles L. Pettigrew to Caroline Pettigrew, Nov. 1, 1860, Pettigrew Papers, SHC.

7. William S. Pettigrew to James Johnston Pettigrew, Nov. 2, 1860, Pettigrew Papers, SHC.

8. *Raleigh Register,* Sept. 1, 1860.

9. Ibid., Nov. 17, 1860.

10. Charles L. Pettigrew to Caroline Pettigrew, Nov. 11, 15, 1860, Pettigrew Papers, SHC; E. B. Haughton to "Aunt," Dec. 20, 1860, Geolet-Buncombe Papers, SHC.

11. Charles L. Pettigrew to Caroline Pettigrew, Nov. 15, 20, 1860, Pettigrew Papers, SHC.

12. Ibid., Nov. 15, 18, 1860.

13. Ibid., Dec. 4, 1860.

14. William S. Pettigrew to brother, Dec. 29, 1860, Pettigrew Papers, SHC.

15. New Bern *Daily Progress,* Feb. 12, 1861. See also the account in J. Carlyle Sitterson, *The Secession Movement in North Carolina* (Chapel Hill: Univ. of North Carolina Press, 1939).

16. On Latham's activities in the North Carolina General Assembly see scattered references in the legislative proceedings recorded in the *Raleigh Register* Dec. 1860 through Feb. 1861.

17. Charles Latham to Henry Short, Feb. 2, 1861, Pettigrew Papers, SHC.

18. S. L. Johnson et al. to William S. Pettigrew, Feb. 1861, Pettigrew Papers, SHC.

19. Ibid.

20. William S. Pettigrew to C. H. Willis, Feb. 14, 1861, Pettigrew Papers, SHC.

21. J. G. N. to Caroline Pettigrew, Feb. 13, 1861, Pettigrew Papers, SHC. "Leveller" was a local term that referred to landless swampers and should be distinguished from another usage that denotes petty property owners. See Christopher Hill, *The World Turned Upside Down: Radical Ideas During the English Revolution* (New York: Penguin Books, 1975), 107–50.

22. J. C. Johnston to William S. Pettigrew, Feb. 11, 18, 1861, Pettigrew Papers, SHC.

23. Caroline Pettigrew to Louise, Feb. 7, 1861, Pettigrew Papers, SHC.

24. William S. Pettigrew to [James S. Johnston], March 12, 1861, Pettigrew Papers, SHC.

25. Ibid.; *Raleigh Register,* Feb. 27, 1861.

26. William S. Pettigrew to [James C. Johnston], March 12, 1861, Pettigrew Papers, SHC.

27. William S. Pettigrew speech at Plymouth, North Carolina, Feb. 19, 1861, Pettigrew Papers, SHC.

28. Ibid.

29. Ibid.

30. William S. Pettigrew to [James C. Johnston], March 12, 1861, Pettigrew Papers, SHC.

31. Caroline Pettigrew to [James] Johnston [Pettigrew], Feb. 23, 1861; William S. Pettigrew to [James C. Johnston], March 12, 1861, Pettigrew Papers, SHC.

32. William S. Pettigrew speech at Cool Spring, Feb. 26, 1861, Pettigrew Papers, SHC.

33. William S. Pettigrew to [James C. Johnston], March 12, 1861, Pettigrew Papers, SHC.

34. Ibid.; William S. Pettigrew speech at Cool Spring, Feb. 26, 1861, Pettigrew Papers, SHC. See an attached note for voting totals by district.

35. *Raleigh Register,* March 6, 1861.

36. Roy P. Basler et al. (eds.), *The Collected Works of Abraham Lincoln,* vol. 2 (New Brunswick, N.J.: Rutgers Univ. Press, 1952): 262–71.

37. Richard H. Wills to William H. Wills, Wills Family Papers, SHC; Caroline Pettigrew to Mamma, March 19, 1861, Pettigrew Papers, SHC.

38. J. G. Randall and David Donald, *The Civil War and Reconstruction,* second ed. (Lexington, Mass.: D. C. Heath, 1969), 163–89.

39. Caroline Pettigrew to Louisa, April 17, 1861, Pettigrew Papers, SHC.

40. R. H. Wills to Brother, April 8, 1861, Wills Family Papers, SHC.

41. *Raleigh Register,* April 20, 1861.

42. H. G. Spruill to William S. Pettigrew, April 25, 1861, Pettigrew Papers, SHC.

43. William S. Pettigrew speech at Cool Spring, April 26, 1861, Pettigrew Papers, SHC.

44. Ibid.; William S. Pettigrew speech at Columbia, May 4, 1861, Pettigrew Papers, SHC.

45. A Statement of the Votes Cast, May 13, 1861, Pettigrew Papers, SHC.

46. *Raleigh Register,* April 24, 1861; H. G. Spruill to William S. Pettigrew, April 25, 1861, Pettigrew Papers, SHC.

47. Caroline Pettigrew to William S. Pettigrew, May 28, 1861; Charles L. Pettigrew to William S. Pettigrew, May 31, 1861, Pettigrew Papers, SHC. The "Morris Guards," the company recruited by Capt. Henry A. Gilliam from around Plymouth was stationed at the village

of Portsmouth just south of Ocracoke Inlet along the Outer Banks seventy miles southeast of Plymouth. New Bern *Daily Progress,* June 11, 17, 1861.

48. R. H. Wills to Mother, May 17, 1861, Wills Papers, SHC.

49. H. G. Spruill to William S. Pettigrew, May 27, 1861, Pettigrew Papers, SHC.

50. R. H. Wills to [William H. Wills], May 30, 1861, Wills Papers, SHC; Malachi J. White to William S. Pettigrew, May 23, 25, 1861, Pettigrew Papers, SHC.

51. William S. Pettigrew to D. G. Cowand, April 23, 1861, Pettigrew Papers, SHC. See Appendix A for a statistical view of who fought for each side.

2. The Yeoman Challenge

1. Deposition of Andrew Bateman, *State v. Ellsberry Ambrose,* January 16, 1862; Deposition of Durham Oliver, *State v. Ellsberry Ambrose,* July 1, 1861; Arrest warrant for Ellsberry Ambrose, *State v. Ellsberry Ambrose,* July 1, 1861; Judgment against Ellsberry Ambrose, Pettigrew Papers, SHC.

2. U.S. Manuscript Census, Agricultural Schedule, 1860, Washington County, N.C., p. 5.

3. Ibid. Durham Oliver is listed number nine on page five; Ellsberry Ambrose number sixteen; and Andrew Bateman number thirty.

4. Ibid., p. 7.

5. Complaint of Durham Oliver against Ellsberry Ambrose, *State v. Ellsberry Ambrose,* July 1, 1861, Pettigrew Papers, SHC.

6. Magistrate's judgment, *State v. Ellsberry Ambrose,* July 1, 1861, Pettigrew Papers, SHC.

7. Bond for Ellsberry Ambrose, *State v. Ellsberry Ambrose,* July 2, 1861, Pettigrew Papers, SHC; U.S. Manuscript Census, Agricultural Schedule, 1860, Washington County, N.C., p. 5.

8. Henderson B. Phelps to William S. Pettigrew, June 23, 1861, Pettigrew Papers, SHC.

9. Ibid.

10. Ibid.; William A. Littlejohn to William S. Pettigrew, June 12, 1861, Pettigrew Papers, SHC.

11. William A. Littlejohn to Governor Henry Clark, Aug. 16, 1861, Governor's Papers, NCA.

12. Ibid.

13. Benjamin F. Butler to John E. Wool, Aug. 30, 1861, U.S. War

Department, *The War of the Rebellion: A Compilation of the Official Records of the Union and Confederate Armies,* ser. 1, vol. 4 (Washington, D.C., 1882): 581–86 (hereafter *ORA*).

14. Ibid.; Colonel Max Weber to Major General Benjamin Butler, Sept. 5, 1861, pp. 589–90; Flag-Officer Samuel Barron (C.S.A.) to Hon. S. R. Mallory, Secretary C.S.A. Navy, Aug. 31, 1861, pp. 592–94; General Order No. 8, C. C. Churchill, p. 594, *ORA,* ser. 1, vol. 4; Rush C. Hawkins, "Early Coast Operations in North Carolina," *Battles and Leaders of the Civil War.* vol. 1 (New York, n.d.); "Hatteras Inlet Expedition," *Report of the Joint Committee on the Conduct of the War,* House of Representatives, Thirty-seventh Congress, Third Session (Washington, D.C., 1863), 280–91.

15. William S. Pettigrew speech to the Constitutional Convention, Sept. [?], 1861, Pettigrew Papers, SHC.

16. Maria H. Hardison to William S. Pettigrew, n.d., Pettigrew Papers, SHC.

17. William S. Pettigrew to [Charles L. Pettigrew], Sept. 5, 1861, Pettigrew Papers, SHC.

18. See "Hatteras Inlet Expedition," *Report,* 280–91; C. B. Hassell Diary, Sept. 2, 1861, vol. 9, p. 1392, Cushing Biggs Hassell Papers, SHC (hereafter Hassell Papers).

19. William S. Pettigrew speech, Sept. 10, 1861, Pettigrew Papers, SHC.

20. Caroline Pettigrew to Mamma, Sept. 3, 1861, Pettigrew Papers, SHC.

21. John G. Barrett, *The Civil War in North Carolina* (Chapel Hill: Univ. of North Carolina Press, 1963), 62–63; William S. Pettigrew to A. L. Chesson and Joshua S. Swift, Oct. 1861; Pettigrew Papers, SHC.

22. Caroline Pettigrew to Mamma, Sept. 3, 1861, Pettigrew Papers, SHC.

23. Pass for William S. Pettigrew, C.S.A. War Department, Sept. 18, 1861; Charles L. Pettigrew to James Johnston Pettigrew, Oct. 2, 1861; William S. Pettigrew to Jefferson Davis, Sept. 21, 1861, Pettigrew Papers, SHC.

24. William S. Pettigrew to James Johnston Pettigrew, Oct. 1, 1861, Pettigrew Papers, SHC.

25. Ibid.

26. D. G. Cowand to William S. Pettigrew, Oct. 8, 1861, Pettigrew Papers, SHC.

27. Ibid.; Asa Biggs to General Gatlin, Oct. 3, 1861, *ORA,* ser. 1, vol. 4, pp. 671–72.

28. New Bern *Daily Progress,* Oct. 2, 1861, p. 2.

29. Caroline Pettigrew to Louise, Sept. 10, 1861, Pettigrew Papers, SHC. For evidence of unionist sentiment in northeastern North Carolina see John E. Wool to Col. E. D. Townsend, Sept. 6, 1861, *ORA,* ser. 1, vol. 4, p. 606; Rush C. Hawkins to Maj. Gen. John E. Wool, Sept. 7, 1861, *ORA,* ser. 1, vol. 4, pp. 607–9; Rush C. Hawkins to Maj. Gen. John E. Wool, Sept. 11, 1861, *ORA,* ser. 1, vol. 4, pp. 609–10; Citizens of Hatteras to the Commander of the Federal Forces at Hatteras Inlet, n.d., *ORA,* ser. 1, vol. 4, p. 611; Rush C. Hawkins to Maj. Gen. John E. Wool, Sept. 19, 1861, *ORA,* ser. 1, vol. 4, pp. 617–19; Rush C. Hawkins to Maj. Gen. John E. Wool, Sept. 21, 1861, *ORA,* ser. 1, vol. 4, pp. 619–20. For a Confederate report on widespread unionist activity see Henry T. Clark [governor of North Carolina] to Hon. J. P. Benjamin [acting Secretary of War], Sept. 24, 1861, *ORA,* ser. 1, vol. 4, p. 657; Henry T. Clark to Hon. J. P. Benjamin, Sept. 25, 1861, *ORA,* ser. 1, vol. 4, p. 658; C. B. Hassell Diary, Sept. 12, 1861, vol. 9, p. 1394, Hassell Papers, SHC. Unionists on the Outer Banks, meanwhile, began taking the federal loyalty oath. New Bern *Daily Progress,* Sept. 23, 1861, p. 3.

30. William S. Pettigrew to Josiah Collins, Nov. 9, 1861, Pettigrew Papers, SHC. For a copy of North Carolina's new ordinance dealing with treason see "Be it ordained by this Convention . . . ," June 18, 1861, *ORA,* ser. 1, vol. 4, p. 659; New Bern *Daily Progress,* May 17, 1861, p. 2.

31. William S. Pettigrew to Josiah Collins, Nov. 9, 1861. Pettigrew Papers, SHC.

32. Ibid.

33. Ibid.

34. William S. Pettigrew speech to the Constitutional Convention, Nov. 1861, Pettigrew Papers, SHC.

35. U.S. Manuscript Census, Agricultural Schedule, 1860, Washington County, North Carolina, p. 8.

36. Ibid., p. 5.

37. Joseph B. Davenport testimony, Oct. 20, 1861; L. B. Davis testimony, Oct. 20, 1861, Pettigrew Papers, SHC.

38. Henderson B. Phelps to William S. Pettigrew, Oct. 20, 1861, Pettigrew Papers, SHC.

39. Ibid.

40. William S. Pettigrew to Henderson Phelps, Oct. 20, 1861, Pettigrew Papers, SHC.

41. William S. Pettigrew to D. H. Hill, Oct. 20, 1861, Pettigrew Papers, SHC.

42. U.S. Manuscript Census, Agricultural Schedule, 1861, Washington County, North Carolina, p. 1.

43. Testimony of Asa Warren, Oct. 26, 1861; testimony of Asa Steely; testimony of Isaac Ambrose; William S. Pettigrew speech to the Constitutional Convention, Nov. 1861, Pettigrew Papers, SHC.

44. William S. Pettigrew speech to the Constitutional Convention, Nov. 1861, Pettigrew Papers, SHC.

45. William S. Pettigrew to Governor Henry Clark, Oct. 24, 1861; testimony of Isaac Ambrose, Oct. 26, 1861, Pettigrew Papers, SHC.

46. William S. Pettigrew to Governor Henry Clark, Oct. 24, 1861, Pettigrew Papers, SHC.

47. U.S. Manuscript Census, Agricultural Schedule, 1860, Washington County, North Carolina, p. 5.

48. Ibid.

49. William S. Pettigrew to Henry Clark, Oct. 24, 1861, Pettigrew Papers, SHC.

50. Ibid., Nov. 3, 1861.

51. Caroline Pettigrew to Mamma, Nov. 12, 1861, Pettigrew Papers, SHC.

52. Ibid.

53. Ibid; C. B. Hassell Diary, Nov. 3, 1861, vol. 9, p. 1408, Hassell Papers, SHC.

54. William S. Pettigrew to Henry Clark, Nov. 7, 1861, Pettigrew Papers, SHC.

55. Ibid.

56. U.S. Manuscript Census, Agricultural Schedule, 1860, Washington County, North Carolina, p. 9.

57. Asa Steely and Lovich W. Steely testimony, Oct. 25, 1861; William L. Smith testimony, Nov. 8, 1861; Isaac Ambrose testimony, Nov. 8, 1861; Asa W. Snell testimony, Nov. 8, 1861; Ann A. Snell testimony, Nov. 8, 1861, Pettigrew Papers, SHC.

58. Caroline Pettigrew to Mamma, Nov. 12, 1861, Pettigrew Papers, SHC.

59. Testimony of L. Harry Spruill, Nov. 6, 1861, Pettigrew Papers, SHC.

60. Testimony of Joseph P. Patrick, Nov. 5, 1861, Pettigrew Papers, SHC.

61. Annie Pettigrew [?] to Brother, May 28, 1861, Pettigrew Papers, SHC.

62. Isaac Ambrose testimony, Nov. 8, 1861, Pettigrew Papers, SHC; U.S. Manuscript Census, Agricultural Schedule, 1860, Washington County, North Carolina, p. 3.

63. Caroline Pettigrew to Mamma, Nov. 12, 1861, Pettigrew Papers, SHC.

64. Untitled speech to the North Carolina Constitutional Convention by William S. Pettigrew, Nov. 1861, Pettigrew Papers, SHC.

65. Hardy Hardison to William S. Pettigrew, Nov. 19, 1861, Pettigrew Papers, SHC.

66. Ibid.

67. James H. Smith to William S. Pettigrew, Nov. 20, 1861, Pettigrew Papers, SHC.

68. Hardy Hardison to William S. Pettigrew, Nov. 14, 1861, Pettigrew Papers, SHC.

69. William S. Pettigrew to James H. Smith, Nov. 23, 1861, Pettigrew Papers, SHC.

70. H. G. Spruill to William S. Pettigrew, Nov. 25, 1861; William A. Littlejohn to William S. Pettigrew, Nov. 25, 1861, Pettigrew Papers, SHC.

71. Malachi White to William S. Pettigrew, Nov. 28, 1861, Pettigrew Papers, SHC.

72. William A. Littlejohn to William S. Pettigrew, Dec. 2, 1861, Pettigrew Papers, SHC.

73. Ibid.

74. Ibid.

75. Ibid.

76. *Raleigh Register,* Nov. 27, Dec. 4, 1861; "An Ordinance in relation to the appointment & commissioning by the Governor of Militia Officers," by William S. Pettigrew, Nov. 23, 1861; "Ordinance sustaining the Gov. in the appointment of the former Militia Officers in the Cool Spring & Germanton Districts in Washington Co.," by William S. Pettigrew, Nov. 1861; Untitled speech to the Constitutional Convention by William S. Pettigrew, Nov. 1861; Untitled seditious language ordinance, by William S. Pettigrew, Nov. 1861, Pettigrew Papers, SHC.

77. H. G. Spruill to William S. Pettigrew, Dec. 6, 1861; Malachi White to William S. Pettigrew, Dec. 7, 1861; William A. Littlejohn to William S. Pettigrew, Dec. 28, 1861, Pettigrew Papers, SHC.

78. William A. Littlejohn to William S. Pettigrew, Dec. 11, 1861, Pettigrew Papers, SHC.

79. Robert McMillen to Governor Henry Clark, Nov. 27, 1861, Pettigrew Papers, SHC.

80. Charles L. Pettigrew to William S. Pettigrew, [n.d.] 1861, Pettigrew Papers, SHC.

3. Removal

1. Major General John A. Wool to Secretary of War Simon Cameron, Sept. 18, 1861, *ORA*, ser. 1, vol. 4, p. 613; Rush C. Hawkins, "Early Coast Operations in North Carolina," in *Battles and Leaders of the Civil War*, vol. 1 (New York: The Century Co., 1884), p. 635.

2. S. H. McRae to William S. Pettigrew, Jan. 6, 1862, Pettigrew Papers, SHC.

3. John Barrett, *The Civil War in North Carolina* (Chapel Hill: Univ. of North Carolina Press, 1963), 66–67. Braxton Bragg Diary, pp. 85–87, Thomas Bragg Papers, SHC; Charles Pettigrew to William S. Pettigrew, Dec. 26, 1861, Pettigrew Papers, SHC. For accounts of local military preparations see, Special Orders, No. 272, Adjt. and Insp'r General's Office, Dec. 21, 1861, *ORA*, ser. 1, vol. 4, p. 715; William S. Pettigrew draft letter, Jan. 1862, Pettigrew Papers, SHC; Richard H. Wills to William H. Wills, Jan. 15, 1862, Wills Papers, SHC; Rush C. Hawkins, "Early Coast Operations," pp. 640–45; C. B. Hassell Diary, Jan. 23, 24, Feb. 2, 8, 9, 1862, vol. 9, pp. 1422–28, 1430–32, Hassell Papers, SHC; New Bern *Daily Progress*, Jan. 18, 1862, p. 2; Jan. 23, 1862, p. 2; Jan. 24, 1862, p. 2; Jan. 25, 1862, p. 3; Jan. 28, 1862, p. 2; Feb. 3, 1862, p. 2; Feb. 7, 1862, p. 2; Feb. 10, 1862, p. 3; Feb. 11, 1862, p. 3; Feb. 12, 1862, pp. 2–3; Feb. 13, 1862, p. 2; Feb. 14, 1862, p. 2; Feb. 17, 1862, p. 2.

4. On the social relations of paternalism see Eugene D. Genovese, *Roll, Jordan, Roll: The World the Slaves Made* (New York: Pantheon, 1974), e.g., 3–7; Charles Joyner, *Down by the Riverside: A South Carolina Slave Community* (Urbana: Univ. of Illinois Press, 1984); Drew Gilpin Faust, *James Henry Hammond and the Old South: A Design for Mastery* (Baton Rouge: Louisiana State Univ. Press, 1982), 69–104; and Michael P. Johnson, "Planters and Patriarchy: Charleston, 1800–1860," *Journal of Southern History*, vol. 46 (Feb. 1980): 45–72.

For studies of masters and slaves during the Civil War see Ira Berlin, Barbara J. Fields, Thavolia Glymph, Joseph P. Reidy, and Leslie S. Rowland (eds.), *Freedom: A Documentary History of Emancipation, 1861–1867*, ser. II, vol. I, *The Destruction of Slavery* (New York: Cambridge University Press, 1985), 663–82; Clarence L. Mohr, *On the Threshold of Freedom: Masters and Slaves in Civil War Georgia* (Athens: Univ. of Georgia Press, 1986), 99–119.

For the objections to what some authors understand as the deterministic implications of Prof. Genovese's argument, see Herbert G. Gutman, *The Black Family in Slavery and Freedom, 1750–1925* (New York: Pantheon, 1976), e.g. 309–20; and Paul D. Escott, *Slavery Re-*

membered: A Record of Twentieth-Century Slave Narratives (Chapel Hill: Univ. of North Carolina Press, 1979), 18–21.

5. Caroline Pettigrew to Charles Pettigrew, March 11, 1862, Pettigrew Papers, SHC.

6. Caroline Pettigrew to Minnie, March 12, 1862, Pettigrew Papers, SHC.

7. Ibid.

8. Ibid.

9. Ibid.

10. Ibid.

11. Ibid.; Caroline Pettigrew to Minnie, March 24, 1862, Pettigrew Papers, SHC.

12. Caroline Pettigrew to Minnie, March 24, 1862, Pettigrew Papers, SHC.

13. Ibid.

14. William S. Pettigrew memo, April 1862; Caroline Pettigrew to ?, March 10, 1862, Pettigrew Papers, SHC.

15. William S. Pettigrew memo, April 1862, Pettigrew Papers, SHC.

16. William Campbell to Mrs. Miller, March 18, 1862, Pettigrew Papers, SHC.

17. William S. Pettigrew to Mr. West, March 28, 1862, Pettigrew Papers, SHC.

18. "Negroes hired in Chatham & Moore Counties in the year 1862," by William S. Pettigrew, March 1862, Pettigrew Papers, SHC.

19. Ibid.

20. William C. Campbell to William S. Pettigrew, May 9, 1862, Pettigrew Papers, SHC.

21. Ibid.; William C. Campbell to William S. Pettigrew, May 22, 1862, Pettigrew Papers, SHC.

22. William C. Campbell to William S. Pettigrew, May 22, 1862, Pettigrew Papers, SHC.

23. Ibid.; "Negroes hired in Chatham & Moore Counties in the year 1862," by William S. Pettigrew, March 1862, Pettigrew Papers, SHC.

24. William C. Campbell to William S. Pettigrew, May 22, 1862, Pettigrew Papers, SHC.

25. William C. Campbell to William S. Pettigrew, May 22, 1862, Pettigrew Papers, SHC.

26. Ibid.

27. Ibid.

28. Ibid.

29. William C. Campbell to William S. Pettigrew, June 10, 1862, Pettigrew Papers, SHC.

30. Ibid.; William S. Pettigrew to William C. Campbell, June 21, 1862, Pettigrew Papers, SHC.

31. "Negroes hired in Chatham & Moore Counties in the year 1862," by William S. Pettigrew, March 1862, Pettigrew Papers, SHC.

32. Angus McLeod to William S. Pettigrew, July 31, 1862, Pettigrew Papers, SHC.

33. Ibid.

34. Ibid.

35. William S. Pettigrew to Angus McLeod, August 9, 1862; William S. Pettigrew to Kennith Worthy, August 9, 1862, Pettigrew Papers, SHC.

36. J. G. N. to Charles Pettigrew, May 4, 1862; J. G. N. to Charles Pettigrew, May 9, 1862, Pettigrew Papers, SHC.

37. Caroline Pettigrew to Charles Pettigrew, June 19, July 16, 1862, Pettigrew Papers, SHC.

38. Caroline Pettigrew to Charles Pettigrew, June 19, 1862, Pettigrew Papers, SHC.

39. Ibid.

40. Caroline Pettigrew to William S. Pettigrew, June 27, 1862, Pettigrew Papers, SHC.

41. Charles Pettigrew to William S. Pettigrew, June 17, 1862; Caroline Pettigrew to William S. Pettigrew, June 27, 1862, Pettigrew Papers, SHC.

42. John M. Hough to William S. Pettigrew, April 20, 1862; Malachi J. White to William S. Pettigrew, May 30, 1862, Pettigrew Papers, SHC.

43. William S. Pettigrew to sister [Annie Pettigrew], July 1, 1862, Pettigrew Papers, SHC.

4. A Question of Sovereignty

1. Caroline Pettigrew to Louise, Feb. 24, 1862; Hardy H. Phelps to William S. Pettigrew, March 4, 1862, Pettigrew Papers, SHC; Richard H. Wills to William Wills, March 7, 1862, Wills Papers, SHC; U.S.N. Commander S. C. Rowan to Flag-Officer Louis M. Goldsborough, March 29, 1862, *Official Records of the Union and Confederate Navies in the War of the Rebellion,* ser. 1, vol. 7, p. 178 (hereafter *ORN*).

2. ? to William S. Pettigrew, March 8, 1862; Caroline Pettigrew to ?, March 3, 1862, Pettigrew Papers, SHC.

3. Hardy Hardison to William S. Pettigrew, Feb. 25, 1862, Pettigrew Papers, SHC.

4. J. M. Hough to William S. Pettigrew, March 18, 1862, Pettigrew Papers, SHC; Commander S. C. Rowan to Flag-Officer Louis M. Goldsborough, March 29, 1862, *ORN,* ser. 1, vol. 7, p. 178.

5. Richard H. Wills to Sister, March 11, 1862, Hunter-Wills Family Papers, Manuscript Department, East Carolina Univ., Greenville, North Carolina: Raleigh *North Carolina Standard* (weekly), April 2, 1862.

6. D. G. Cowand to William S. Pettigrew, March 29, 1862, Pettigrew Papers, SHC; Richard H. Wills to Brother Norman, April 9, 1862, Wills Papers, SHC.

7. John M. Hough to William S. Pettigrew, April 20, 1862, Pettigrew Papers, SHC.

8. Ibid.; William S. Pettigrew to Sister, April 23, 1862, Pettigrew Papers, SHC; Richard H. Wills to William Wills, April 19, 1862, Wills Papers, SHC.

9. H. G. Spruill Memorandum, May 15, 1862, pp. 2–3 (typescript used), Pettigrew Papers, SHC. The H. G. Spruill Memorandum is a daily record of interviews Spruill held with various people, including the federal officers stationed at Plymouth. The typscript version consists of seventy-nine pages covering the period from May 1 to Dec. 10, 1862, except for six weeks from Aug. 1 through Sept. 15. This typescript will be referred to in the notes as the Spruill Memorandum. The original manuscript is also available in the Pettigrew Papers. There is also a manuscript filed separately in the Pettigrew Papers that covers the period Aug. 1 through Sept. 15. I will refer to this document as the Spruill Manuscript. This portion of Spruill's record became separated from the main body when Spruill lent it to a certain A. G. Garrett, who did not return it. The two were reunited in the Pettigrew Papers only in recent years.

10. Spruill Memorandum, May 15, 1862, pp. 3–5, Pettigrew Papers, SHC; C. B. Hassell Diary, May 14, 1862, vol. 9, p. 1452, Hassell Papers, SHC.

11. New Bern *Daily Progress,* May 23, 1962. In the event, President Lincoln countermanded Hunt's order and reserved to himself the power to alter slavery.

12. Ibid., May 15, 1862, p. 6; S. C. Rowan to Louis M. Goldsborough, May 15, 1862, *ORN,* ser. 1, vol. 7, p. 372; Francis M. Manning Copybook, May 16, 1862, Francis Manning Papers, Manuscript Department, East Carolina Univ., Greenville; Richard H. Wills to ?, May 19, 1862, Wills Papers, SHC.

Gilliam did break his parole, but he had no choice in the matter. The assistant adjutant general of the Department of North Carolina, R. H. Riddick, issued a special order Jan. 10, 1862, commanding all prisoners captured at Hatteras and recently exchanged to report to the nearest military post for duty and reassignment. New Bern *Daily Progress,* January 16, 1862.

13. C. W. Flusser to S. C. Rowan, May 18, 1862, *ORN,* ser. 1, vol. 7, p. 384; Spruill Memorandum, May 17, 1862, p. 7, Pettigrew Papers, SHC.

14. Spruill Memorandum, May 15, 1862, p. 6, Pettigrew Papers, SHC.

15. Ibid., May 17, 1862, p. 8.

16. Ibid., pp. 7–8.

17. Ibid., May 18, 1862, pp. 9–10; C. B. Hassell Diary, May 19, 1862, vol. 9, pp. 1453–54, Hassell Papers, SHC.

18. C.S.A. to William S. Pettigrew, May 24, 1862, Pettigrew Papers, SHC; C. W. Flusser to S. C. Rowan, May 19, 1862, *ORN,* ser. 1, vol. 7, pp. 391–92.

19. C.S.A. to William S. Pettigrew, May 24, 1862, Pettigrew Papers, SHC.

20. Richard Wills to ?, May 19, 1862, Wills Papers, SHC; C.S.A. to William S. Pettigrew, May 24, 1862, Pettigrew Papers, SHC; S. C. Rowan to Louis M. Goldsborough, May 22, 1862, *ORN,* ser. 1, vol. 7, pp. 415–16; C. B. Hassell Diary, May 20, 1862, vol. 9, p. 1454, Hassell Papers, SHC.

21. Spruill Memorandum, May 20, 1862, pp. 13, 14, Pettigrew Papers, SHC.

22. Ibid., May 23, 1862, pp. 15–16.

23. Ibid., pp. 16–17.

24. Ibid., pp. 17–18.

25. Ibid., June 3, 1862, pp. 20–21.

26. Ibid., June 8, 1862, p. 23.

27. Rush C. Hawkins, *An Account of the Assassination of Loyal Citizens of North Carolina for Having Served in the Union Army which Took Place at Kingston in the Months of February and March 1864* (New York: 1897), 7–8.

28. Spruill Memorandum, June 12, 1862, p. 24, Pettigrew Papers, SHC. Beth G. Crabtree and James W. Patton (eds.), *"Journal of a Secesh Lady": The Diary of Catherine Ann Devereux Edmondston, 1860–1866* (Raleigh, N.C.: Division of Archives and History, Department of Cultural Resources, 1979), July 13, 1862, p. 213; Hawkins, *An Account of the Aassassinations,* pp. 8–9.

29. S. C. Rowan to Louis M. Goldsborough, June 12, 1862, *ORN,* ser. 1, vol. 7, p. 476; Hawkins, *An Account of the Assassinations,* pp. 9–10.

30. Hawkins, *An Account of the Assassinations,* pp. 9–10.

31. Ibid.

32. Rush C. Hawkins, "Early Coast Operations in North Carolina," *Battles and Leaders of the Civil War,* vol. 1, p. 658; Spruill Memorandum, June 14, 1862, p. 26, Pettigrew Papers, SHC.

33. Spruill Memorandum, June 16, 25, 1862, pp. 29–30; William S. Pettigrew to Joshua S. Swift, July 1, 4, 1862, Pettigrew Papers, SHC.

34. New Bern *Daily Progress,* June 11, 1862; Spruill Memorandum, June 29, 1862, p. 33, Pettigrew Papers, SHC. From spring 1862 through 1865, the New Bern *Daily Progress* operated as the semi-official newspaper of the Union army in eastern North Carolina. The editors, of course, took a distinctly unionist position in their politics and coverage. On Stanly's career and appointment see New Bern *Daily Progress,* April 23, 1862. Stanly's appointment was not the federal government's first attempt to establish a provisional government in North Carolina. See New Bern *Daily Progress,* July 20, 1861, and Dec. 12, 1861; and Norman C. Delaney, "Charles Henry Foster and the Unionists of Eastern North Carolina," *North Carolina Historical Review,* vol. 37 (July 1960): 348–66.

35. New Bern *Daily Progress,* June 20, 1862; Spruill Memorandum, July 2, 1862, p. 35, Pettigrew Papers, SHC. This issue of the *Daily Progress* contained a reprint of Stanly's speech at Washington, North Carolina, which, according to H. G. Spruill, is the same speech the governor gave at Plymouth on July 2. The printed speech confirms Spruill's account. Meetings such as the one at Plymouth were held throughout the North Carolina coastal plain. In May, one such meeting in Carteret County called upon "all Union-loving men to meet & speak their Union sentiments." The meeting also resolved to request "protection by our Federal friends." New Bern *Daily Progress,* May 12, 1862. For Craven County see New Bern *Daily Progress,* May 15, 1862.

36. Spruill Memorandum, July 2, 1862, p. 37, Pettigrew Papers, SHC.

37. Ibid., pp. 37–38.

38. C. W. Flusser to S. C. Rowan, July 11, 1862, pp. 556–57; Thomas J. Woodward to C. W. Flusser, July 11, 1862, p. 557; John MacDiarmid to C. W. Flusser, July 10, 1862, *ORN,* ser. 1, vol. 7, p. 588; Spruill Memorandum, July 12, 1862, p. 40, Pettigrew Papers, SHC; New Bern *Daily Progress,* July 13, 1862. There was also an expedition to Williamston by Flusser's gunboats. See C. B. Hassell Diary, June 30, 1862, vol. 9, pp. 1464–65, Hassell Papers, SHC.

39. Spruill Memorandum, July 17, 1862, p. 43, Pettigrew Papers, SHC.

40. Ibid., July 18, 1862, pp. 44, 46.

41. New Bern *Daily Progress,* October 6, 1862.

42. Ibid., July 21, 1862; Spruill Memorandum, July 14, 1862, p. 42, Pettigrew Papers, SHC.

43. Spruill Memorandum, July 15, 1862, p. 43, Pettigrew Papers, SHC.

44. Ibid., July 19, 1862, p. 45. The rule requiring local residents to take a Union oath was sanctioned four days later by General Orders No. 11 issued by General Pope at Washington, D.C., on July 23, 1862. The order was printed in the New Bern *Daily Progress,* July 29, 1862.

45. Spruill Memorandum, pp. 44–45, Pettigrew Papers, SHC.

46. George Patterson, "First Visit of the Yankees to Somerset Place, Lake Scuppernong, North Carolina, July 21, 1862," Josiah Collins Papers, NCA.

47. Ibid., pp. 1, 2; C. W. Flusser to H. H. Davenport, Aug. 4, 1862, *ORN,* ser. 1, vol. 7, pp. 622–23.

48. Patterson, "First Visit," p. 3.

49. Ibid., p. 4.

50. George Patterson, "Second Visit of the Yankees to Somerset Place, Lake Scuppernong, July 27th, 1862," p. 1, Josiah Collins Papers, NCA.

51. Ibid., p. 2; Spruill Memorandum, Aug. 1, 1862, p. 46; Caroline Pettigrew to William S. Pettigrew, Aug. 28, 1862, Pettigrew Papers, SHC.

52. Caroline Pettigrew to William S. Pettigrew, Aug. 28, 1862, Pettigrew Papers, SHC.

53. Crabtree and Patton (eds.), *"Journal of a Secesh Lady,"* July 30, 1862, pp. 226–27.

54. Spruill Manuscript, Aug. 17, 18, 1862, pp. 4, 9, Pettigrew Papers, SHC.

55. Ibid., Aug. 17, 1862, p. 5.

56. D. G. Cowand to William S. Pettigrew, July 19, Aug. 4, 1862, Pettigrew Papers, SHC. For over a year, some secessionists had argued in favor of waging a guerrilla war. An editorial from the *Richmond Dispatch* and reprinted in the New Bern *Daily Progress* put it this way: "Guerilla Warfare. Nothing can be more important than the general adoption of this mode of warfare in the South." New Bern *Daily Progress,* June 3, 1861.

57. ? to William S. Pettigrew, July 30, 1862; "Parpatharkies" [George Patterson] to Mrs. [Charles L.] Pettigrew, Aug. 26, 1862, Pettigrew Papers, SHC. "Parpatharkies" was George Patterson's last name before he Anglicized it. He was born in Greece.

58. Spruill Manuscript, Sept. 3, 1862, pp. 14–15, Pettigrew Papers, SHC.

59. New Bern *Daily Progress,* Sept. 18, 1862.

60. Spruill Manuscript, Sept. 16, 1862, p. 47, Pettigrew Papers, SHC; C. B. Hassell Diary, September 18, 1862, vol. 9, p. 1483, Hassell Papers, SHC.

61. Spruill Manuscript, Sept. 23, 1862, pp. 49–50, Pettigrew Papers, SHC.

62. Ibid.

63. New Bern *Daily Progress,* Oct. 17, 1862.

5. The Emancipation Proclamation

1. ? to William S. Pettigrew, March 8, 1862, Pettigrew Papers, SHC.

2. Spruill Memorandum, July 19, 1862, p. 45, Pettigrew Papers, SHC.

3. Caroline Pettigrew to William S. Pettigrew, Aug. 28, 1862, Pettigrew Papers, SHC; Patterson, "First Visit of the Yankees to Somerset Place, Lake Scuppernong, N. Carolina, July 21st 1862," p. 5, Josiah Collins Papers, NCA.

4. Patterson, "First Visit," p. 5.

5. Patterson, "Second Visit of the Yankees to Somerset Place, Lake Scuppernong, July 27th 1862," p. 3, Josiah Collins Papers, NCA.

6. John A. Hedrick to Brother, Sept. 25, 1862, Benjamin Hedrick Papers, Duke Univ., Durham, North Carolina (hereafter DU); Spruill Memorandum, Oct. 2, 1862, p. 51, Pettigrew Papers, SHC.

7. Spruill Memorandum, Oct. 3, 1862, p. 51, Pettigrew Papers, SHC. The full text of the Emancipation Proclamation was first published in the Albemarle area in the New Bern *Daily Progress,* Sept. 29, 1862.

8. William S. Pettigrew to Charles Pettigrew, Oct. 2, 1862, Pettigrew Papers, SHC.

9. Spruill Memorandum, Oct. 7, 1862, p. 52, Pettigrew Papers, SHC.

10. C. W. Flusser to H. K. Davenport, Oct. 12, 1862, *ORN,* ser. 1, vol. 8, p. 129; Spruill Memorandum, Oct. 7, 1862, p. 56, Pettigrew Papers, SHC.

11. C. W. Flusser to H. K. Davenport, Oct. 15, 1862, *ORN,* ser. 1, vol. 8, pp. 139–40.

12. Spruill Memorandum, Oct. 18, 22, 25, 1862, pp. 55–57, Pettigrew Papers, SHC.

13. Ibid., October 25, 1862, p. 57.

14. William S. Pettigrew to sister, Oct. 13, 1862, Pettigrew Papers, SHC.

15. S. P. Lee to Gideon Welles, Secretary of the Navy, Oct. 25, 1862, *ORN,* ser. 1, vol. 8, pp. 145–46; W. J. Hotchkiss to S. P. Lee, Oct. 18, 1862, *ORN,* ser. 1, vol. 8, p. 146; H. K. Davenport to S. P. Lee, Oct. 18, 1862, *ORN,* ser. 1, vol. 8, pp. 157–58; C. W. Flusser to S. P. Lee, Oct. 18, 1862, *ORN,* ser. 1, vol. 8, p. 159; J. Innis Randolph (C.S.A.) to C. H. Dimmock (C.S.A.), Oct. 3, 1862, *ORN,* ser. 1, vol. 8, pp. 185–87; W. G. Bender (C.S.A.) to J. I. Randolf (C.S.A.), Oct. 28, 1862, *ORN,* ser. 1, vol. 8, pp. 187–88; W. G. Bender (C.S.A.) to Z. T. Adams (C.S.A.), Nov. 1, 1862, *ORN,* ser. 1, vol. 8, p. 188.

16. C. W. Flusser to S. P. Lee, Oct. 18, 1862, *ORN,* ser. 1, vol. 8, p. 158; S. P. Lee to Gideon Wells, Secretary of the Navy, Oct. 28, 1862, *ORN,* ser. 1, vol. 8, p. 157.

17. S. P. Lee to H. K. Davenport, Oct. 24, 1862, *ORN,* ser. 1, vol. 8, pp. 147–48; H. K. Davenport to S. P. Lee, Oct. 28, 1862, *ORN,* ser. 1, vol. 8, pp. 160–61.

18. Z. B. Vance to the Honorable General Assembly, Nov. 17, 1862, *ORN,* ser. 4, vol. 2, p. 188; S. G. French to Zebulon B. Vance, Nov. 16, 1862, *ORA,* ser. 1, vol. 18, p. 778; S. G. French (C.S.A.) to Zebulon Vance, Oct. 22, 1862, *ORA,* ser. 1, vol. 18, p. 760; Spruill Memorandum, Oct. 29, 30, 31, Nov. 2, 1862, pp. 59–60, Pettigrew Papers, SHC; Beth G. Crabtree and James W. Patton (eds.), *"Journal of a Secesh Lady,"* Nov. 2, 1862, pp. 290–91; C. B. Hassell Diary, Oct. 30, 1862, vol. 9, p. 1496, Hassell Papers, SHC.

19. U.S. Manuscript Census, 1860, Agricultural Schedule, Washington County, North Carolina, p. 5; Deposition of Thomas S. Hassell; Deposition of Wilson A. Ambrose; Deposition of James A. Wilson, Records of the General Accounting Office, Records of the Third Auditor's Office, Southern Claims Commission Case Files, 1877–83, Box 233, Entry 732, Record Group 217, National Archives (hereafter cited as Southern Claims Commission, RG 217, NA); John Pool to Zebulon B. Vance, Sept. 18, 1862, *ORA,* ser. 1, vol. 18, pp. 745–77.

20. S. P. Lee to Gideon Welles, Nov. 14, 1862, *ORN,* ser. 1, vol. 8, p. 180; H. K. Davenport to S. P. Lee, Nov. 10, 1862, *ORN,* ser. 1, vol. 8, pp. 181–83.

21. S. P. Lee to Gideon Welles, Secretary of the Navy, Nov. 14, 1862, *ORN,* ser. 1, vol. 8, pp. 181–82; H. K. Davenport to S. P. Lee, Nov. 10, 1862, *ORN,* ser. 1, vol. 8, pp. 181–82; J. G. Foster to C. W. Flusser, Nov. 1, 1862, *ORN,* ser. 1, vol. 8, pp. 184–85; W. G. Bender (C.S.A.) to General Gwynn (C.S.A.), Nov. 4, 1862, *ORN,* ser. 1, vol. 8,

p. 188; Francis S. Wells to H. K. Davenport, Nov. 5, 1862, *ORN,* ser. 1, vol. 8, pp. 188–90; H. K. Davenport to S. P. Lee, Nov. 15, 1862, *ORN,* ser. 1, vol. 8, pp. 211–12; John G. Foster to Maj. Gen. H. W. Halleck, Oct. 30, 1862, *ORA,* ser. 1, vol. 18, p. 447; John G. Foster to Henry W. Halleck, Nov. 12, 1862, *ORA,* ser. 1, vol. 18, pp. 20–22; C. B. Hassell Diary, Nov. 3, 1862, vol. 9, p. 1497, Hassell Papers, SHC; New Bern *Daily Progress,* Nov. 15, 1862, p. 2.

22. S. G. French to Zebulon Vance, Oct. 22, 1862, *ORA,* ser. 1, vol. 18, p. 760.

23. Spruill Memorandum, Nov. 6, 8, 10, 11, 1862, pp. 62–64, Pettigrew Papers, SHC.

24. Ibid.; A. G. Jones to father, Dec. 3, 1862, Abraham G. Jones Papers, East Carolina University, Manuscript Department, Greenville, North Carolina (hereafter ECU); C. B. Hassell Diary, Nov. 4, 13, 1862, vol. 9, pp. 1496, 1498–1500, Hassell Papers, SHC.

25. Spruill Memorandum, Nov. 12, 1862, p. 67, Pettigrew Papers, SHC.

26. Spruill Memorandum, Nov. 8, 1862, p. 63, n.d., p. 72, Pettigrew Papers, SHC; J. G. Foster to H. W. Halleck, Sept. 12, 1862, *ORA,* ser. 1, vol. 18, p. 6; Edward E. Potter to Capt. Southard Hoffman, Sept. 5, 6, 1862, *ORA,* ser. 1, vol. 18, pp. 6, 7.

27. (C.S.A.) Major General S. G. French to General J. G. Foster, U.S.A., Nov. 27, 1862, *ORA,* ser. 1, vol. 18, p. 466.

28. Ibid.

29. J. G. Foster to (C.S.A.) Maj. Gen. S. G. French, Dec. 4, 1862, *ORA,* ser. 1, vol. 18, p. 470; J. G. Foster to (C.S.A.) Brig. Gen. J. G. Martin, Dec. 4, 1862, *ORA,* ser. 1, vol. 18, p. 471.

30. S. G. French to J. G. Foster, Dec. 13, 1862, *ORA,* ser. 1, vol. 18, p. 481.

31. Caroline Pettigrew to Charles Pettigrew, Oct. 22, 1862; Spruill Memorandum, Nov. 12, 1862, p. 64, Pettigrew Papers, SHC.

32. Spruill Memorandum, n.d., p. 71, Pettigrew Papers, SHC.

33. Ibid.

34. Spruill Memorandum, Nov. 15, 1862, pp. 67–68, Pettigrew Papers, SHC; Crabtree and Patton (eds.), *"Journal of a Secesh Lady,"* Dec. 14, 1862, p. 316.

35. Spruill Memorandum, Nov. 19, 1862, p. 70, Pettigrew Papers, SHC.

36. Ibid., November 17, 1862, p. 68; John M. Hough to William S. Pettigrew, Aug. 12, 1864, Pettigrew Papers, SHC.

37. John M. Hough to William S. Pettigrew, Aug. 12, 1864, Petti-

grew Papers, SHC. For Lincoln's proclamation and the second Confiscation Act see *U.S. Statutes at Large*, vol. 12, pp. 589–92, 1266.

38. Deposition of Jeremiah P. Newberry; Deposition of John B. Chesson, Jr.; Deposition of William Atkinson, Box 233, Southern Claims Commission, RG 217, NA; U.S. Manuscript Census, 1860, Agricultural Schedule, Washington County, North Carolina, p. 17.

39. Deposition of Isaac Harrison; Deposition of Joseph Alexander; Deposition of C. C. Brundy, Box 233, Southern Claims Commission, RG 217, NA; U.S. Manuscript Census, 1860, Agricultural Schedule, Washington County, North Carolina, p. 11.

40. Spruill Memorandum, n.d., pp. 73, 75, Pettigrew Papers, SHC; Edward Stanly to Maj. Gen. J. G. Foster, Dec. 29, 1862, *ORA*, ser. 1, vol. 18, p. 498.

41. C. F. W. Behm to Captain C. W. Flusser, Dec. 10, 1862, *ORN*, ser. 1, vol. 8, pp. 276–77; Chas. F. W. Behm to Acting Rear-Admiral S. P. Lee, Dec. 29, 1862, *ORN*, ser. 1, vol. 8, pp. 278–80; C. B. Hassell Diary, Dec. 10, 1862, vol. 9, p. 1509, Hassell Papers, SHC.

42. B. Ewer, Jr., to General Foster, Dec. 10, 1862, *ORA*, ser. 1, vol. 18, pp. 45–46; B. Ewer, Jr., to General Foster, Dec. 11, 1862, *ORA*, ser. 1, vol. 18, p. 46; B. Ewer, Jr., to Colonel Richmond, Dec. 30, 1862, *ORA*, ser. 1, vol. 18, p. 47; C. W. Flusser to Maj. Gen. J. G. Foster, Dec. 30, 1862, *ORA*, ser. 1, vol. 18, p. 48; J. T. Mizell to Col. E. E. Potter, Dec. 16, 1862, *ORA*, ser. 1, vol. 18, pp. 48–49; New Bern *Daily Progress*, Dec. 12, 1862.

43. Crabtree and Patton (eds.), *"Journal of a Secesh Lady,"* Dec. 14, 1862, p. 316.

44. Spruill Memorandum, n.d., pp. 77–79, Pettigrew Papers, SHC; Ed. Stanly to Maj. Gen. J. G. Foster, Dec. 29, 1862, *ORA*, ser. 1, vol. 18, p. 498; Crabtree and Patton (eds.), *"Journal of a Secesh Lady,"* Dec. 12, 1862, pp. 314–15.

45. [Henry?] Phelon to Josephine, Dec. 20, 1862, Phelon Papers, SHC; C. W. Flusser to Commander H. K. Davenport, Dec. 12, 1862, *ORN*, ser. 1, vol. 8, p. 282.

46. J. G. Foster to Maj. Gen. S. G. French, Dec. 27, 1862, *ORA*, ser. 1, vol. 18, p. 495; J. G. Foster to Maj. Gen. S. G. French, Dec. 31, 1862, *ORA*, ser. 1, vol. 18, pp. 497–98; Ed. Stanly to Maj. Gen. J. G. Foster, Dec. 29, 1862, *ORA*, ser. 1, vol. 18, p. 498; S. G. French to Maj. Gen. J. G. Foster, U.S.A., Jan. 7 [6], 1863, *ORA*, ser. 1, vol. 18, pp. 505–7.

47. Hardy Hardison to Josiah Collins, Sr., March 27, 1863; Girard W. Phelps to [Josiah Collins], March 14, 1863; George Patterson,

"List of Adults & Chil*n* left at the Lake," Oct. 30, 1862, Josiah Collins Papers, NCA; Charles Pettigrew to Caroline Pettigrew, April 1863, Pettigrew Papers, SHC.

48. Hardy Hardison to Josiah Collins, Sr., March 27, 1863, Josiah Collins Papers, NCA; Charles Pettigrew to Caroline Pettigrew, April 1863, Pettigrew Papers, SHC.

49. Wilson A. Norman to Josiah Collins, June 28, 1863, Josiah Collins Papers, NCA.

50. George Spruill to Josiah Collins, May 16, 1863; Girard W. Phelps to Josiah Collins, March 14, 1863; Joseph W. Murphy to Josiah Collins, May 30, 1863, Josiah Collins Papers, NCA; Spruill Memorandum, n.d., p. 71, Pettigrew Papers, SHC.

51. George Spruill to Josiah Collins, May 16, 1863; B. B. Ainsley to Josiah Collins, May 4, 1863, Josiah Collins Papers, NCA.

52. George Spruill to Josiah Collins, May 16, 1863, Josiah Collins Papers, NCA.

53. John M. Hough to William S. Pettigrew, Aug. 4, 1864, Pettigrew Papers, SHC.

54. Ibid.

55. Ibid.

56. Ibid.

57. George F. Weston to sir, Feb. 2, 1863, New Berne Occupation Orders and Papers, SHC.

6. Refugeeing

1. "List of Adults & Chil*n* to be carried up the Country," Oct. 30 1862; "List of Adults & Chil*n* left at the Lake," Oct. 30, 1862; "A List of the names & ages of the Servants at Hurry Scurry—Nov. 1862," Josiah Collins Papers, NCA; Bennett interview, F.S.A. Papers, NCA; Joseph Blount Cheshire, *The Church in the Confederate States* (New York: Longman's, Green & Co., 1912), 128–29.

2. Alfred A. Watson to Josiah Collins, Jan. 13, 1863; "Family List," n.d. [1860]; "List of Adults and Chil*n* left at the Lake"; "Estate of Josiah Collins in Account Current with Mrs. Mary Collins, Ex, June 1863–July 1867," Josiah Collins Papers, NCA.

3. J. G. Moore to Josiah Collins, Jan. 7, 13, 1863; E. Alethea Warren to Josiah Collins, April 21, 1863; Receipt No. 17, Dec. 31, 1863, by Josiah Collins, Josiah Collins Papers, NCA.

4. William S. Pettigrew to [John B. Chesson], Jan. 28, 1863, Chesson Papers, DU.

5. William S. Pettigrew notice, Jan. 2, 1863, Pettigrew Papers, SHC; William S. Pettigrew to [John B. Chesson], Jan. 28, 1863, Chesson Papers, DU. A few slaves, probably house servants, were hired out in the town of Winston in Forsyth County adjacent to Davie County. See John A. Campbell to William S. Pettigrew, Jan. 19, 1863, Pettigrew Papers, SHC.

6. William S. Pettigrew to T. J. Sumner, Jan. 19, 1863; William S. Pettigrew to John Hall, Jan. 4, 1863, Pettigrew Papers, SHC; William S. Pettigrew to [John B. Chesson], Jan. 28, 1863, Chesson Papers, DU.

7. Charles Pettigrew to Caroline Pettigrew, Jan. 12, 1863, Pettigrew Papers, SHC.

8. W. A. Eaton to Josiah Collins, March 4, 1863, Josiah Collins Papers, NCA.

9. Caroline Pettigrew to Charles Pettigrew, Jan. 26, 1863, Pettigrew Papers, SHC.

10. Ibid.

11. Ibid., March 27, 1863.

12. Emanuel Fisher to William S. Pettigrew, Jan. 27, 1863, Pettigrew Papers, SHC.

13. Ibid.

14. Ibid.

15. Charles Pettigrew to Caroline Pettigrew, Jan. 23, 1863, Pettigrew Papers, SHC.

16. Ibid.

17. Ibid.

18. Ibid.

19. Josiah Collins to William S. Pettigrew, March 9, 1863, Pettigrew Papers, SHC. West had addressed his letter to Josiah Collins. Pettigrew evidently had left Greensboro for Cherry Hill without telling West where he could be found. Therefore, the slaves' friend wrote to Collins hoping that the planter would know Pettigrew's whereabouts.

20. Charles Pettigrew to Caroline Pettigrew, April 3, 1863, Pettigrew Papers, SHC.

21. Ibid.

22. Ibid.

23. Charles Pettigrew to Caroline Pettigrew, Aug. 6, 1863, Pettigrew Papers, SHC.

24. Caroline Pettigrew to Charles Pettigrew, July 31, 1963, Pettigrew Papers, SHC.

25. Ibid., Aug. 6, 1863.

26. Ibid.

27. Ibid.

28. Ibid.

29. Ibid.

30. Charles Pettigrew to Caroline Pettigrew, Aug. 6, 1863, Pettigrew Paper, SHC.

31. Lloyd Bateman to Josiah Collins, June 1, 1863, Collins Papers, NCA.

32. Ibid.

33. Ibid.

34. Ibid.

35. W. A. Eaton to Josiah Collins, June 2, 1863, Collins Papers, NCA.

36. Hugh McNair to W. A. Eaton, June 9, 1863; E. D. McNair to Josiah Collins, June 9, 1863; W. A. Eaton to Josiah Collins, June 14, 1863, Josiah Collins Papers, NCA.

37. Hugh McNair to Josiah Collins, June 16, 1863; E. D. McNair to Josiah Collins, June 16, 1863, Josiah Collins Papers, NCA.

38. E. D. McNair to Josiah Collins, June 16, 1863, Josiah Collins Papers, NCA.

39. Em. S. Fisher to William S. Pettigrew, Feb. 27, 1863, Pettigrew Papers, SHC.

40. Ibid.; Em. S. Fisher to William S. Pettigrew, April 3, 1863, Pettigrew Papers, SHC.

41. William S. Pettigrew to John A. Campbell, May 18, 1863, Pettigrew Papers, SHC.

42. Jack to William S. Pettigrew, July 21, 1863, Pettigrew Papers, SHC. Unlike letters dictated by Henry and Glasgow to Pettigrew's white neighbor, Malachi White, Jack's letter shows no signs of having been written out by someone else. In the absence of other evidence, we must assume that Jack was literate and perhaps educated to some extent. The diction and handwriting are very fine.

43. Ibid.

44. "$25 Reward," copy of a public notice by William S. Pettigrew, July 18, 1863, Pettigrew Papers, SHC.

45. Caroline Pettigrew to Charles Pettigrew, Dec. 25, 1863, Pettigrew Papers, SHC.

46. Charles Pettigrew to Caroline Pettigrew, Dec. 23, 1863, Pettigrew Papers, SHC.

47. Ibid.; Thomas, *Confederate Nation,* pp. 264–65.

48. Charles Pettigrew to Caroline Pettigrew, Dec. 26, 1863, Pettigrew Papers, SHC.

49. Lloyd Bateman to Josiah Collins, Nov. 11, 1863, Josiah Collins Papers, NCA.

50. Caroline Pettigrew to Charles Pettigrew, Jan. 4, 1863, Pettigrew Papers, SHC.

51. Ibid., March 29, 1864.

52. Charles Pettigrew to William S. Pettigrew, Aug. 22, 1864; Caroline Pettigrew to Charles Pettigrew, Sept. 16, 1864, Pettigrew Papers, SHC.

7. Guerrilla War

1. Charles Pettigrew to Caroline Pettigrew, Jan. 23, 1863; George Parpatharkies to Caroline Pettigrew, Feb. 3, 1863, Pettigrew Papers, SHC; Alfred A. Watson to Josiah Collins, Jan. 13, 1863, Josiah Collins Papers, NCA.

2. John M. Hough to William S. Pettigrew, Aug. 12, 1864, Pettigrew Papers, SHC.

3. Ibid.

4. Ibid.

5. U.S. Manuscript Census, 1860, Population Schedule, Washington County, North Carolina.

6. James A. Smith to Mary, Martha, and Lucy, Jan. 19, 1863, Chesson Papers, DU; Girard W. Phelps to Josiah Collins, March 3, 1863, Collins Papers, NCA.

7. C. W. Hollowell to James C. Johnston, Feb. 12, 1863, Hayes Collection (Johnston Series), SHC.

8. Abigail Brothers Stanley Memoir, p. 10, ECU.

9. M. Bowan to Charles L. Pettigrew, March 1, 1863, Pettigrew Papers, SHC.

10. Ibid.

11. Robert S. Geolet to mother, June 23, 1863, Geolet-Buncombe Papers, SHC.

12. C. W. Flusser to Commander A. Murray, Feb. 6, 1863, *ORN*, ser. 1, vol. 8, p. 508.

13. Samuel D. Hines to Commander A. Murray, Feb. 12, 1863, *ORN*, ser. 1, vol. 8, p. 524; C. W. Flusser to Commander A. Murray, March 1, 1863, *ORN*, ser. 1, vol. 8, p. 580; I. N. Palmer to Lieut. Col. Southard Hoffman, March 5, 1863, *ORA*, ser. 1, vol. 28, p. 552; H. G. Spruill to Josiah Collins, March 11, 1863, Josiah Collins Papers, NCA.

14. A. Murray to Acting Rear-Admiral S. P. Lee, March 4, 5, 1863, *ORN*, ser. 1, vol. 8, pp. 586–87.

15. H. G. Spruill to Josiah Collins, March 11, 1863, Josiah Collins Papers, NCA.

16. Ibid., March 16, 1863.

17. Ibid.

18. Jasper Spruill to Josiah Collins, April 22, 1863, Josiah Collins Papers, NCA.

19. Barrett, *Civil War in North Carolina*, pp. 149–52.

20. D. H. Hill to Hon. James A. Seddon, Feb. 23, 1863, *ORA*, ser. 1, vol. 28, pp. 809–91.

21. J. G. Foster to Maj. Gen. H. W. Halleck, Jan. 20, 1863, *ORA*, ser. 1, vol. 28, pp. 524–25; J. G. Foster to Maj. Gen. H. W. Halleck, March 11, 1863, *ORA*, ser. 1, vol. 28, pp. 556–57; J. G. Foster to Maj. Gen. H. W. Halleck, March 17, 1863, *ORA*, ser. 1, vol. 28, p. 562; Barrett, *Civil War in North Carolina*, pp. 152–62. For an eyewitness account of the New Bern campaign see James J. Iredell to Sam [Iredell?], March 17, 1863, Hayes Papers (Johnston Series), SHC.

22. J. G. Foster to Maj. Gen. H. W. Halleck, March 12, 1863, *ORA*, ser. 1, vol. 28, pp. 549–50; J. G. Foster to Maj. Gen. H. W. Halleck, March 11, 1863, *ORA*, ser. 1, vol. 28, pp. 556–57; I. N. Palmer to Maj. Gen. J. G. Foster, April 5, 1863, *ORA*, ser. 1, vol. 28, pp. 584–85; Josiah Pickett to Lieut. W. L. Wheaton, April 12, 1863, *ORA*, ser. 1, vol. 28, pp. 602–3; J. G. Foster to Maj. Gen. H. W. Halleck, April 16, 1863, *ORA*, ser. 1, vol. 28, p. 623; Josiah Pickett to Lieut. Col. Southard Hoffman, April 18, 1863, *ORA*, ser. 1, vol. 28, p. 640; G. Moxley Sorrell to Maj. Gen. D. H. Hill, April 1, 1863, *ORA*, ser. 1, vol. 28, p. 953; R. B. Garnett to Maj. Gen. D. H. Hill, April 2, 1863, *ORA*, ser. 1, vol. 28, pp. 955–56.

23. J. G. Foster to Rear-Admiral S. P. Lee, April 22, 1863, *ORA*, ser. 1, vol. 28, pp. 647–48; D. H. Hill to General G. T. Beauregard, April 29, 1863, *ORA*, ser. 1, vol. 28, p. 1030.

24. General Orders, No. 62, by (Southard Hoffman) Assistant Adjutant-General, Hdqrs. Eighteenth Army Corps, New Berne, April 23, 1863, *ORA*, ser. 1, vol. 28, p. 652; General Orders No. 64, by (Southard Hoffman) Assistant Adjutant-General, Hdqrs, Eighteenth Army Corps, New Berne, April 23, 1863, *ORA*, ser. 1, vol. 28, pp. 659–60; Abstract from Tri-monthly Return of the Eighteenth Army Corps, Maj. Gen. John G. Foster commanding, for April 30, 1863, *ORA*, ser. 1, vol. 28, pp. 678–79; S. P. Lee to Maj. Gen. J. G. Foster, May 1, 1863, *ORA*, ser. 1, vol. 28, pp. 681–82; J. G. Foster to Rear-Admiral S. P. Lee, May 13, 1863, *ORA*, ser. 1, vol. 28, p. 715; J. G. Martin to Maj. Archer Anderson, May 16, 17, *ORA*, ser. 1, vol. 28, pp. 1064–65.

25. Barrett, *Civil War in North Carolina*, pp. 162–70; Crabtree and Patton (eds.), *"Journal of a Secesh Lady,"* July 23, 1863, pp. 439–40.

26. H. B. Short to William S. Pettigrew, May 19, 1863, Pettigrew Papers, SHC.

27. Ibid.

28. Thomas J. Norman to Josiah Collins, June 23, 1863, Josiah Collins Papers, NCA.

29. Wilson A. Norman to Josiah Collins, June 28, 1863, Josiah Collins Papers, NCA.

30. Ibid.; L. W. Gooding to R. B. Gooding, n.d., 1863, Gooding Papers, DU; Nate Lampheur to L. C. Newton, June 15, 1863, Nate Lampheur Papers, DU; J. S. Kiester to Father, August 21, Sept. 4, 1863, Jacob S. Kiester Papers, ECU.

31. Joseph W. Murphy to Josiah Collins, May 30, 1863, Thomas J. Norman to Josiah Collins, June 23, 1863, Josiah Collins Papers, NCA.

32. Deposition of Harmon Harrison; Deposition of Horton H. Waters; Deposition of George Woodward, Box 233, Southern Claims Commission, RG 217, NA.

33. H. B. Short to William S. Pettigrew, May 19, 1863, Pettigrew Papers, SHC.

34. John Pool to Governor Zebulon Vance, July 25, 1863, Governor's Papers, NCA. On deserters see L. Gooding to Richard, March 13?, 1863, Gooding Papers, DU; and Jesse Hill to Emeline Hill, March 16, 1864, Jessie Hill Papers, ECU.

35. John Pool to Governor Zebulon Vance, July 25, 1863, Governor's Papers, NCA.

36. Joseph W. Murphy to Josiah Collins, May 30, 1863, Thomas J. Norman to Josiah Collins, June 23, 1863, Josiah Collins Papers, NCA.

37. Charles L. Pettigrew to Caroline Pettigrew, April 2, 1864; William S. Pettigrew to Sir, Jan. 5, 1864; D. G. Cowand to William S. Pettigrew, March 1, 1864; John B. Chesson to William S. Pettigrew, April 8, 1864, Pettigrew Papers, SHC.

38. William S. Pettigrew to Sir, Jan. 5, 1864, Pettigrew Papers, SHC; William S. Pettigrew to James C. Johnston, Aug. 9, 1864, Hayes Collection (Johnston Series), SHC.

39. Charles Pettigrew to William S. Pettigrew, April 12, 1864, Pettigrew Papers, SHC.

40. William S. Pettigrew to James C. Johnston, Aug. 9, 1864, Hayes Collection (Johnston Series), SHC.

41. New Bern *North Carolina Times,* Jan. 16, 23, 1864. The *North Carolina Times* was published in New Bern as the semi-official newspaper of the federal army.

42. New Bern *North Carolina Times,* Jan. 23, 1864. The announcement is dated Jan. 2, 1864. Presumably it first appeared on that day.

43. Ibid.
44. Ibid.
45. William S. Pettigrew to Sir, Jan. 5, 1864, Pettigrew Papers, SHC.

8. The Battle of Plymouth

1. Jefferson Davis to His Excellency Z. B. Vance, Feb. 29, 1864, *ORA,* ser. 1, vol. 51, pt. 2, pp. 809–10. On the peace movement see A. Sellew Roberts, "The Peace Movement in North Carolina," *Mississippi Valley Historical Review,* 9 (June 1924): 190–99.; Michael Honey, "The War Within the Confederacy: White Unionists of North Carolina," *Prologue,* vol. 18 (summer 1986): 75–94; Horace W. Raper, *William W. Holden: North Carolina's Political Enigma* (Univ. of North Carolina Press, 1985), 45–58.

2. William T. Auman and David D. Scarboro, "The Heroes of America in Civil War North Carolina," *North Carolina Historical Review,* vol. 53, no. 4 (Oct. 1981): 327–63; J. G. de Roulhac Hamilton, "The Heroes of America," *Publications of the Southern History Association,* vol. 11 (Jan. 1907): 10–19; Richard E. Yates, *The Confederacy and Zeb Vance* (Tuscaloosa, Ala.: Confederate Publishing Co., Inc., 1958), 33–49, 85–107; Memory F. Mitchell, *Legal Aspects of Conscription and Exemption in North Carolina, 1861–1865* (Chapel Hill: Univ. of North Carolina Press, 1965).

3. J. J. Sloan to Hon. James A. Seddon, Feb. 2, 1864, *ORA,* ser. 1, vol. 51, pt. 2, pp. 815–16.

4. Jefferson Davis to His Excellency Z. B. Vance, Jan. 8, 1864, *ORA,* ser. 1, vol. 51, pt. 2, pp. 808–10; Jefferson Davis to the Senate and House of Representatives, Nov. 9, 1864, in Allan Nevins and James D. Richardson (eds.), *The Messages and Papers of Jefferson Davis and the Confederacy, 1861–1865,* vol. 1 (New York: Chelsea House, 1966): 498.

5. Z. B. Vance to His Excellency Jefferson Davis, March 9, 1864, *ORA,* ser. 1, vol. 51, pt. 2, pp. 830–33; W. N. H. Smith to Hon. James A. Seddon, Feb. 16, 1864, *ORA,* ser. 1, vol. 51, pt. 2, p. 821.

6. Braxton Bragg to Brig. Gen. Robert F. Hoke, April 12, 1864, *ORA,* ser. 1, vol. 51, pt. 2, pp. 857–58.

7. Ibid.

8. James A. Seddon to General Braxton Bragg, April 17, 1864, *ORA,* ser. 1, vol. 51, pt. 2, pp. 864–65.

9. On Bragg's reputation see Grady McWhiney, *Braxton Bragg and*

Confederate Defeat: Field Command (New York: Columbia Univ. Press, 1969).

10. Henry Phelon to Josephine, Feb. 26, 1863, Phelon Papers, SHC; Dwight[?] Gooding to brother Richard, March 23, 1864; Dwight Gooding to sister, March 9, 1864; Dwight Gooding to brother Richard, March 30, 1864, Gooding Papers, DU; H. W. Wessells to Captain Judson, April 13, 1864, *ORA*, ser. 1, vol. 23, p. 281; John J. Peck to Maj. Gen. B. F. Butler, April 19, 1864, *ORA*, ser. 1, vol. 23, p. 282.

11. Thomas Jones to William S. Pettigrew, April 4, 1864, Pettigrew Papers, SHC.

12. Walter Clark (ed.), *Histories of the Several Regiments and Battalions from North Carolina, in the Great War, 1861–65*, vol. 5 (Goldsboro: Nash Brothers, 1901).

13. John A. Reed, *History of the 101st Regiment Pennsylvania Veteran Volunteer Infantry, 1861–1865* (Chicago: L. S. Dickey & Co., 1910), p. 125; Capt. R. D. Graham, "Map of Plymouth and Defences, April 17–20, 1864," n.p., in Clark, *Histories of the Several Regiments*, vol. 5.

14. Reed, *History of the 101st Regiment*, p. 126.

15. Ibid.; On Wessells's career see Bvt. Maj.-Gen. George W. Cullum, *Biographical Register of the Officers and Graduates of the U.S. Military Academy at West Point, N.Y. from Its Establishment, in 1802, to 1890* . . . , third edition, vol. 1 (Boston: Houghton Mifflin Company, 1891), pp. 560–61.

16. Reed, *History of the 101th Regiment*, pp. 125–26; Nate Lanpheur, "Fall of Plymouth, North Carolina" pp. 2–3, Nate Lanpheur Papers, DU.

17. Reed, *History of the 101st Regiment*, p. 125.

18. Ibid., pp. 126, 128; Ira B. Sampson Diary, p. 56, Ira B. Sampson Papers, SHC.

19. Lanpheur, "Fall of Plymouth," pp. 8–10, Lanpheur Papers, DU; H. W. Wessells to Maj. Gen. J. J. Peck, Aug. 18, 1864, *ORA*, ser. 1, vol. 23, p. 298; Capt. Charles W. Loehr, "Plymouth Campaign," pp. 2–3 in John W. Darden, "The Story of Washington County," unpublished typescript, North Carolina Collection, University of North Carolina Library. John Darden was a journalist, amateur historian, and resident of Washington County who in the 1920s and 1930s collected various written and oral accounts of the community's history.

20. Reed, *History of the 101st Regiment*, pp. 130–31; H. W. Wessells to Maj. Gen. J. J. Peck, Aug. 18, 1864, *ORA*, ser. 1, vol. 23, p. 298.

21. L. A. Butts to Brig. Gen. H. W. Wessells, April 1, 1865, *ORA,* ser. 1, vol. 23, pp. 301–3.

22. Ibid.; Lanpheur, "Fall of Plymouth," pp. 14–15; Lanpheur Papers, DU; Loehr, "Plymouth Campaign," pp. 3–5.

23. L. A. Butts to Brig. Gen. H. W. Wessells, April 1, 1865, *ORA,* ser. 1, vol. 23, pp. 301–3.

24. Ibid., p. 303.

25. n.a., "Construction of the Ram," p. 2, Miscellaneous Records, A-H, 1867–1933, Washington County Records, NCA; J. W. Cooke to Hon. S. R. Mallory, April 23, 1864, *ORN,* ser. 1, vol. 9, pp. 656–58; J. N. Maffett to George Davis, Aug. 17, 1874, George Davis Papers, DU; A. M. Waddell, *An Address Before the Association Army of Northern Virginia . . .* (Richmond: Wm. Ellis Jones, 1888), 11.

26. C. W. Flusser to Acting Rear-Admiral S. P. Lee, April 18, 1864, *ORN,* ser. 1, vol. 9, pp. 636–67; C. W. Flusser to Commander H. K. Davenport, April 18, 1864, *ORN,* ser. 1, vol. 9, p. 667; G. W. Barrett to Commander H. K. Davenport, April 21, 1864, *ORN,* ser. 1, vol. 9, pp. 643–44.

27. Charles A. French to Acting Rear-Admiral S. P. Lee, April 19, 1864, *ORN,* ser. 1, vol. 9, p. 638; Frank W. Hackett to Commander H. K. Davenport, April 19, 1864, *ORN,* ser. 1, vol. 9, pp. 638–39; Wm. N. Welles to Acting Rear-Admiral S. P. Lee, April 23, 1864, *ORN,* ser. 1, vol. 9, pp. 639–40; Charles A. French to Acting Rear-Admiral S. P. Lee, April 21, 1864, *ORN,* ser. 1, vol. 9, pp. 641–42; J. W. Cooke to Hon S. R. Mallory, April 23, 1864, *ORN,* ser. 1, vol. 9, pp. 656–58; Crabtree and Patton (eds.), *"Journal of a Secesh Lady,"* Apr. 22, 26, 1864, pp. 550–51.

28. Charles A. French to Acting Rear-Admiral S. P. Lee, April 21, 1864, *ORN,* ser. 1, vol. 9, pp. 641–43; J. W. Cooke to Hon S. R. Mallory, April 23, 1864, *ORN,* ser. 1, vol. 9, pp. 656–58.

29. Reed, *History of the 101st Regiment,* p. 132.

30. H. W. Wessells to Maj. Gen. J. J. Peck, Aug. 18, 1864, *ORA,* ser. 1, vol. 33, p. 299; Reed, *History of the 101st Regiment,* p. 132; Edwin G. Moore, "Ransom's Brigade," in R. A. Brock (ed.), *Southern Historical Society Papers,* vol. 36 (1908): 365. This article was reprinted from the *Richmond Dispatch,* Feb. 26, 1901. Moore was a member of Ransom's brigade and an eyewitness to the attack on the east side of Plymouth.

31. Moore, "Ransom's Brigade," p. 366; Waddell, *An Address,* p. 13.

32. Moore, "Ransom's Brigade," p. 367; Reed, *History of the 101st Regiment,* p. 133; Waddell, *An Address,* p. 13.

33. Lanpheur, "Fall of Plymouth," p. 21, Lanpheur Papers, DU.

34. Reed, *History of the 101st Regiment,* p. 134.

35. H. W. Wessells to Maj. Gen. J. J. Peck, Aug. 18, 1864, *ORA,* ser. 1, vol. 23, p. 299; Alonzo Cooper, *In and Out of Rebel Prisons* (Oswego, N.Y.: H. J. Oliphant, 1888), 30.

36. Ira Berlin, Joseph P. Reidy, and Leslie R. Rowland (eds.), *Freedom: A Documentary History of Emancipation,* ser. I, *The Black Military Experience* (New York: Cambridge Univ. Press, 1982), 539–48.

37. H. W. Wessells to Maj. Gen. J. J. Peck, Aug. 18, 1864, *ORA,* ser. 1, vol. 23, p. 299; Cooper, *In and Out of Rebel Prisons,* p. 32.

38. H. W. Wessells to Maj. Gen. J. J. Peck, Aug. 18, 1864, *ORA,* ser. 1, vol. 23, p. 299; Reed, *History of the 101st Regiment,* p. 134.

39. H. W. Wessells to Maj. Gen. J. J. Peck, Aug. 18, 1864, *ORA,* ser. 1, vol. 23, pp. 299–301.

40. Charles Loehr, "Plymouth Campaign," p. 6. This account was written by one of Hoke's own officers who personally witnessed the general's remarks and the rush of soldiers and civilians.

41. Loehr, "Plymouth Campaign," pp. 6–7; Reed, *History of the 101st Regiment,* pp. 135–36; Cooper, *In and Out of Rebel Prisons,* pp. 33–34; Crabtree and Patton (eds.), *"Journal of a Secesh Lady,"* Apr. 23, 26, 1864, p. 551.

42. Loehr, "Plymouth Campaign," p. 7; Cooper, *In and Out of Rebel Prisons,* p. 33; "Addenda" to a letter from H. W. Wessells to Maj. Gen. J. J. Peck, Aug. 18, 1864, *ORA,* ser, 1, vol. 23, p. 301. The "Addenda" is incorrectly labeled a "Return of Casualties."

43. John A. Hedrick to brother, May 8, 1864, Hedrick Papers, DU.

44. Reed, *History of the 101st Regiment,* p. 135.

45. Ibid.; New Bern *North Carolina Times,* April 27, 1864, p. 2; Samuel Johnson deposition, July 11, 1863 enclosed in Benj. F. Butler to Lieut. Gen. U. S. Grant, July 12, 1864, *ORA,* ser. 2, vol. 7, pp. 459–60; Crabtree and Patton (eds.), *"Journal of a Secesh Lady,"* Apr. 22, 26, 1864, p. 551.

46. Darden, "The Story of Washington County," p. 8. The elder Darden, father of the author John W. Darden, was stationed at Rainbow Banks on the James River with the 10th North Carolina Volunteers in April 1864 but happened to be at home in Washington County on sick leave. The Darden story appears under the subtitle "Legend," and is a recollection recounted in the 1920s by the elder Darden who witnessed these events.

47. Darden, "The Story of Washington County," p. 8; Reed, *History of the 101st Regiment,* pp. 136–37; Cooper, *In and Out of Rebel*

Prisons, p. 34; Berlin et al., *The Black Military Experience,* pp. 588–89.

48. Darden, "The Story of Washington County," pp. 8–9; Cooper, *In and Out of Rebel Prisons,* pp. 33–34.

49. *Richmond Examiner,* April 28, 1864, quoted in the New Bern *North Carolina Times,* May 21, 1864, p. 2; Crabtree and Patton (eds.), *"Journal of a Secesh Lady,"* Apr. 22, 26, 1864, p. 551.

50. E. Ransom to William S. Pettigrew, May 6, 1864, Pettigrew Papers, SHC; Edw. H. Ripley to Major-General Peck, April 22, 1864, *ORA,* ser. 1, vol. 23, pp. 948–49.

51. William S. Pettigrew to James C. Johnston, Aug. 9, 1864, Hayes Collection (Johnston Series), SHC.

52. William S. Pettigrew speech at Williamston, July 12, 1864, Pettigrew Papers, SHC.

Epilogue

1. William S. Pettigrew to James C. Johnston, Aug. 9, 1864, Hayes Collection (Johnston Series), SHC.

2. Ibid.

3. Ibid.

4. E. Ransom to William S. Pettigrew, April 5, 1864; D. G. Cowand to William S. Pettigrew, May 2, 1864, Pettigrew Papers, SHC.

5. E. Ransom to William S. Pettigrew, May 5, 1864, Pettigrew Papers, SHC; William S. Pettigrew to James C. Johnston, Aug. 9, 1864, Hayes Collection (Johnston Series), SHC.

6. William S. Pettigrew speech, July 12, 1864, p. 2, Pettigrew Papers, SHC.

7. Ibid., p. 3.

8. Ibid., pp. 4–16.

9. William S. Pettigrew to James C. Johnston, Aug. 9, 1864, Hayes Collection (Johnston Series), SHC; C. B. Hassell to William S. Pettigrew, July 22, 1864, Pettigrew Papers, SHC; Untitled broadside including letters C. B. Hassell to Capt. Thomas J. Norman, July 23, 1864 and William S. Pettigrew to Rev. C. B. Hassell, July 23, 1864, North Carolina Collection, University of North Carolina Library.

10. "To the Voters of Washington and Martin Counties," broadside dated July 18, 1864, in the Pettigrew Papers, SHC; New Bern *North Carolina Times,* Aug. 23, 1864.

11. J. W. Edmondson to Miss Bettie, Nov. 5, 1864, Wright-Herring Papers, SHC.

12. Charles Pettigrew to Caroline Pettigrew, April 24, 1864, Pettigrew Papers, SHC.

13. Ibid.

14. Ibid.

15. Ibid.

16. Jno M. Hough to William S. Pettigrew, Aug. 12, 1864, Pettigrew Papers, SHC.

17. Ibid.; Jno M. Hough to William S. Pettigrew, Aug. 20, 1864, Pettigrew Papers, SHC.

18. Joshua S. Swift to William S. Pettigrew, Sept. 2, 1864; William S. Pettigrew to Joseph Calhoon, Sept. 27, 1864, Pettigrew Papers, SHC.

19. Charles D. Boynton, *The History of the Navy during the Rebellion,* vol. 2 (New York: D. Appleton and Company, 1868): 506–9; J. W. Edmondson to Miss Bettie, Nov. 5, 1864, Wright-Herring Papers, SHC. On plans to attack the *Albemarle* see Henry Phelon to Josephine, April 26, 1864, Phelon Papers, SHC. See also Crabtree and Patton (eds.), *"Journal of a Secesh Lady,"* Oct. 31, 1864, p. 628–30; Colonel George Wortham, Confederate post commander at Plymouth, had complained to his superiors in June about the small size of the garrison and demanded more troops. His request was marked "File, no action." See Geo. Wortham to the Ast. Adgt. Gen. Com[manding], Genl. Winders Staff, June 2, 1864, Theophilus H. Holmes Papers, DU; W. H. Macomb to Rear-Admiral D. D. Porter, Nov. 1, 1864, *ORN,* ser. 1, vol. 11, pp. 12–15; Crabtree and Patton (eds.), *"Journal of a Secesh Lady,"* Nov. 2, 1864, p. 633.

20. J. W. Edmondson to Miss Bettie, Nov. 5, 1864, Wright-Herring Papers, CHS; Crabtree and Patton (eds.), *"Journal of a Secesh Lady,"* Nov. 2, 1864, p. 634.

21. Charles Pettigrew to [William S. Pettigrew], Nov. 8, 1864, Pettigrew Papers, SHC.

22. William S. Pettigrew untitled dream, Feb. 2, 18, 1864, Pettigrew Papers, SHC. Pettigrew's dreams are all grouped together at the end of the undated folder for 1864 in the Pettigrew Papers.

23. William S. Pettigrew untitled dream, April 1, 1864, Pettigrew Papers, SHC.

24. William S. Pettigrew untitled dreams, March 17, July 17, Aug. 16, 1864, Pettigrew Papers, SHC.

25. Testimony of Benjamin E. Bailey, 6 July 1876; testimony of Richard Iredell Hassell, 6 July 1876, Washington County NC case files, Southern Claims Commission, RG 217, NA.

26. New Bern *North Carolina Daily Times,* July 28, 1865.

Bibliographic Note

The story of Washington County, North Carolina, during the Civil War can be recovered in the main through the use of two primary sources—the Pettigrew Papers and the printed *Official Records* of the armies and navies during the War of the Rebellion (as the War Department called the conflict in later years).

The Pettigrew Papers proved invaluable for two reasons. First, they contain the letters of two brothers, Charles and William, who operated three plantations a few miles distant from each other in the Scuppernong neighborhood. They regularly moved slaves among the plantations, and therefore each had to keep abreast of the operations of the other. This they did by exchanging letters several times each week. Charles's wife, Caroline, also frequently wrote very detailed letters about life on the plantations to her sister in South Carolina. Second, during the war, the Pettigrew brothers acted as a kind of clearinghouse of information for planters, in part because the county had no newspaper. They received regular written reports from fellow planters around the county and dispatched news in return from the Scuppernong neighborhood—including their own plans and opinions, various rumors circulating in the neighborhood, and observations about the activities of yeoman farmers, white wage laborers, and their own slaves. In sum, the Pettigrews wrote often and in great detail about themselves and their neighbors. The result is a detailed and continuous record of the Civil War in a plantation community.

The Pettigrew Papers also include a memorandum or daily diary kept by H. G. Spruill, a planter who resided in Plymouth, where he served as mayor of the town and general for the state militia around the Albemarle Sound. The Spruill Memorandum is over one hundred pages of close handwriting and is especially important for its daily record of Spruill's conversations with various federal officers in command at Plymouth. Those conversations trace in detail the evolution of federal military policy toward Confederates, unionists, and fugitive slaves in Washington County.

The *Official Records* of the armies—both Confederate and Union—and of the U.S. Navy form the second major source for this study. Using the massive general indexes for each set, I located over one thousand pages of information concerning Plymouth and its environs. As might be expected, these records chronicle military policy at the district and department levels in great detail. More surprising was the multitude of letters and reports written by low-level officers—often captains and even lieutenants—dealing with the daily affairs of a post, company, or gunboat. These documents proved to be important because post commanders and gunboat commanders dealt personally with planters, unionists, and fugitive slaves. The officers' letters concern local politics, the confiscation of personal property and plantations, controversies over political allegiance, and accounts of guerrilla operations and other violence. In short, they are the raw materials for writing a social history of the Civil War.

Other manuscript and printed sources mainly filled gaps here and there in the narrative. But a few deserve special mention because they yielded information of an unusual or crucial nature. The printed histories of several regiments—both Union and Confederate—often contained firsthand accounts of daily life in occupied Plymouth, of soldiers' experiences on picket duty or during forays into the upcountry, and of the terrors of living in the midst of a local guerrilla war. The records of the Southern Claims Commission at the National Archives yielded biographical information on a few men who remained in the county, including direct testimony of extraordinary quality by the claimants and their friends. Finally, there are two diaries—the manuscript diary of Cushing Biggs Hassell, a wealthy planter and elder in the Primitive Baptist Church who resided in Martin County; and the published diary of Catherine Ann Devereux Edmondston, a planter's wife who lived further up the Roanoke River. Hassell's diary runs to several thousand pages written over the span of at least three decades and includes daily entries during the war. Hassell wrote about all manner of public and private affairs but paid particularly close attention to the activities of fugitive slaves beginning to stream down the Roanoke River in mid-1862. The Edmondston diary focuses on the local politics of the Albemarle Sound region and the ill-fortunes of her planter friends.

These sources, while few in number, yielded a wealth of stories about rich and poor, black and white, unionists and secessionists, soldiers and civilians. They suggest that a close examination of similar sources elsewhere—in eastern Virginia, coastal South Carolina, West Virginia, Kentucky, Missouri, Tennessee, Arkansas, Louisiana, and Texas—would reveal conflicts over land and labor similar to those that raged in Washington County, North Carolina, during the Great Rebellion.

Index

281